STEP BY STEP
ELECTRONIC TECHNIQUES DESIGN

ELECTRONIC DESIGN TECHNIQUES

Edited by

Talitha Harper and Sara Booth

Step-By-Step Electronic Design Techniques
Edited by Talitha Harper and Sara Booth

Peachpit Press
1249 Eighth Street
Berkeley, CA 94710
510 524-2178
800 283-9444
510 524-2221 fax
Find us on the World Wide Web at:
http://www.peachpit.com

Peachpit Press is a division of Addison Wesley Longman.

Publisher *Step-By-Step Electronic Design:*
    Michael Hammer
Editorial Director *Step-By-Step Electronic Design:*
    Talitha Harper
Editor *Step-By-Step Electronic Design:*
    Sara Booth
Art Director *Step-By-Step Electronic Design:*
    Michael Ulrich
Cover Illustration: Ray Koleczek
Cover Design: Amy Changar
Index: Steve Rath

ISBN 0–201–69672–X

Printed and bound in the United States of America

ELECTRONIC ✦ DESIGN

In this book, you'll see some of the most exciting projects we've featured in past issues of *Step-By-Step Electronic Design,* a 20-page monthly newsletter from Step-By-Step Publishing. Coming up with exciting digital projects every month can be a challenge, but we've developed a fairly simple formula for unearthing cutting-edge techniques. We look for outstanding projects from the most innovative electronic designers and illustrators. Invariably, we've discovered, people who do great work have developed great working techniques.

You'll recognize the names of many of our writers, too: Linnea Dayton, co-author of *The Photoshop Wow! Book* and editor of the Wow! series, is the founding editor of *Step-By-Step Electronic Design,* and she set the standards we strive to meet in each monthly issue of the newsletter; Janet Ashford, author of *Start with a Scan,* helped mold the newsletter's in-depth reporting style; Lynda Weinman, author of *Designing Web Graphics,* has contributed ahead-of-the-trends tips on Web design; and Cher Threinen-Pendarvis, author of *The Painter Wow! Book,* has shared her insights with our readers.

In addition to hundreds of software tips, you'll find a trove of inspiration in this book — and it's just a fraction of the information we've delivered to our subscribers. Each month, *Step-By-Step Electronic Design* presents dozens of tips and techniques in the leading graphic arts applications — Photoshop, Illustrator, FreeHand, Painter, QuarkXPress, and PageMaker. After all, we look for the best work from the leading design professionals, so we're always making exciting discoveries.

Talitha Harper
Editorial Director
Step-By-Step Electronic Design

For subscription information, call 800-255-8800
or e-mail us at sbspub@dgusa.com.

1 TECHNIQUES

BITMAP

POSTSCRIPT **89** STRATEGIES

More POSTSCRIPT STRATEGIES

170 POSTSCRIPT

BITMAP MEETS

BITMAP TECHNIQUES

publishers: r.j. miller / j.c

aging editor: lisa derketsch

editor: freddy j. nager

ting editors: keith gorman +

+ robbie snow + stacey

art direction: tim

n / creation of amplbook: dav

contributing designer: toda

technology con

When the Hiebing Group of Madison, Wis., produced the startling image shown below, the designers relied on sophisticated color handling as well as seamless collage techniques to give the scene its drama. To find out more about how the Hiebing Group uses Photoshop to produce photorealistic fantasy images, see "Building a New Reality," page 11. (This image, like the one featured on the cover, was created as part of an advertising campaign for a client specializing in environmental control.)

Eldon Doty's humorous "portraits" of imaginary people get a lot of their punch from the contrast between the rich textures of the characters' clothing and surroundings and the cartoonish expressions of the characters themselves. In this illustration, Doty added sheen to the ribbons and the satin of the skirt by using Photoshop's dodge-and-burn tool to generate strong highlights. He painted in the lacework using the airbrush tool — first using a large, soft brush to cover the entire lace area with white at a low opacity, then increasing the opacity, reducing the brush size, and painting in the loops and dots that make up the lace pattern. The medallions on the skirt were created using Terrazzo, a pattern-generating Photoshop plug-in. For more on Doty's electronic portrait gallery, see "Cloning a Humorous Portrait" on page 59.

Skeptical designers may wonder whether the World Wide Web really brings in business, but the partners at Canary Studios are convinced. Representatives of the Internet search firm Yahoo saw Canary's Web site (www.canary-studios.com /~ canary) and were so impressed that they hired Canary to develop icons for their Los Angeles site (see "Breaking the Boundary" on page 114).

Ken Roberts of Canary used a roundabout method to give the site's opening image a distressed look. Starting with a scanned photograph, he applied the blur filter to knock the image out of focus, then used the Color Halftone filter to generate the dots around the edges of the image. This approach gave Roberts a chance to have some fun with one of the frustrations of Web design: the dithering effect caused by the limited palettes available to browsers.

Softness and texture were Elliott Park's goals when he created the Eiffel Tower illustration above. The South Lake, Texas, illustrator captured texture from the very beginning by laser-printing the linework he had created in Illustrator and using a photocopier to enlarge and reduce it repeatedly until the lines began to break down — a process he hastened by rubbing the copies with steel wool.

The resulting image, when he scanned it and opened it in Photoshop, looked as if it had been drawn with a pastel crayon. To create a similar texture in some of the color areas (especially the shrubs below the tower), Park wanted to be able to add noise without affecting other shapes. So he modified his scan so that he had three layers: the linework in front, the dark-blue background in back, and a color layer sandwiched between the two. That way, he could create the shrub shapes on the color layer and easily apply the Add Noise filter to them without affecting the background or the linework.

To make the white pixels transparent in his scanned linework — so the color would show behind it — Park selected all in the linework layer, copied, and pasted the scan into a new channel. Then he deleted everything from the linework layer, loaded the selection he had just created, and filled the linework with a rich black. For more on Park's Photoshop techniques, see "Painting with Light," page 175.

PHOTOSHOP

Creating Convincing Light

■ *by Sara Booth*

WITH PHOTOSHOP, IT's relatively simple to combine elements from different photographic sources. But a successful photo composite depends on developing realistic relationships among those elements, and one of the most critical tools is light. To make a fantasy scene look like reality, Bryan Allen and Wayne Roth planned the scene carefully, took most of the photographs in a single session, then turned to Photoshop's contrast adjustment tools to adjust the light until the scene looked believable.

One of the greatest challenges was to create the look of captured lightning. "You can't just use photos of lightning," Allen says. "That ends up looking like little sticks in a jar." So the model for the shot offered a machine from his collection of

When Wayne Roth and Bryan Allen, partners in the imaging firm Chisel-Vision, created a promotion for the firm, they wanted to showcase "not so much our technical prowess as our abilities in idea generation," Allen says. Photoshop helped them transform fair weather to storms.

❶

1 To simulate the electricity in the jars, Allen used a machine that sent electricity crawling across a metal surface. Taking the device into his darkroom, he placed raw film on the metal and contact-exposed a variety of prints to use in all the jars.

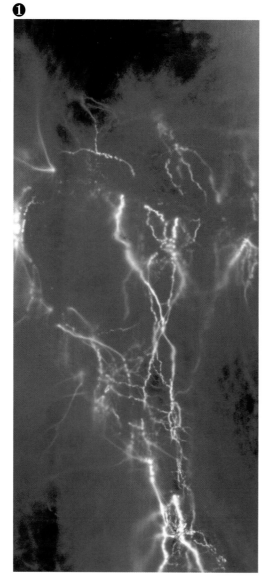

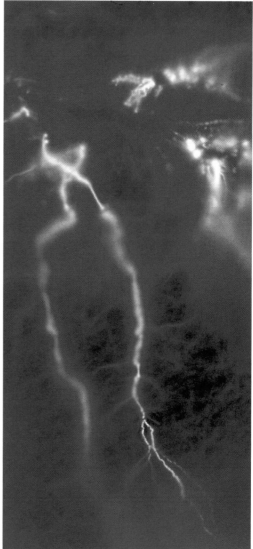

gadgets: a device, originally designed to detect leaks in neon tubing, which sent a current creeping across any metal surface it touched **❶**.

When Allen photographed the man holding the jars, he wanted them to cast a realistic light on the face, so he lit up the jars using small light bulbs attached to a lantern battery, with white paper to diffuse the light. But when lightning was added to the jars, the result "looked fake," Allen says. "It had no depth. And when we tried to make the electricity layer transparent, it didn't help because there was nothing to see" **❷**. So a third layer — this one of the jars lying on the flannel shirt, with lights but no paper — was added to the equation for a more realistic look **❸**.

Once the lightning was in the jars, though, the partners didn't feel that it was shedding enough light on the man's face and body. To make the lighting more realistic, Allen used the same tech-

nique repeatedly: He made rough selections with the marquee or lasso, used the Color Range dialog box to narrow these selections, feathered slightly, then used a variety of Photoshop tools, including Curves, Hue/Saturation, and Selective Color, to alter the color. By this process, he brightened the areas around the eyes and nose and under the chin and added light to the shirt above the belt and parts of the sleeve and jeans.

Since the day of the photo shoot was sunny, the partners had waited until dusk so that the light would be as close as possible to the light in a thunderstorm. However, when they placed the background behind the man, they had to make changes to give it a stormy look. Allen began by darkening the landscape **❹** to match the sky, which was constructed from several photographs from an earlier photo shoot **❺**. Allen added a fence from another file photo (using the Perspective command to

❷

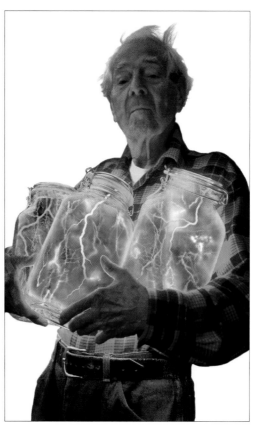

2 The model was photographed holding jars lit from inside, with white paper in them to soften the light (left). Allen first pasted in the electricity on its own layer, with a layer mask to allow the image to appear only inside the jars, but he didn't feel that the results looked real.

3 To allow the man's shirt to show through, Allen photographed the jars on the flannel shirt, this time with lights but no paper, and again masked out everything except what would appear through the jars. He placed the shirt layer behind the electricity layer, then worked on the lightning with the eraser tool in airbrush mode, brushing in partial transparency where the shirt layer would be visible.

❸

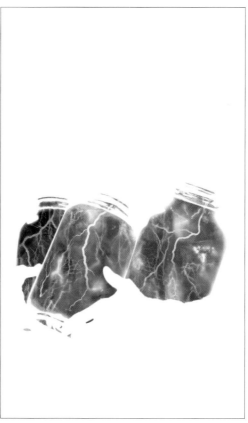

4 After Allen cloned in a hill on the right side of the background, he began working on giving the background realistic light for a thunderstorm. Using Quick Mask to select the land, he chose Image, Adjust, Hue/ Saturation, then moved the Lightness slider left to darken the image and moved the Saturation slider right to bump up the colors.

5 Allen began work on the sky by copying one sky photograph onto its own layer (left). A second photograph was placed on a layer above the first, and Allen reduced its opacity to 45% for a more realistic composite. Finally, he cloned in lightning from other photos, then used the airbrush tool to adjust the clouds and add the appearance of falling rain in the distance.

❹

❺

make it follow the slope of the field), then used the lasso to select the curve on the upper left part of the landscape and copied it into the right side of the shot to add a rolling hill.

By the time the woman was photographed, it was nearly dark. Allen and Roth placed a strobe near the end of the "lightning rod" (which is actually a rake handle, to which the partners attached a tapering piece of wood and a glass ball used to transport gases for neon signs), but not enough light reached the grass and the surroundings. So to make the woman seem to be lit by the bolt of lightning she's capturing, Allen selected areas of the background and used Curves and Levels to lighten them. To make the fence appear to be lit by the same glow, he used the dodge and burn tool on the posts nearest to the woman.

The bright light had burned out the details in the woman's face and body. Allen used the Color Range command to select the highlights, then used Levels and Curves to boost the contrast there. Then he selected the woman, added a small amount of noise, and applied the Gaussian Blur filter with a low setting. "This can help add tone and texture without looking too obvious," he says.

The light in the jars cast a "fringe" of light around the edge of the man's hands. To accentuate that effect, Allen used the lasso to select the backs of the hands, feathered the selection, and used the Curves dialog box to darken it. Allen wanted to give the jars more of a glow, too, so he used the airbrush to stroke white over the lightest parts of the electricity. In the same way, he added glow to the lightning in the sky. He wanted the effect to be subtle, so he used an opacity of only 6% and a brush about half again as wide as the streams themselves. He painted the glow into its own layer so he could adjust its opacity later. ◼

Painting with Natural Media

■ *by Talitha Harper*

WITH THE COMPUTER, you can think of your environment as palette and brush," says illustrator Jim Carroll of Old Chatham, N.Y. Carroll draws freely from his surroundings to compose lush, bitmapped paintings. His favorite "brush" is Photoshop's rubber stamp tool, and he uses it to soak up color and texture from scanned elements (photographs, hand drawings, and found objects) and apply them to his illustrations. This blend of painting, photography, and collage is a style that could only be produced electronically, but Carroll's work rarely has a computer-generated look.

When the United Methodist Church wanted an illustration for a fund-raising drive, the planning committee turned to Carroll. The theme of the drive was the civil war in Somalia, and committee members wanted an image that evoked the suffering of the war's victims yet captured the spirit of hope.

MANAGING HIGH-MEMORY FILES

The illustration was to be printed in several sizes, on pamphlets, booklets, ads, and posters. So Carroll sized the illustration to accommodate the largest format, the 17 x 30-inch poster. At that size, a resolution of 266 dpi (the optimum resolution for the 133-lpi line screen that would be used to print the poster) would have produced a mammoth 137.7MB file in CMYK mode — and Carroll always works in CMYK. "It's the only way I can get an accurate feel for the printed color," he says. But Carroll has de-

Jim Carroll relies on collage techniques — rather than brush-work — to produce his painterly images. He uses Photoshop's rubber stamp tool to add texture to his illustrations and to blend the colors in his pasted-in elements with the tones on the underlying layer.

1 Carroll worked from photographs to create the woman's face, but he didn't want a photorealistic image. So he constructed it from three photos, using Photoshop's lasso tool to select the chin, ear, and lips from one photo, the nose and eye from another, and the hair from the third.

2 Using the rubber stamp tool, Carroll cloned skin from one of the scanned photos and applied it to the composite image. He chose large, soft-edged brushes to fill in big areas like the chin and cheeks and smaller, soft edged brushes to clone skin tone up to the hairline.

3 After applying a wash of color over the image, Carroll scaled the face disproportionally. "When I'm working with photography, I almost always distort," Carroll says. "If I don't, the image looks too literal to be effective."

4 Starting with a quick computer sketch of the boy's face, Carroll used the rubber stamp tool to apply skin tone and hair sampled from a photo, then added color and scaled the image.

5 When Carroll scanned a crumpled piece of tissue paper, he left the top of the scanner bed open, turning the background black. And because the background contrasted dramatically with the image, it was easy to create a silhouette selection by selecting the background with the magic wand tool and choosing Select, Inverse.

❶

❷

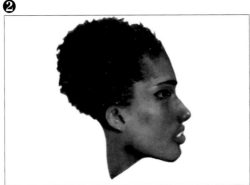

❸

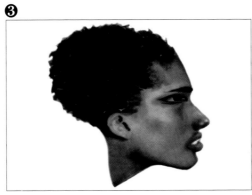

❹

❺

veloped a strategy for reducing the working size of his Photoshop images. He often creates his paintings at a relatively low resolution (150 to 200 dpi) and increases the resolution at the end of the process through the Image, Image Size dialog box. Carroll chose 150 dpi for this illustration, which gave him a file size of just under 44MB. "With my style, I don't sacrifice quality by upping the resolution at the end," he says. ☞ *When you open a new Photoshop document, the file size is listed at the top of the dialog box. So you can adjust the dimensions or the resolution if you need to keep the file to a manageable size.*

Carroll also reduced processing time by working on individual elements, honing each image in a separate file and combining them later.

COMPOSING THE FACES

To create the woman in the illustration, Carroll began by asking a friend to pose for photographs. Although he works with a color scanner — and he used color film when he shot the pictures — the photos were scanned in grayscale. Carroll planned to combine several photographs into a composite image, and he knew that eliminating the color information would downplay any discrepancies in lighting or skin tone. He selected sections from three different photos and pasted the elements into a new Photoshop file ❶. Using one of the scanned photos as his source file, he Option-clicked with the rubber stamp tool to sample skin tones from the source photo, then "painted" the skin texture into the composite image ❷.

Once he was satisfied that the composition looked convincing, Carroll was ready to add color. He converted the grayscale file to CMYK mode, selected a warm, rosy brown as his foreground color, and chose the Color option in the Brushes palette pop-out menu. The Color setting produced a sheer paint that didn't obscure the tonality in the underlying grayscale image. Carroll also used a light touch with his pressure-sensitive tablet to soften the color even more.

Carroll scaled the composite (Image, Effects, Scale) to add drama to the face. First, he selected the eye and enlarged it to roughly three times its original size, using the Hide Edges command (Select, Hide Edges or Command-H) as he scaled the eye to turn off the selection border, giving himself a clear view of the effect. After blending the eye into the surrounding skin with the smudge tool, he selected the entire head with the marquee tool and scaled, stretching the head horizontally ❸.

A similar technique was used to paint the child, but in this case, Carroll began with a quick computer sketch. First, he opened a new grayscale file and roughed in the head, using a soft-edged brush and a pressure-sensitive tablet. With the rubber stamp tool, he cloned skin tone from one of the scanned photos — the same photo he had used to fill in the skin texture in the composite image of the woman — and applied it to the drawing ❹.

ASSEMBLING THE ILLUSTRATION

Working in his poster-size file, Carroll filled the canvas with a luminous shade of blue. (Throughout the illustration, Carroll selected clear, vibrant tones, reminiscent of the colors used in African textiles.) He selected clouds from scanned snapshots and pasted them into the file.

To intensify the color in the clouds, Carroll adjusted the Hue/Saturation settings (Command-U) and the Levels controls (Command-L). First, he selected the clouds by clicking on the background with the magic wand tool and choosing Select, Inverse. He used the same technique — selecting the solid-colored background and inverting — to produce silhouette selections of the other images before pasting them into the background file.

Carroll planned to unify the woman and the boy by wrapping a blanket around their shoulders, and he created this blanket from a piece of tissue paper, placed directly on the scanner bed. Carroll opened the scan in Photoshop and used the burn tool (activated by pressing the Option key while the dodge and burn tool is selected) to intensify the shimmering colors the scanner light had infused into the tissue ❺.

Then Carroll pasted the woman's head into the sky-and-clouds file, rotating it (Image, Rotate, Free) to turn the face upward. While the selection was still active, Carroll returned to one of his original scanned photos, selected the arm, and clicked on the poster-size image to activate it. He chose Edit, Paste Behind to place the arm behind the head. While the arm was still selected, he could drag it into the position he wanted. Here again, he used the Hide Edges command in order to see the effect clearly. He selected the shoulder from another scan and pasted it on top of the composite, then added the boy's head. Finally, he pasted the blanket into the illustration ❻.

PAINTING WITH FOUND OBJECTS

A scanned dandelion "fresh from the yard" was used to create the pattern on the blanket. Carroll drew a circle around the dandelion by creating a selection with the oval marquee tool and choosing Select, Border. He drew additional circles, then used the rubber stamp to transfer the pattern onto the blanket. As he applied the design, he set the opacity at 80 percent in the Brushes palette, and he varied the stylus pressure to soften sections of the cloned pattern even more. "When I put components together, I like the tone to vary," says Carroll, "or they look like they've been pushed to-

❻

❼

❽
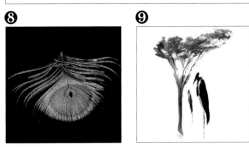

❾

❿
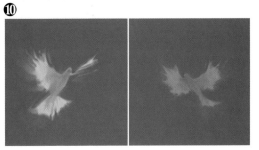

6 Carroll pasted the figures into the background, then added the blanket. He used the smudge tool and the rubber stamp to smooth the seams where the woman's head, shoulder, and arm had been pasted together.

7 Carroll used a broad, soft-edged brush to paint a dove in Photoshop. Inverting the file (Image, Map, Invert or Command-I) gave him a white dove on a black background.

8 After scanning a peacock feather, Carroll selected the background with the magic wand tool and inverted to select the feather. He used the rubber stamp tool to apply the feather texture to the dove, setting the opacity in the Brushes palette at 25 percent and applying gentle pressure with the stylus so that only a hint of the peacock coloring was painted onto the dove.

9 The vultures and the tree were drawn in a separate Photoshop file, then pasted into the illustration.

10 Carroll drew two small doves on the computer, then used the Invert command (Command-I) to change the original black doves to white. Coloring from the peacock feather was cloned and applied to the birds before they were pasted into the illustration.

11 After scanning a pear, Carroll used the Levels controls to adjust the color in the scan to give the pear a hand-painted look.

12 The pear, branch, and leaves were pasted into the illustration. Carroll then set the opacity at 10 percent in the Brushes palette and used the rubber stamp tool to produce a pale clone of the elements.

13 A freeform design was drawn on tracing paper with a black marker and scanned. After coloring the design, Carroll pasted it into the illustration and scaled it to fit the image perfectly.

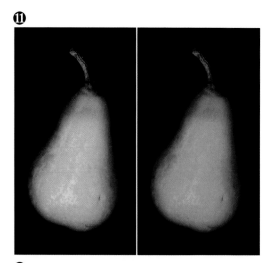

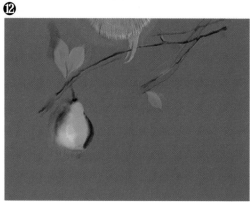

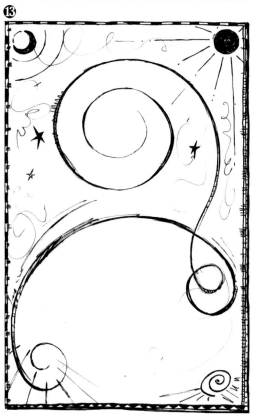

gether." He scaled the dandelion design periodically as he worked, and he occasionally bypassed some of the elements in the rubber stamp process to keep the clones from looking identical.

Carroll also used the rubber stamp tool to paint feathers on a dove. After working out the design in a few quick pencil sketches, Carroll painted the dove in a new Photoshop file ❼. He scanned a peacock feather he had found on a trip to a petting zoo with his children and cloned the texture from the scanned feather onto the dove ❽.

FINISHING THE DESIGN
Several of the elements Carroll added to the illustration were drawn directly in Photoshop ❾ ❿. Others (a pear ⓫ a twig, and two leaves) were scans of real objects.

Carroll assembled the scanned elements, made a silhouette selection of the assembled image, and copied. In order to paste the copied image into the dove's beak, he used the magic wand tool to select the orange beak before choosing Edit, Paste Behind. Then he used the rubber stamp tool to clone the pear, the twig, and the leaves, creating ghostly duplicates of the images ⓬

Once he was satisfied with the composition, Carroll added a border design to the illustration. He created the border by hand, drawing a sun, moon, and stars and adding free-flowing swirling lines ⓭ After scanning the design, he selected the background, inverted to select the linework, and hid the selection borders (Command-H). He painted inside the selection with the brush tool, changing the paint color frequently to produce a vibrant, multi-colored design. Finally, he copied the selected linework and pasted it into the poster-sized file. ☞ *Copying and pasting large elements can slow down processing time, because the copied selection remains in the clipboard until you copy again. You can remove the memory-intensive element from the clipboard — and free up RAM — by making a tiny selection and copying. The new element will replace the image stored in the clipboard.*

As he pasted elements, Carroll often used the rubber stamp tool — set to revert — to bring back some of the underlying color. "This softens the pasted-in effect," Carroll says, "and that keeps the image from looking too constructed." To set the rubber stamp to revert, he double-clicked on its icon in the toolbox to open the Rubber Stamp Options dialog box and selected Revert To Saved.

As a final refinement, Carroll imported the illustration into Fractal Design Painter and added thin washes of color with the Water Color brush. Then he returned to Photoshop in order to output the file in CMYK format so that the image could be placed into QuarkXPress. ■

Building a New Reality

■ *by Talitha Harper*

PHOTOSHOP is often used as a compositing tool to create fantasy collages. But Ray Koleczek, computer graphics manager of the Hiebing Group in Madison, Wis., relies on the same collage techniques to assemble realistic photographs of impossible scenes.

When the Hiebing Group was asked to produce a series of ads for Siebe, a company that develops environmental controls for offices and industrial sites, Koleczek worked in Photoshop to illustrate "solutions" to hopeless environmental challenges — letting a parakeet breathe under water, for example. To create the scene, Koleczek began with three separate photos, each set up to capture one of the key ingredients he needed for the collage: a parakeet perched on a bird swing, a fishbowl filled with water, and rising air bubbles ❶.

PREPARING THE BASE IMAGE

The photo of the fishbowl filled with water was used as the basis of the composition, and other elements were pasted into this image to build the scene. But before the collage work began, Koleczek made some modifications to his base image.

When the fishbowl was photographed, Koleczek hung a bird perch from the lip of the bowl so the photo would display the effects of light refraction where the legs of the perch pierced the surface of the

The Hiebing Group of Madison, Wis., used a variety of Photoshop collage techniques to create this fantasy scene, then adjusted the color in each CMYK channel to make the image even more dramatic.

❶

1 Koleczek combined three photographs to create the montage. For the first, he suspended a bird swing inside a fishbowl, placed a parakeet into the bowl, and set a wire rack on top to keep the parakeet from flying away. (By putting the parakeet in the fishbowl, Koleczek captured the reflection of the bird, an important element in the finished montage.)

For the second photo, water was added to the bowl and the legs of the bird perch were hung from the rim to capture the refraction of the wire legs where they met the water.

For the third photo, an aerator was placed inside the bowl to create bubbles in the water.

water. But the photo of the parakeet also included the bird perch, and Koleczek wanted to paste the bird and the perch into the image as a single selection. (That way, he could position the two as a unit without having to worry about bringing them into alignment.) So Koleczek used the rubber stamp tool to "erase" the legs of the perch where they fell below the surface of the water, covering them up with color sampled from the water (by Option-clicking with the rubber stamp to "pick up" color from the water and then clicking with the tool to stamp the color over unwanted elements). The rubber stamp tool was also used to "remove" the putty that had been used to hold the legs of the perch in place during photography.

The fishbowl had been photographed at a dramatic angle, looking up from a position off to one side the bowl, and at this angle, the surface of the water appeared to fall at a slant. So Koleczek used the Skew command (Image, Effects, Skew) to raise one side of the water, making it look level. First, he used the pen from the Paths palette to create a selection that followed the surface of the water. Then he chose Make Selection from the palette menu and skewed the selection **❷**. (The skewed selection included highlights and shadows defining one side of the bowl, and the rubber stamp tool was later used to smooth out the transition between the skewed highlights and shadows and those in the original photo.) ☞ *After performing a Photoshop function that requires interpolation (the Image, Rotate command or the Scale, Skew, Perspective, and Distort functions in the Image, Effects submenu), it's a good idea to apply the Unsharp Mask filter (Filter, Sharpen, Unsharp Mask) to bring the interpolated image into clearer focus.*

PLACING THE BIRD IN THE WATER

Once he had touched up the base illustration, Koleczek was ready to add the parakeet. Each of the three photos he used to build the scene had been photographed against the same background so that Koleczek could place elements from one photo into another without worrying about tonal distinctions. So when he pasted the parakeet into the base photo, he was able to create a fairly rough selection border because he didn't have to worry about discrepancies in the background color between the base photo and the pasted-in selection.

There were two sections of the selection, however, that had to be carefully defined. One was the tip of the bird's tail, which extended into a background highlight; Koleczek didn't want to include this highlight in the selection. The other was the parakeet's reflection; the original photo included two reflections of the bird (see Figure 1), and Koleczek planned to use only one in the collage.

So he used the pen tool to create a selection path that outlined the tail and the reflection tightly. But as he defined the rest of the path, he clicked quickly with the pen tool to select the background surrounding the parakeet.

When he created the selection, Koleczek cropped the wire legs of the bird perch close to the parakeet to make sure the wires wouldn't rise above the surface of the water when the selection was pasted into the base photo. Then, once the parakeet had been pasted into position, the rubber stamp tool was used to "raise" the cropped-off wires to water level ❸.

FINE-TUNING THE IMAGE

After pasting the parakeet into the bowl of water, Koleczek turned to the rubber stamp tool to perfect the image. In some cases, the tool was used to correct problems — to remove hot reflections on the fishbowl, for example, and to delete many of the tiny bubbles that had formed on the inside of the glass when water was poured into the bowl.

In other cases, Koleczek used the rubber stamp to add drama to the image. He repositioned segments of the bird perch with the rubber stamp, heightening the effect of refracted light ❹. And air bubbles, sampled from the third photo (see Figure 1), were stamped into the collage to make it look as if the parakeet had exhaled them ❺.

The fishbowl was reflected at the bottom of the composition, and Koleczek applied the Distort function (Image, Effects, Distort) to exaggerate the perspective of the reflected bowl. First, he selected the reflected image, using the pen tool and the Make Selection command in the Paths palette menu. He carefully traced the bottom of the bowl where it met the reflection, but selecting the sides of the reflected bowl wasn't as critical, so at the sides, he drew the path on top of the background rather than following the shape of the bowl precisely.

Koleczek wanted a radical distortion, and he knew the effect called for dragging the two bottom handles (which became visible when the Distort function was activated) far outside the Photoshop window. So before selecting Distort, he zoomed out (Command-Option-spacebar), reducing the size of the on-screen image and giving himself plenty of room on the desktop to drag the handles.

As a final touch, Koleczek chose white as the foreground color and used a tiny brush to paint bubbles (like those that had formed naturally on the marbles at the bottom of the bowl) into the bird and the perch.

ADJUSTING THE COLOR

Although the color in the original photography was bright and distinct, Koleczek adjusted the

❷

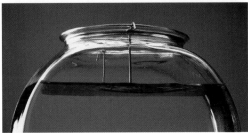

❸

❹

2 Photoshop's Skew command was used to level the surface of the water. Before skewing the selection, Koleczek created a floating copy (Command-J). Because the original photo remained intact beneath the floating copy, skewing didn't open up an expanse of white canvas (as it does when the original selection, rather than the copy, is skewed).

3 The bird, along with its reflection, was pasted on top of the photo of the bowl of water. While the bird was still selected, Koleczek enlarged it (Image, Effects, Scale) to make it fill most of the bowl.

4 Enlarging the bird and the perch made the distance between the legs of the perch wider, diminishing the effect of light refraction. After enlargement, the front wire formed a nearly straight line above and below the water. And a segment of the back leg, which bent dramatically where it entered the water, no longer matched up to rest of the wire leg. So Koleczek used the rubber stamp tool to reposition two segments of the wire legs (stamping copies into new positions and then stamping out the original segments).

5 Bubbles from the photo of the fishbowl with the aerator (see Figure 1) were rubber stamped into the montage.

6 Koleczek wanted to brighten the yellows and greens in the bird while deepening the purple tones in the rest of the image. So he selected the parakeet and the perch in order to adjust the color separately inside (and outside) the selection. With a complex shape, it's often easier to make the selection in one of the color channels where the contrast is more distinct than it is in the composite image. In this case, the contrast between the parakeet and the background was most pronounced in the yellow channel (bottom left).

7 Koleczek used the Levels controls (Image, Adjust, Levels or Command-L) to modify the tonality in the individual channels. In the cyan channel (top left) and the magenta channel (top right), he increased contrast in the parakeet and darkened the shadow tones in the rest of the image. In the yellow channel (bottom left), he intensified highlights and shadows in the bird, but in the fishbowl and the background, he raised the white Input slider to a point that bleached out the highlights and midtones. And in the black plate (bottom right), he lightened shadows and highlights in the bird, while increasing contrast in the rest of the image.

❺

❻

❼

tonality in the composite image to make the parakeet stand out against background. He began by using the marquee tool to select the parakeet, along with a section of the water. Then he Command-clicked with the magic wand tool on the background to remove it from the selection so that only the parakeet and the perch remained selected. Koleczek wanted the selection to include every part of the perch that fell inside the water — but his original marquee selection had been drawn well below the water's surface. So Koleczek pressed the Shift key while using the lasso to trace around the legs of the perch where they met the top of the water, adding them to the selection ❻. (Pressing the Option key let Koleczek click from point to point with the lasso tool to create straight selection paths along the length of the wires, and dragging the lasso let him trace the rounded contours at the top of the wires.)

Koleczek opened the Levels dialog box and worked in the individual CMYK channels to adjust the colors precisely inside the selection, moving the black Input Levels slider toward the center of the bar when he wanted to darken the shadows and shifting the white Input Levels slider toward the center when he wanted to brighten the highlights. When Koleczek was satisfied with the effect, he clicked OK to close the dialog box and finalize the changes. The Select, Inverse command reversed the selection, allowing Koleczek to fine-tune the Levels settings in the rest of the image while the adjustments he had made to the parakeet and the perch were unaffected ❼. ☞ *In the Levels and Curves dialog boxes (accessed through the Image, Adjust submenu or by choosing Command-L for Levels or Command-M for Curves), you can keep the composite image in view while adjusting the color in the individual channels. Just choose one of the color channels from the pop-out menu in the dialog box or use the keyboard shortcut to select a channel (Command-1 through Command-4 for each component color in a CMYK image, Command-1 through Command-3 for the RGB channels, and Command-0 for the composite channel in any color file). But if you want to see the individual channel — and not the composite image — as you make the adjustment, you must activate the channel before opening the dialog box.*

Before releasing the selection (Command-D), Koleczek converted it to a path and stored it in the Paths palette (by choosing Make Path and then Save Path from the palette's pop-out menu) so that he could reactivate the selection (by clicking on the path's name in the palette and choosing Make Selection) in case he needed to make additional color corrections later. ∎

Turning Images into Texture

■ *by Talitha Harper*

THE IMAGERY ITSELF is secondary for Margaret Carsello of Carsello Creative, Inc., in Hinsdale, Ill. She concentrates on color and texture when she designs a collage, using Adobe Photoshop's Duotone function and layering modes to turn scanned photography and public domain illustrations into textural elements that enhance the brushwork of her hand-painted backgrounds.

But that's not to say Carsello chooses graphics haphazardly. "I build a strong background surface before I put any specific imagery down," she says, "and I put a lot of time and thought and research into the pieces I add to a collage." Selecting the imagery was a particularly demanding process when Carsello was asked to design a scrapbook cover for Whim Wham, Inc., because the client wanted Carsello to weave together a wide range of topics — and restrictions were placed on almost all the subjects that were to be illustrated. The scrapbook was targeted to high school students, and Whim Wham wanted Carsello's collage to include everything from sports and schoolwork to ecological awareness and romance. But sports had to be depicted as an opportunity for personal fulfillment, not a school activity, and education had to be shown at its most exciting (no pencils or stacks of books allowed). Allusions to the environment had to avoid regionalism, and symbols of romance had to be subtle and "unmushy."

Margaret Carsello strives to bring "a fine arts feel" to her Photoshop collage work. She starts with a hand-painted background and converts many of the photos she uses to duotones so that she can control the color precisely when she builds the composition.

1 Carsello worked with brushes, brayer, and palette knife to build up texture in the acrylic painting she created as a background for the collage.

2 To intensify the texture in the background, Carsello scanned a public domain pattern (only a small swatch of the design is shown) and a photo she had taken of a deserted beach. Although she relies on a professional scan to maintain the color of the background painting, Carsello isn't so cautious with the photos she adds to a collage. "I use my desktop scanner for them," she says. "But then, I know I can use the modes to pull color from the background into the imagery."

3 Layering the pattern over the background in Lighten mode at 60 percent opacity leached color from the base painting. And setting the sand photo (on the right side of the canvas in the center) to Saturation mode added a rippled texture to the background color.

4 A stylized emblem, drawn in Illustrator, was placed in the center of the collage. After opening the Illustrator image in a separate Photoshop file, Carsello copied it into a new channel and inverted. She activated the channel selection, used the Command key and the marquee tool to deselect half the emblem, and gave the remaining half a gradient fill. She repeated the process to apply a gradient to the other half of the design (left). The selection was loaded into the composite channel and filled with color (center). Finally, Carsello pasted the emblem into a new layer in the collage file and chose Overlay in the Layers palette to make the color in the emblem interact dramatically with the background (right).

❶

❷

❸

❹

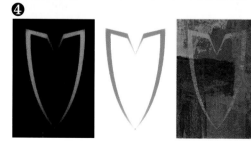

CONTROLLING COLOR

Carsello's collage work always begins with a hand-painted oil or acrylic background, and the colors she chooses for the painting dominate the entire composition. "Color is such an important part of my work, I need client approval from the beginning," Carsello says. "I can't afford to have the client come back later and tell me, 'I don't like orange.'" So she talks to the client at length before creating the background painting to find out what mood the piece should express — and to get the client's opinion about the colors that suggest that mood. And once she paints the background, Carsello shows the painting to the client before she proceeds with the collage work to make sure the palette is acceptable ❶.

Because color is vital to Carsello, she sends the painting to a color separation house for drum scanning. "I can't trust the accuracy of a desktop scanner," she says. The shop converts the scan to a CMYK Photoshop file, which Carsello uses as the backdrop for the collage. She also asks the separation shop to provide a color proof, and she refers to the proof rather than the monitor when she makes additional color choices.

Many of the images Carsello adds to a collage are scans of public domain line art, drawn in black-and-white, and when she adds color to the drawings, she uses swatch books to choose tones that enhance the colors in the proof. To color the illustrations, Carsello opens each scanned image in Photoshop, converts it to CMYK mode, and places the image into an alpha channel by selecting the black channel in the Channels palette and choosing Duplicate Channel from the palette's pop-out menu. Working in the duplicate channel, she uses the Invert command (Image, Map, Invert or Command-I) to turn the black linework into a white-filled selection area. Then she returns to the composite channel, selects all, and deletes, producing an empty white canvas. Finally, Carsello loads the channel selection and Option-deletes to fill it with the foreground color. ☞ *To load a Photoshop selection channel without going through the Select, Load Selection submenu, Option-click on the channel's name in the Channels palette or press the Command and Option keys, along with the number key for the channel you want to load.* ☞ *You can work within Photoshop's Layers palette (rather than channels) to add color to a black-and-white scan. First, place the scan on its own layer and use the magic wand tool and the Select, Similar command to select the black tones. Then choose New Layer from the Layers palette. The magic wand selection will be active in the new (empty) layer, and you can press Option-delete to fill the selection with the foreground color. As a last step, delete the layer that holds the original black-and-white art. (If you don't move to a new layer to fill the selection — and simply change the color on the black-and-white layer instead — some anti-aliased edges from the black-and-white image will remain.)*

"It's easy to control the color in line art," says Carsello, "but color photos are more challenging." So she often uses Photoshop's Duotone function to reduce the range of tones before pasting the image into the collage. She selects Mode, Duotone (first converting the image to grayscale so she can access the Duotone function) and works through the Duotone Curves dialog box to recolor the photo, referring to the color proof as she selects tones from a swatch book. (She doesn't need to convert the image back to CMYK; the conversion takes place automatically when the duotone is pasted into the CMYK collage.)

ASSEMBLING THE COLLAGE

Once Carsello is satisfied with the color in individual images, she's ready to begin constructing the collage. The first images she adds to the composition are chosen to intensify the texture of the painted background ❷, and she often manipulates the layer mode settings so that only the texture of the graphics — without their color — is incorporated into the design ❸.

As she builds the collage, Carsello refers to a pencil sketch, created early in the process, when the images were selected. "I always do a rough sketch for placement, but positions change once I start assembling the images because of the way colors affect each other," she says. ☞ *To select a layered element in Photoshop without its transparent background, activate the layer and press Command-Option-T. To reposition a layered element without selecting it, activate the layer and press the V key to access the move tool.*

Carsello usually works from the center of the design out, selecting images from the individual Photoshop files and pasting each one onto a new layer in the collage document. With the line art, she can activate the channel selection (which she created when she colored the image) to produce clean-edged selections ❹. But with the photos, she uses the Select, Feather command to give the selection soft edges that will fade into the background ❺. "I go by eye when I set the feathering," she says. "I usually start with a 10-pixel feather and then add more if I need it."

After arranging the imagery, Carsello fine-tunes the color by experimenting with the layer modes ❻. She finishes a piece by adding a few accent elements to bring highlight colors to the composition ❼, choosing Normal mode to retain the original color of the pasted-in image ❽. ■

❺

❻

❼

❽

5 Photos were pasted into the collage in Normal mode at 100 percent opacity so that Carsello could see them clearly as she positioned them. Several of the photos began as rectangular selections, but Carsello used the lasso tool to delete "chunks" from some of the rectangles to keep images from overlapping too much.

6 Carsello used several different layer mode settings (at opacities of about 50 to 80 percent) for the photos, choosing Hard Light for the flower and CD discs (for an effect similar to Normal, but with "electrified" color), Color for the woman's eye (so that only the colored pixels, with none of the whites, were added to the collage), Overlay for the sea urchins, soccer ball, and computer keyboard (to preserve detail in the photos but pick up color from the background), Multiply for the basketball photo (so that tonality in the photo was used to intensify background tones), and Normal for the musical notes and the clock face.

7 Scanned line drawings were layered into the collage at 70 to 100 percent opacity to add accent color. Carsello also used the words *Awareness, Love, Peace, Future,* and *Friendship* to bring more color to the design, typing each word on its own layer and then adjusting the layer's opacity.

8 Carsello chose Normal as the layer mode for most of the line art in the collage. An exception was the drawing of a group of Egyptian women. Setting the image to Overlay mode held fine lines that would have been lost in Normal mode and softened the densest tones in the illustration.

Art In Progress

■ *by Sara Booth*

WHEN CLIENTS BEGAN ASKING for photos that looked like paintings, Judy L. Miller knew it was time for her self-promotions to reflect her skill in this area. The Tucson, Ariz., illustrator is best known for photo manipulation and photocollage, but she had developed a Photoshop filter sequence to produce a painterly effect, and her collage techniques helped her put together an image that communicates the whole photo-to-electronic-paint process.

Miller began by lining up the four scans that she would combine to make up the collage ❶. She took a photograph of the sunflowers on color transparency film, then had it professionally drum scanned. But for the canvas texture, frame, and paintbrush (complete with yellow paint), she simply placed each item directly on her scanner bed. "Depending on the object, I can take a scan that's as sharp as a photo or sharper," she says. "And sometimes for a project, there's not time to wait for film processing."

"Often, art directors want to use a photo, but they want it to look more artful," says Tucson, Ariz., illustrator Judy L. Miller. Miller used a variety of Photoshop filters to achieve the look of painting and sketching, then used layer masks and other photo compositing techniques to create a self-promotional collage.

1 Miller opened her scans in Photoshop and chose Filter, Sharpen, Unsharp Mask, setting the Amount to between 35 and 50 pixels. She prefers highlights to contain three to five percent color, so she chose Image, Adjust, Curves (Command-M) and adjusted the curve, checking the readings in the Info palette.

CREATING ELECTRONIC PAINT

The first step in producing the "watercolor" effect was to reduce the resolution of the sunflower photo from the original 350 pixels per inch to 250 ppi by choosing Image, Image Size and entering a new resolution. By removing some of the sharpness of the scan, this resampling gave her softer results from her filters. (Most Photoshop users avoid resampling because it can damage sharpness, but for this image, that loss of sharpness was actually the goal.)

Miller tried a variety of filter effects, applying them to a copy of her image cropped to 2 inches square to speed her work and keeping a record of her settings, until she got the results she wanted to use on her final image. She used the Noise, Facet, and Gaussian Blur filters, as well as the Angled Strokes filter from Adobe Gallery Effects, to give the image the appearance of paint ❷.

FINE-TUNING COLOR

The resulting image had the softness Miller wanted, but the color needed work. She first chose Image, Adjust, Hue/Saturation (Command-U). While Master was checked, she dragged the Lightness slider to +31 to lighten the image overall. Then she cooled down the greens (by choosing the green component and dragging the Hue slider to +50) and warmed up the yellows (by choosing the yellow component and dragging the Hue slider to -6).

Miller had a background color in mind, chosen from a spot color swatchbook. After defining that color as her foreground color, she used the pen tool to outline the flowers, converted the path to a selection, inversed the selection (Filter, Select, Inverse) to select the fabric background, and chose Edit, Fill. She filled the background with her custom color, setting the opacity at 45% and the mode to Color so that the background would take on the chosen hue and saturation but keep its original gray values. ☞ *Feathering Photoshop selections, even with an amount as small as 1 pixel, can make transitions smoother. If you use the selection icon at the bottom of the Paths palette, rather than choosing Make Selection from the palette's popout menu, Photoshop normally doesn't give you the opportunity to feather your selection. But pressing the Option key as you drag a path onto the selection icon will open the Make Selection dialog box, where you can set the desired feather.*

Next, Miller adjusted the color in the centers of the sunflowers: She first used the magic wand to select the centers of the sunflowers (setting the tolerance to about 35 pixels so the wand would pick up most, but not all, of the centers), then opened the Hue/Saturation dialog box and dragged the Hue slider to -31. Then she chose Image, Adjust, Color Balance (Command-Y) and dragged the top slider toward the red side.

To adjust the entire image, Miller chose Image, Adjust, Curves (Command-M) and dragged the center of the curve downward to lighten the image

2 To produce a painted effect, Miller used a series of filters: Add Noise with an Amount of 25 pixels (top left), Facet (top right), Gaussian Blur with a Radius of 2 pixels (bottom left), and Gallery Effects Angled Strokes (bottom right).

❷

overall while keeping darker shadows. Then, seeing that the shadow-to-midtone balance still didn't satisfy her, she chose Image, Adjust, Variations, selected Shadows, and chose a lighter version of the image. Finally, she opened the Hue/Saturation dialog box again to boost saturation overall; this gave her a final result she was happy with ❸.

Miller now returned to the original sunflower file, applied the Find Edges filter ❹, and saved the resulting image as *Line Drawing* so she could use it to add definition to the painting ❺. She saved this file with the name *Painting*. ☞ *To create a new Photoshop layer as you paste from the clipboard, choose Edit, Paste Layer.*

CREATING THE COMPOSITE PAINTING

Next, Miller opened her scanned canvas, copied it to the clipboard, and pasted it into a new layer in the *Line Drawing* image, setting its mode to Darken so only its shadows would be added, creating the look of texture. She used the line tool to add a graph-paper grid ❻. Knowing that registration on lines this small could become "a printer's nightmare" if she used more than one color, she chose 100 percent cyan as her foreground color. She set the line width to 1 pixel and varied the opacity, creating the impression of graph paper.

Different opacity settings produced lines that appeared thicker or thinner. Holding down the Shift key constrained the lines to vertical and horizontal. She saved this file as *Sketch*.

To combine the two into a final composite painting, Miller copied the *Sketch* image to the clipboard. Then she opened the *Painting* image and used the lasso to select areas where she wanted the sketch to show. Using the Edit, Paste Into command, she pasted the sketch into selections until she had the look she wanted ❼ and saved the file as *Composite Painting*. Finally, Miller used the Image Size dialog box to sample the image back up to its original resolution so that all the elements of the collage would have the same resolution. ☞ *If you repeatedly use a Photoshop function for which there is no keyboard shortcut, you can add it to a custom Commands palette. First display the palette by choosing Window, Palette, Show Commands. Then choose New Command from the palette's popout menu, choose your desired command, and assign it to an unassigned function key.*

PUTTING IT ALL TOGETHER

Returning to the original sunflower photo, Miller drew a path to crop the image, made of straight

❸

❹

❺

❻

❼

3 Miller used a variety of Photoshop's color and contrast adjustment tools to lighten the painting overall while boosting the impact of some of the colors.

4 She applied the Find Edges filter (Filter, Stylize, Find Edges) to the sunflower photo and saved the resulting file as *Line Drawing.* It would be used both for the "sketch" in the center of the image and to add details to the painted image.

5 To restore detail lost in the filter process, Miller made a new layer in the painting image, copied the *Line Drawing* file, and pasted it on the new layer, setting its mode to Darken and its opacity to 55%.

6 A canvas texture and a grid transformed the *Line Drawing* file into a "sketch."

7 Miller initially intended to use more of the sketch in her final painting, but "it was getting too confusing," she said.

segments except where it followed the curve of a leaf. Turning the path into a selection, she chose Select, Inverse and deleted everything outside the selection, then rotated the image before adding a layer mask (by choosing Add Layer Mask from the popout menu of the Layers palette) filled with a black-to-white blend to fade the edges. She saved this as a new document called *Final.* ☞ *To view a layer's mask in Photoshop, rather than the layer itself, Option-click the mask thumbnail.*

The next step was to copy the composite painting into *Layer 2* of the *Final* file. Miller wanted the painting to appear to be moving into the frame. So she chose Image, Effects, Scale to stretch it horizontally, then chose Image, Effects, Perspective and adjusted the perspective.

Miller opened her picture frame scan and drew a path outlining it, making subpaths for carved-out areas. She turned the path into a selection and copied the frame, pasting it into *Layer 3* of the *Final* file. A layer mask was used to make the left side of the frame fade out. Similarly, she used a path to outline the paintbrush she had scanned, then pasted into *Layer 4* with a layer mask.

To add a shadow behind the paintbrush, Miller duplicated the paintbrush layer, checked Preserve Transparency in the Layers palette, then filled the layer with 100 percent black. To soften the edge, she deselected Preserve Transparency and applied the Gaussian Blur filter, setting the radius to 8 pixels. She rotated the shadow layer, placed it behind the paintbrush layer (by dragging its icon down in the Layers palette), and set its opacity to 30% and its mode to Multiply. ☞ *Like many of Photoshop's filters, the Gaussian Blur filter behaves differently depending on the image's resolution. High-resolution images require a higher pixel setting to achieve the same degree of softness.* ∎

PHOTOSHOP
Controlling Transparency

■ *by Michael Ryznar*

In a series of insect drawings, I combined traditional hand-drawing techniques with Photoshop work. For each piece, I spent four hours on the pen-and-ink drawing and four hours adding color in Photoshop.

PHOTOSHOP LAYERS are a great time saver, but going a step beyond layers can speed up your work even more. Little-known shortcuts offer precise, pixel-by-pixel control over how the layers interact in the final illustration. For a series of insect drawings for the pond life section of Science World British Columbia's "Mine Games" exhibition, I used layer masks, blend controls, and layer transparency to add color to scanned pen-and-ink drawings. Without the computer, the project would have taken much longer, and some of the effects couldn't have been accomplished at all.

The first step was to scan the ink drawing and place it on its own layer ❶. I then created a new layer below the linework where I could paint color. A layer mask kept the color inside the boundaries of the black linework, allowing me to paint freely without worrying about the paint going outside the lines — but when I made the mask, I wanted to be certain that the black linework would cover the "seam" between the color areas and the white background. So I set a high tolerance in the Magic Wand Options palette and checked the Antialiasing box. When I clicked on the white background, the wand made a selection a pixel or two from the edge of the black linework ❷. ☞ *To open the Options palette for a selected tool, press Return.*

To use this selection to create a layer mask, I activated the color layer and chose Add Layer Mask from the popout menu of the Layers palette. I Option-clicked the layer mask icon in the Layers palette to display the mask rather than the layer. Then I switched to the Channels palette and selected the Layer 1 Mask channel (Command-~). The magic wand selection was still active, so I

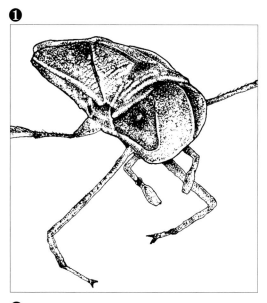

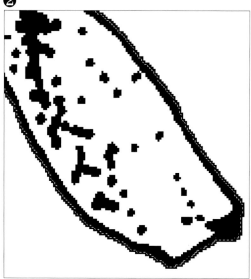

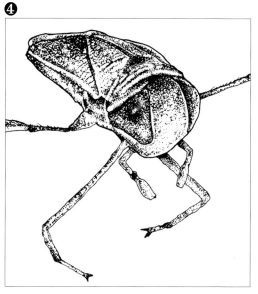

1 I drew the water boatman (an aquatic insect) in pen-and-ink and scanned it at 300 dpi. After opening the line art in Photoshop, I converted it to RGB mode.

2 Before adding color, I used the magic wand tool, with antialiasing turned on, to select the background. I usually set the tolerance for 130 to 200 pixels. Because of this high tolerance, the selection overlapped the line art by one or two pixels, so the linework would trap the color.

3 I added color with the airbrush, varying the brush size and the pressure setting (using brushes between 17 and 65 pixels in diameter) and working generally from dark to light. The layer mask cropped away colors outside the boundary.

4 After checking Preserve Transparency in the Layers palette, I airbrushed a white highlight and a bit of the red background color onto the linework layer. The airbrush affected only the black pixels, leaving the transparent areas unchanged.

typed *X* to return the foreground and background colors to their default black and white, then pressed Option-Delete to fill the selection with black.

On the linework layer, I wanted all the white areas to be transparent so the color would show through. I double-clicked the layer's icon in the Layers palette to open the Layer Options dialog box. On the This Layer scale in the Blend If area, I dragged the right slider from 255 to 254. This made the white areas transparent. ☞ *The Blend If sliders in Photoshop control a layer (when they are accessed through the Layer Options dialog box) or a floating selection (when accessed by choosing Select, Float Controls). ☞ The Blend If sliders can be used to make all pixels with a certain brightness value transparent, either in the active layer or selection or in the background. Entering 254 on the top slider, for example, makes the pixels with a value of 255 (white) transparent by instructing Photoshop to take information for those pixels from the background, rather than from the active layer or selection.*

Finally, I airbrushed the background colors onto the color layer **3**. ☞ *When Photoshop's airbrush tool is active, the pressure can be changed by typing a number: 1 for 10%, 2 for 20%, and so on. For 100% pressure, type 0.*

To add a highlight and a little color to the insect's eye, I activated the linework layer and checked the Preserve Transparency box in the Layers palette. Ordinarily, the airbrush sprays the foreground color over all pixels, even transparent ones. With the Preserve Transparency box on, the airbrush only affected the non-transparent pixels on the target layer **4**. ■

The Human Touch

■ *by Sara Booth*

FOR MOST DESIGNERS, indexed color mode is a compromise — a way to reduce the color depth of an image for multimedia, animation, or other applications for which 8-bit color is standard. But for Albuquerque designer Maggie Macnab, indexed color is a way to transform a grayscale image into unexpected color combinations. When the American Society of Radiologic Technologists hired Macnab to design a poster for its annual convention, the headline, "Technology with a Human Touch," was already chosen. So Macnab used custom color tables to give a lively glow to X-rays of a hand and a seashell.

After having the X-rays drum scanned, Macnab opened the hand and shell files separately, so that she could apply a different custom color table to each one. Photoshop used these tables to map a color to each shade of gray ❶. ☞ *Any Photoshop image can be used to create a custom color table. First convert the image to indexed color mode (choosing Adaptive in the Palette area), then choose Mode, Color Table and click Save.*

To add a glow to the shell, Macnab selected it with the lasso, chose Select, Modify, Expand, feathered the selection, and filled with pink. A similar technique was used to add a halo around the small letters that spelled out the conference dates ❷.

"Of course, it would be a violation of medical ethics to X-ray somebody's hand just for a poster," says Albuquerque designer Maggie Macnab. So when she needed an X-ray for a poster for the American Society of Radiologic Technologists, Macnab went to Bob Fosbinder, head of radiology at the University of New Mexico School of Medicine, who gave her access to the school's teaching images and also X-rayed a seashell for the project. Custom color tables were used to map color to the grayscale X-rays in Photoshop, and a bit of the resulting color image was applied as a pattern to scanned calligraphy.

To combine the hand and shell, Macnab first used the lasso to select the shell and delete the background. She copied the shell into a new layer in the hand document, rotated it, and resized it using the Image, Effects, Scale command, then dragged it into place and saved the selection as a channel. To mask out the area where the fore-finger overlaps the shell, she displayed the hand layer, then loaded the shell channel. Switching to Quick Mask mode, she used the paintbrush to paint out areas of the selection, then returned to the shell layer, copied, and pasted the shell onto the hand layer. ☞ *To toggle between normal and Quick Mask modes, type the letter* q.

The next step was to make channels that would be used to darken the background. To create the "1996" behind the hand, Macnab set numerals in Illustrator, chose Type, Create Outlines, used the scale tool to distort the numbers, then pasted them into Photoshop and saved the selection. To add a shadow to the hand and shell, she loaded the selections, expanded and feathered, then saved the new selection. She loaded the number and shadow selections, subtracted the original hand and shell selections, and filled the resulting selection with black at 20% opacity. Finally, she added the headline, hand-lettered by Albuquerque calligrapher Fred Yost, and filled it with a pattern ❸. ∎

❶

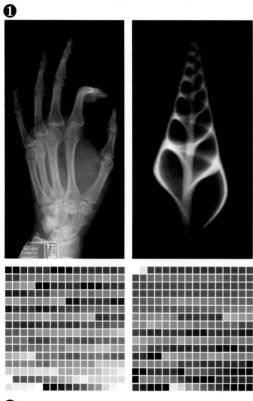

❷

❸

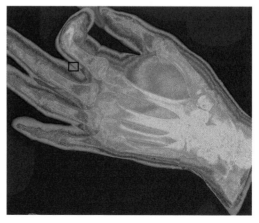

1 Macnab has gotten a variety of custom color tables from fellow designer and computer enthusiast Paul Gallegos. To add color to X-rays, she converted them to indexed color mode, then chose Mode, Color Table and clicked the Load button to load a color table.

2 Macnab set the type in Illustrator, placed it in Photoshop, and saved the selection as a channel. To add a glow, she chose Select, Modify, Expand to broaden the selection, then Select, Feather to soften it. She loaded the original letter selection again, choosing Subtract From Selection in the Load Selection dialog box to select only the glow, then filled the selection with the glow color. To add a highlight, she chose Select, Modify, Contract, feathered slightly, and filled with her highlight color.

3 To add texture to the calligraphy, Macnab selected a rectangle of the green glow around the hand and chose Edit, Define Pattern. Then she loaded the headline selection and filled it with this pattern. A diagonal blue area became a subtle stripe.

Perfection is easy to achieve on the computer, but messiness is a bit more of a challenge. To make a poster look like a wall of sloppily glued handbills, Michael Holmes took advantage of Photoshop's ability to show part of a layer (with layer masks) or a ghost of a layer (with layer transparency).

PHOTOSHOP

Masks for Partial Transparency

■ *by Sara Booth*

WHEN MICHAEL HOLMES began working on a promotional poster for a new multimedia firm, Eagle River Interactive, he wanted an image with "the feel of a Soviet propaganda wall" — layers of posters, roughly attached with glue. So he attacked royalty-free sources using Photoshop's layers and masks to create a multi-layered, multi-textured poster.

Holmes began with an image from the Bolshevik Posters CD from Planet Art: three frames of a shouting man's face. After using the rubber stamp tool to remove part of the Cyrillic lettering at the bottom of the illustration and adding the firm name and a slogan, he copied the image onto a new layer, which he named *Top Poster*. Returning to the background layer, he opened the Levels dialog box (Image, Adjust, Levels or Command-L) and dragged the gray input slider to the left, darkening the entire image.

The next step was to create a layer mask that would allow this darker version to show through, creating the effect of brushed-on glue. On Photo/Graphic Edges from Auto F/X, a CD of edge effects intended to be applied to photographs, Holmes found an edge effect that could serve as a starting point.

Since Holmes wanted to use the brushstroke effect at large scale, he retrieved the image at the highest resolution available on the CD, then copied it into a new channel and began manipulating to get the rough look he wanted ❶. Then he added a mask to the *Top Poster* layer, activated the mask, loaded the new channel he had created, and filled with black ❷.

Once a single copy of the faces image was saved in grayscale, the next step was to multiply the image for the final poster. Holmes created a new document the size of the full-size poster. He first tried simply filling it with several copies of the image, but he found the repetition too obvious. So he went back to the original file and saved several duplicates. In each of the copies, he reflected the layer mask — vertically in one, horizontally in another, and along both axes in the third. When he flattened the images and combined them, the different edges gave a random effect.

The text used in the center of the poster was typed in an Illustrator file. Holmes placed this file on its own layer above the background, called *Type,* then began to work on giving the layer different levels of opacity. His goal was to make the central section look like a handbill that was saturated with glue and placed haphazardly on the wall by someone in too much of a hurry to be concerned with perfect adhesion.

Holmes copied the layer mask he had used in the faces image and applied it as a layer mask to the *Type* layer, making some adjustments for variety. A second copy of the *Type* layer, set at 40% opacity and without a mask, boosted the white, making the text stand out. ☞ *To copy a layer mask from one Photoshop file to another, display both files, then activate the masks (by Option-clicking their icons in the Layers palette). Select All in your source document, then drag and drop into your target document. When you drop the floating selection, the copied image will become a layer mask.*

Holmes wanted one area at the bottom of the white section to look as though it stood away from the wall, so he used Photoshop's selection tools to make a selection that was feathered in some areas and not in others ❸. Similarly, he created the crease along the middle of the white section by airbrushing into a selection with a feather of 10 on one side and a feather of 2 on the other. ■

❶

❷

❸

1 To create the layer mask used on the faces in the background, Holmes began with a border from Auto F/X's Photo/Graphic Edges CD. By the time he had finished with it — cloning some sections, airbrushing out others — it looked as though it had been painted with a wallpaper brush.

2 Holmes applied his mask to the image, then placed a darkened copy of the same image on a layer behind the first image. Bits of the dark image show in the brush-strokes around the edges.

3 To simulate a raised edge, Holmes needed to place a soft shadow under the white outline of the paper. He first used the lasso, with a feather of 10 to 15 pixels, to select a rough area. Then he set the lasso's feather to 0 and used the Command key to delete an area from the selection. Once this area was selected, he used the airbrush tool to brush a shadow into the area, using a metal ruler on his pressure-sensitive tablet to guide his hand along a straight line.

Feathered selections, low opacity settings, layer masks, and Photoshop blending modes were used to merge the various elements used in this poster, made up of images from Planet Art's European Posters CD-ROM. The headline and tagline were imported from Illustrator and treated with a glow and a drop shadow, respectively, built up with three layers in Overlay mode.

■ *by Jack Davis and Linnea Dayton*

Making Montages

1 The train was separated from its background using Select, Color Range, then dragged and dropped to make a new layer above the alpine background. In a new layer between train and background, the train's transparency mask was loaded as a selection (Command-Option-T); the selection was feathered and filled for a glow.

2 The Matterhorn image was dragged, dropped, and scaled to fit over part of the train. A layer mask was added. With the layer mask active but the main image in view, mask-building began with a feathered lasso selection. Black streaks were added to the mask with the airbrush at low opacity to let the train show through the slopes.

ECOND ONLY TO CHOOSING the right composition to communicate an idea, the most important factor in making a successful photo montage is what happens at the edges where the parts blend. A smooth but dynamic merging of images can make the difference between a unified, effective collage and an awkward "cut and pasted" look.

To make a traditional vignette, you can frame the subject with the ellipse or rectangle selection tool with a feathered border. For objects with smoothly rounded edges, the pen tool does a good job of silhouetting. For elements with detailed or straight-edged outlines, the lasso with the Option key is ideal. For subjects that are very different from their background, you can select (or at least begin the selection) with the magic wand or the Select, Color Range command. In some cases the selection may be almost ready-made in one of the individual color channels (red, green, or blue). ☞ *To shrink a selection to eliminate any fringe of background around the edges, load the selection and choose Select, Modify, Contract. Or, if your selection is saved as an alpha channel, use the Gaussian Blur filter to soften the edge, adjust the contrast (with Image, Adjust, Brightness/Contrast) to reduce the blur to an antialiasing effect, and then move the Brightness slider to the left to shrink the white part of the mask.*

To put the elements together in the montage, a feather at the selection border or a layer mask can help blend the images. A gradient mask lets objects fade at one edge. And hand-painting a mask can soften edges or create a ghosting effect so that one object seems to float partly in front of and partly behind another. For more global layer effects, adjust transparency — overall (with the Opacity control) or to create special blending effects (with the Layer Options dialog box).

For this image advertising a series of posters, the first step was to look at the resources the client had provided in Photo CD format. Rather than copy and montage half a dozen rectangular posters, a better approach seemed to be to isolate elements from several posters and combine them. Looking at thumbnails of the posters inspired several sketches, experiments with contrasts in color, size, and shape. With the elements selected and dimensions of the final image set, the layout began to take shape. The general flow of the piece would be down and to the right, with elements arranged to sweep the viewer's attention into the center. Under this scheme, some elements fell into place almost automatically — the driver, for instance, would fit well only in the lower right corner, and the cigarettes were a natural for the lower left. ■

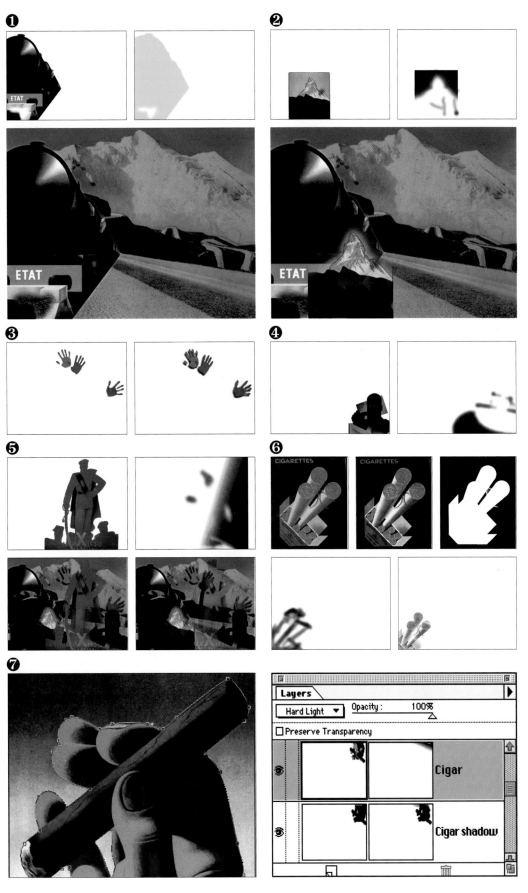

3 Shadows for the hands were created on a layer between the hands and the Matterhorn by loading the transparency mask for the hands, filling the selection with black, blurring the layer slightly, setting the Opacity to 75 percent, and then choosing the move tool and pressing arrow keys to offset the shadows down and left.

4 A feathered lasso was used to make the shape that masks the driver's lower left corner. "Transparency" was airbrushed into the wind-shield with layered strokes of low-opacity black paint.

5 The general and the man with the pipe were both masked with black-to-white gradients made by dragging the gradient tool over short distances. For the general, black and white strokes were added the mask to cre-ate ghosting. When the blending mode for the layer was changed from Normal (left) to Hard Light (right), the ghosting effect was complete.

6 The first step in selecting the cigarettes was to use Image, Adjust, Levels to in-crease the contrast. The Se-lect, Color Range command in the red channel created a fairly good outline, which was stored in a new channel and improved further by blurring, increasing contrast to sharpen the edge, and re-ducing brightness to choke the white area. Low-opacity airbrushing on the mask and setting the layer's mode to Hard Light completed the ghosting effect.

7 The curves of the hand holding the cigar made it an ideal candidate for selection with the pen tool. It was dropped into the image file and rotated to fit the com-position. A mask and a masked shadow on the layer below allowed this element to be composited in Hard Light without the black shadow showing through the hand.

Imitating Paint and Canvas

■ *by Jack Davis and Linnea Dayton*

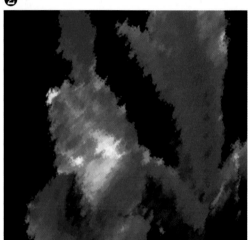

PHOTOSHOP FILTERS such as Facet and Crystallize and third-party filters such as Gallery Effects and Paint Alchemy can automatically create some pretty amazing painterly effects. But no single filter provides control over all of the attributes you might like to include in a painting: the gestural brushstrokes, the built-up texture of thickly applied paints, and the texture of the white canvas that shows through in areas where paint is thin or absent.

You can do it all in Photoshop, though, with the right combination of filters. ☞ *Painterly filters and lighting effects can be RAM- and time-hogs. If you plan to do a lot of this kind of imitation of natural media, it would be worth investigating MetaCreations Painter, which has built-in, easy-to-use functions for a wide variety of painterly effects.*

To turn a stock photo in Kodak Photo CD format (from Digital Stock Corporation's *Flowers* CD-ROM) into a painting, we used version 1.0.2 of Xaos Tools' Paint Alchemy filter, which is included on the CD-ROM that comes with *The Photoshop 3 Wow! Book,* to produce brushstrokes. (The new Paint Alchemy 2 filter is faster and has an easier-to-use interface and more preset brush functions.) We used Photoshop's Lighting Effects filter to give the strokes the thickness of paint. Finally, we applied the Offset filter and Lighting Effects again to make and apply the custom canvas texture. ☞ *Don't miss the 75 tiling patterns in the Textures folder (inside the Goodies folder on the Adobe Photoshop Deluxe CD-ROM).* ∎

1 We applied Image, Adjust, Auto Levels to adjust the tonal range and Image, Adjust, Variations to push midtones toward magenta.

2 To "paint" the photo, we applied the Paint Alchemy filter, using the Oil Canvas Wide style and the Oil Tip brush, and leaving Color, Size, Angle, and Transparency at their defaults.

3 We studied color channels by turning off the Channels palette's eye icon for all but one channel at a time. The green channel held the most brushstroke detail.

4 The Lighting Effects filter "embossed" the brushstrokes: We used a Spotlight with a wide focus to add drama, choosing green as the Texture Channel and turning off White Is High, since we wanted to raise the paint above the white canvas. We used a low Height so the paint wouldn't look too thick.

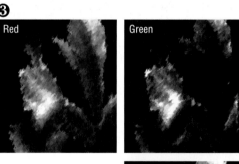

Red

Green

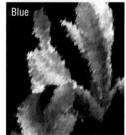

Blue

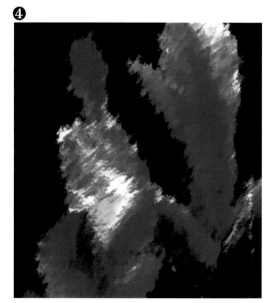

❺ ❻

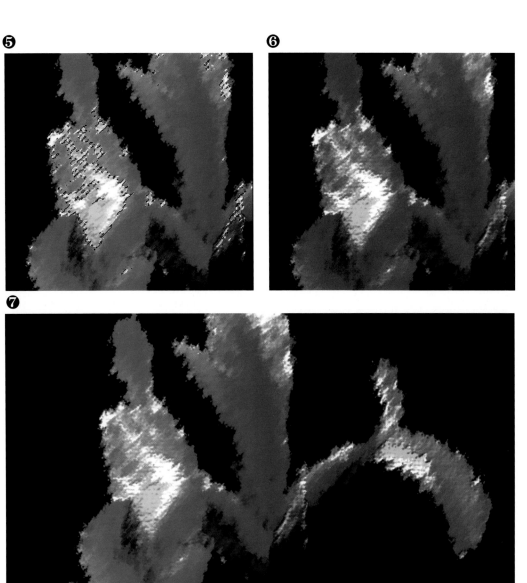

❼

5 We scanned a small piece of canvas, selected a square of it, and used the Offset filter to reveal "seams" so we could eliminate them by cloning with the rubber stamp. We clicked the New Channel icon at the bottom left of the Channels palette to make an alpha channel to hold the canvas texture. We activated the new channel (by clicking its name in the Channels palette or pressing Command-channel number) and applied the Render, Texture Fill filter, choosing our canvas as the fill pattern.

6 We wanted to select white areas of the image so that when we applied the Lighting Effects filter again, the canvas texture would appear only there. Sometimes — as in this case — we can make this kind of a selection just by choosing the best color channel and loading it as a selection (here, we loaded the green channel by typing Command-Option-3). If none of the channels had made a good selection of the white areas, we could have chosen Select, Color Range and clicked the left eyedropper on a white area.

7 We used Lighting Effects again, this time turning on White Is High (since white areas of the canvas texture were the raised areas), reducing the Height even more, and setting channel 4 as the Texture Channel. (The Lighting Effects preview shows the effect over the entire preview area, not just in selected areas. When we applied the texture, the preview showed it just as strongly in painted areas; but after the filter was used, the image showed a much stronger canvas texture in the selected white spaces.)

Maximum Masking

■ *by Steve Greenberg*

A WHILE AGO a client of mine asked me if I could do a shoot involving a Slinky. It would have been a good project for my digital camera, but by the time the concept made it to his client, the creative direction had changed. The idea of a Slinky shot still appealed to me, and when I had a break in the action at the studio I decided to put it to pixel.

The first thing I did was brave the toy stores a week before Christmas to find a Slinky. To thin out the crowds a bit, I yelled from deep in the aisles, "I found a Tickle-Me Elmo!" and I had the checkout counters to myself.

The next step was to shoot the Slinky. (Did you know that they're made of plastic nowadays? But my 5-year-old can still tangle one up in less than five seconds.) To keep my sanity and take advantage of the wonderful world of digital cameras, I used a bluescreen set. The bluescreen paint is manufactured by Rosco and is the same paint used in the movie and television industries. I shot several pictures with the Slinky in shapes that

interested me, then ran the files through Photo-Fusion, a Photoshop plug-in that makes it easy to generate bluescreen silhouettes.

I decided to test-drive the new Photoshop 4.0 for this job. (It's always a good idea to learn new software when a client isn't sitting next to you.) I wanted to try out the new Free Transform command. To me this is the most important improvement in 4.0, and I used it every time I needed to move, rotate, or resize an element.

I started out with a yellow-filled background layer — because this was going to be a portfolio piece, I picked a color that worked well with my existing "portfolio palette." The next thing I did was to bring the S-shaped Slinky shot in on its own layer. I also made a layer mask (using the channel generated by PhotoFusion) so that I could use the Slinky's silhouette and shadow. Each element I added would have its own layer and layer mask from now on.

The red Slinky was next. The colors were not sending me yet, so I decided to start having fun. I started playing with the blending modes for the *S*

❶

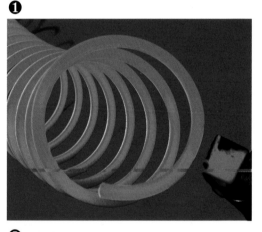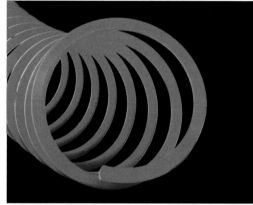

1 I shot several photos of a Slinky on a bluescreen, then used the PhotoFusion plug-in to silhouette them. The difference between PhotoFusion and just using Photoshop's magic wand tool is that PhotoFusion removes only the blue from the image and not the shadow detail, whereas the magic wand would remove everything.

❷

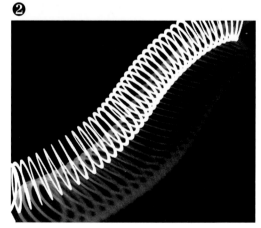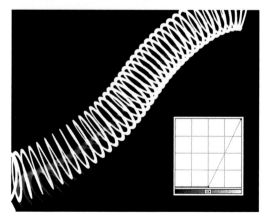

2 I played around with the color on the *S*-shaped Slinky shot, but its shadow was still gray and I thought it would be nice if that had some color too. I duplicated the layer mask for the *S* shape layer, calling the new channel *Duplicate.* I then went into the original layer mask and called up my Curves controls (Image, Adjust, Curves or Command-M). I brought the shadow end of the curve to the center. This drove all of the gray areas (the shadow) to black.

shape, and decided to use Exclusion. Now I was getting some funky color. This is why I chose to use Photoshop instead of Live Picture: You can't do layer manipulations in Live Picture.

Once I'd figured out a way to use channels to select only the shadow of the *S* shape so I could do some color manipulation, I had most of the image done except for the space in the upper left. I held a Slinky in front of my screen and decided what shape I wanted, then went back to the digital camera and shot it, then placed it on its own layer with a mask. I set the opacity to 12% and used the Multiply layer mode. Nice, but why not another? So I duplicated the layer and moved it over a bit. I also changed its hue and saturation with the Image, Adjust, Hue/Saturation dialog box. ■

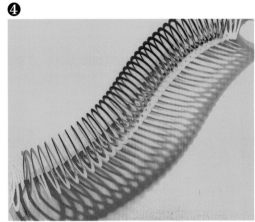

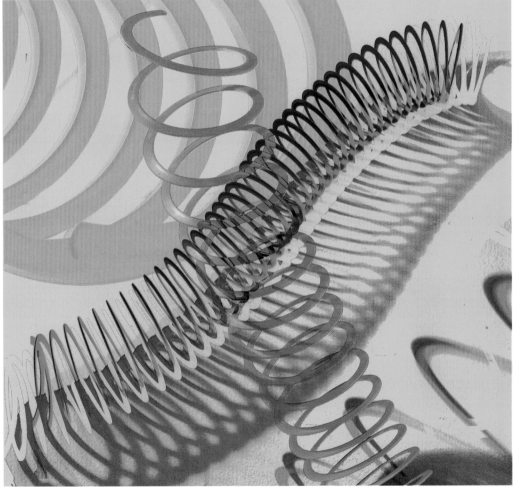

3 Now that I had created a mask for only the *S* shape, I went into the *Duplicate* channel and used the magic wand (with a tolerance of about 20) to select the white area. I saved the selection as a channel called *Slinky Only*. I went into that new channel and ran the Maximum filter at a radius of 1 pixel to enlarge the white areas, then saved as a new channel called *Slinky Maximum*. I loaded the *Slinky Maximum* channel as a selection into the *Duplicate* channel (follow me now) and filled it with black. This left only the shadow detail.

4 I created a new layer called *Shadow* and filled it with the purple color (I could change the color later if I wanted to) and brought the *Duplicate* channel in as a mask. I now had a colored shadow that could be put anywhere I wanted it.

5 The pieces came into the lower right by accident. I had an element floating around that I was trying to use somewhere else. I moved it out of the frame except for its shadow and really liked its placement. Again I wanted to use color, so I once again used channels to delete the "real" object and kept the shadow. I adjusted the opacity and chose the Multiply option on the colored shadow layer.

Photoshop Marbling

■ *by Susan Liston*

HAVE ALWAYS been fascinated by the feathery, swirling patterns of marbled paper, and I've made several attempts to duplicate the effect in Photoshop. I thought it would be easy: Choose some rich colors, apply a few filters, and watch a pattern appear (with none of the mess of real marbling). But the process wasn't as effortless as I expected. No matter how I varied the experiments, I ended up with consistent, computerized repeating patterns. Many of the designs were beautiful, but they didn't have the free-flowing look I wanted. When I hit on the solution, I was almost embarrassed by its simplicity: Take those repeating patterns that are so easy to produce in Photoshop and use the Twirl filter judiciously, in small selections, to introduce some random twists and turns into the design.

To speed the process up, I do the early stages of the work in a small, fast-acting file, a square or rectangle no larger than two inches on each side. And I work in RGB mode (with Mode, CMYK Preview selected) because I need to use the Offset filter later to "erase" seam lines in the pattern, and the Offset filter can't be applied in CMYK mode.

The basis of a marbled design is a striped canvas — and to produce it, I often start by selecting a single row of pixels from a design I've already created. I choose Single Row as the Shape option in the Marquee Options palette, copy the row of pixels I've selected, and paste them into a new file. Then, when I choose Image, Canvas Size and enlarge the vertical dimension of the canvas, that row of pixels is stretched out into thin vertical stripes. I use the Ripple filter to introduce lacy

1 To create a marbled paper design in Photoshop, I begin with a striped pattern and apply the Ripple and Polar Coordinates filters (both in the Filter, Distort submenu). I can get interesting results with almost any Ripple setting, but my favorite choice is Medium at an Amount of 100.

2 I used a vertical offset and the Wrap Around function (Filter, Other, Offset) to bring the top and bottom of the design together in the center of the canvas. To disguise the seam where they met, I made two elliptical selections in the "bottom" section and enlarged them (Image, Effects, Scale) to make them extend across the seam into the top of the design. Then I selected the center of the design with the rectangular marquee and applied the Ripple filter again.

3 The Twirl filter (in the Distort submenu) disguised the center line even more. After applying the filter, I offset the pattern horizontally, and twirled it again.

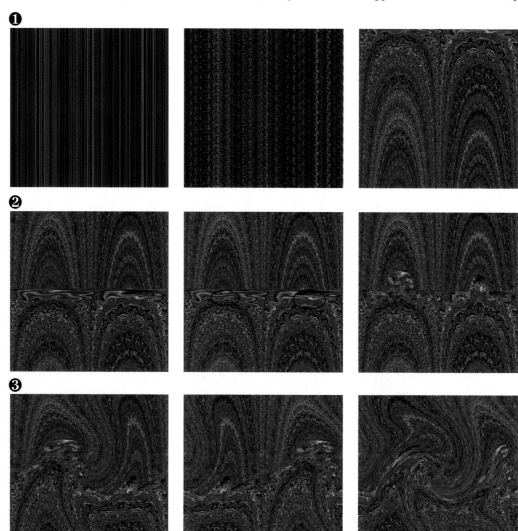

❶

❷

❸

twists into the design and the Polar Coordinates filter, set at Polar To Rectangular, to add dramatic, sweeping curves.

When I first apply the Offset filter, I enter a vertical offset to bring the top and bottom edges of the pattern together, but I set the horizontal offset at zero. (I don't need to worry about matching up the sides of the design because the Polar Coordinates filter has already done that for me.) At this point, the seam where the top and bottom of the design meet is a sharp, distinct line, and I use the Twirl filter to "twist" the seam line into a fluid shape. The Twirl filter acts on the center of a selection. So when I apply it, only the center of the seam line is distorted — at the outside edges of the pattern, the seam is still obvious. So I use the Offset filter, set for a horizontal shift, to slide the design over and place the outside edges of the pattern in the center of the canvas. Then I apply the Twirl filter again to reshape another section of the seam line. ☞ *The Twirl filter "stretches out" the pixels in the center of the design — and detail can be lost. If you want to create a large twirl, you can keep the loss to a minimum by setting a small amount in the Twirl dialog box and reapplying the filter.*

When I'm happy with the design, I use it as a repeating pattern to fill a new Photoshop file. And finally, I apply the Twirl filter to random selections in the overall design to introduce differences into the repeating elements. ☞ *Pressing the Shift key and then pressing Delete opens Photoshop's Fill dialog box where you can choose Pattern, Saved, or Snapshot as the fill options.* ∎

❹

4 The design was used as a pattern tile to fill a larger canvas. First, I selected the design and chose Edit, Define Pattern. Then I opened a new (larger) Photoshop file, selected all, and filled the canvas with the pattern tiles by choosing Edit, Fill and selecting Pattern in the Fill dialog box. The pattern repeated precisely — and marbled paper doesn't. So I made several small selections and applied the Twirl filter each one to create random variations.

Perfecting a Pattern

■ *by Kathy López*

1 Scanned paint spatters were used as the basis of a Photoshop pattern.

2 The Offset filter's Wrap Around function brought the edges of the scan together.

3 Windows, Color Range controls (set to a fuzziness of 100) were used to select the background in order to fill it with a consistent color.

4 After the seams were touched up with the rubber stamp and brush tools, I chose Edit, Define Pattern.

5 To fill a selection with the repeating pattern, I chose Edit, Fill and set Pattern as the Contents option.

6 To draw a seamless Photoshop pattern, I began in the center of the window, leaving the outer edges free.

7 The Offset filter, set to Wrap Around, brought the outer edges of the design into the center of the window. (Option-clicking on the file size on the scroll bar at the bottom of the window displayed the file's height and width in pixels. I divided these measurements by two to find the Offset settings I needed to move the outer edges of the design into the exact center of the window.)

8 I continued working on the design (top left), using the Offset filter as needed to reposition the art so that I was always working well within the edges of the window (top right). After completing the pattern segment, I applied the Define Pattern command and used the Fill dialog box to produce the pattern (bottom). As a last step, I applied the KPT Hue Protected Noise filter to add some texture to the design.

TURNING SCANNED ART into a repeating pattern is a simple process in Photoshop: Just select the scan (or part of it), choose Define Pattern from the Edit menu, and then use the pattern to fill other selections. Creating smooth, seamless edges between the repeating segments isn't that easy, though. Perfecting a repeating pattern calls for a few extra steps.

First, select the art that will be used to create the pattern and apply the Offset filter, entering Horizontal and Vertical offset values and clicking Wrap Around in the Offset dialog box. (Activating the Preview option in the dialog box will let you set the Horizontal and Vertical values interactively, making it easy to find an offset that works well.)

The Offset filter's Wrap Around function makes the selection fold in on itself, letting you see how the edges will meet when the image is turned into a repeating pattern so that you can touch up these edges to make the seam invisible once you define the pattern and use it as a fill.

Because retouch work is required to produce a seamless pattern, this process is easiest when the original scan has a lot of open areas with a solid color (or colorless) background. The denser the image and the more tonal variation it has, the more touch-up you'll need to do to make the edges match up smoothly.

PRODUCING YOUR OWN PATTERN

When you're creating an original pattern — rather than working from a scanned image — it's usually easier to design the pattern segment in a PostScript draw program (where features like the Snap-To controls and the duplication functions give you precise control over the placement of the elements) and then import it into Photoshop. But don't try to bring a PostScript tile pattern into Photoshop. Photoshop can't recognize PostScript tiles, and the fill will become solid black.

There may be times, though, when the effect you have in mind simply can't be produced in PostScript, and you need to use Photoshop's painting tools or filters. In that case, you can create the design seamlessly by working from the center out, using the Offset filter to recenter the design as it progresses. This way, there are no seams to worry about, because the pattern is created in unbroken expanses. ■

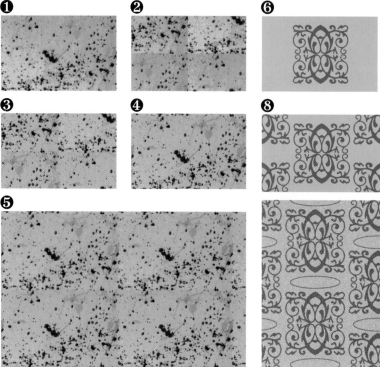

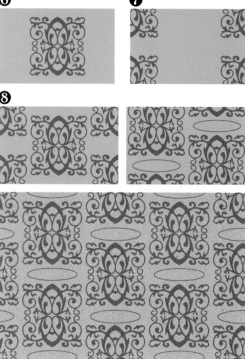

Playing
with Paint

■ *by Sara Booth*

L ORI OSIECKI uses her computer like a box of crayons. The Mesa, Ariz., illustrator uses handmade scratchboard drawings as a basis for her images. After she adds colors with Photoshop's paintbucket tool, she uses the painting tools to fill the shapes with playful scribbled textures, creating a surprising variety of surfaces by using Dissolve as a painting mode, applying the Add Noise filter, or using the paintbucket to pour color into areas where she has already scribbled.

Osiecki finds that placing the scratchboard directly on the scanner bed results in an inferior scan, because the scanner picks up shadows and fattens lines. Instead, she photocopies her scratchboard drawings and scans the copies. She rarely touches up her scans in Photoshop, preferring a rougher scan that captures the spirit of her scratchboard art.

Lori Osiecki is a Photoshop minimalist: "Most of the time I use six tools — pencil, airbrush, magic wand, paintbucket, paintbrush, and eyedropper — and ignore all the rest," she says. In this self-promotional illustration, she gave the shirt a finger-paint effect with pencil, paintbrush, and airbrush.

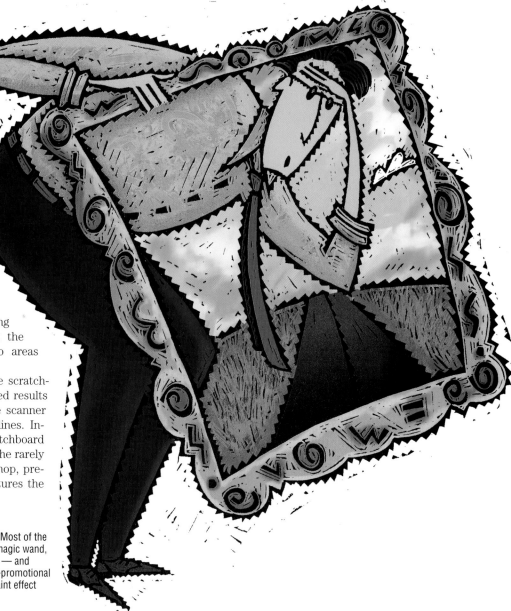

❶ For a look that resembles batik, Osiecki first used the paintbucket to fill the dress with dark blue. She airbrushed loops of lighter blue, then used the paintbucket to dump an even lighter shade between scribbles. Finally, a small, harder brush was used to draw more loops in the lightest shade.

❷ Osiecki used a pattern fill for this background. She filled a new document with yellow, added scribbles and dots with the paintbrush and airbrush, selected the area, and chose Edit, Define Pattern. When she filled the background of the main image with the pattern (by choosing Edit, Fill and choosing Pattern in the Contents popout menu), the repetition was too obvious. So she added more pencil scribbles for a random look.

Osiecki works on a single layer in Photoshop. To make adding color easier, she begins by defining each area that will be filled with a particular color. After using a pencil with her fill color to stop up any gaps in her scanned lines, she uses the paintbucket to pour color into each area. Next, she uses the magic wand and the Select, Similar command to select all the pixels of that color, then saves the selection in a channel. When selections are saved for all the important areas, she is ready to add color.

Osiecki doesn't define a palette at the beginning of a drawing; instead, she tries different combinations as she goes along. When she finds colors she likes, she adds them to Photoshop's Swatches palette (by clicking in any swatch in the palette). To add final colors to her shapes, she loads a selection, then uses the paintbucket to dump in flat color before airbrushing highlight and shadow colors along the edges.

To add textures, Osiecki combines Photoshop tools that mimic traditional drawing tools — pencil, airbrush, paintbrush — with strictly electronic functions such as painting modes and patterns. For example, when she updated a black-and-white illustration (first used to illustrate a humor column in *New Orleans* magazine on packing for vacations), Osiecki created a texture by "scribbling" with the airbrush tool, then filling some areas with the paintbucket ❶. She took a different approach in an editorial illustration for a nursing magazine, using Photoshop's pattern fill to create a basic background, then adding more scribbles for a less mechanical look ❷.

In *Frame It,* a self-promotional illustration (see page 37), Osiecki used the airbrush in Normal mode to brush white and light blue on a darker blue background for the clouds. For the grass, she used a large airbrush in Dissolve mode to paint gold over the green background; the rest is layer after layer of pencil scribbling in different shades of gold and green.

After filling the shirt with pink and scribbling on it with the painting tools, Osiecki used the paintbucket to add broad areas of lighter pink. Then she used the airbrush, selecting a large brush and setting the mode to Dissolve, to add grainy highlights and shadows before applying the Add Noise filter for even more grain.

After Osiecki has created a texture with many shades of the same color, she sometimes wants to select one shade so she can add noise or another effect. To make this easier, she sometimes uses a temporary color when she first paints the texture ("one of those you can't possibly print," she says). Then she uses the magic wand to select all the pixels in that color, saves the selection as a channel, and fills the selection with the final color. ∎

PHOTOSHOP

Pencil Virtuosity

■ *by Sara Booth*

PHOTOSHOP'S HUMBLE PENCIL tool gets center stage in the artwork of Elizabeth Brandt. The Holland, Mich., illustrator creates a scratchboard look using the pencil almost exclusively. Varying the brush size and changing the image's resolution allows her to create a variety of textures with a single tool.

Brandt does much of her work in black-and-white for newsletters, newspapers, and other publications, but she has a growing number of clients who want color. So when she designed a self-promotional piece, she did both black-and-white and color versions. To give her color illustration more depth, she added texture using one of Painter's paper textures.

Beginning with a scanned pencil sketch in bitmap mode, Brandt immediately changed the feel of the piece by tracing it in Photoshop with a heavy black pencil, filling large areas with black and obliterating many details. Then she changed her foreground color to white, chose a smaller brush size, and began "etching away" at the black. She continued to switch between black and white, using smaller and smaller brushes to add detail and to carve up smooth edges. ☞ *To exchange Photoshop's foreground and background colors, type the letter X.*

To achieve the roughness that she wanted, Brandt began the piece at a resolution of 200 ppi at half its final size. "It's like a thumbnail at that point," she says. When she was ready to add more detail, she used the Image, Image Size command to enlarge the illustration, then continued working with smaller and smaller brush sizes, alternating black and white, until the woodcut effect had all the detail she wanted. "Changing the resolution gives it a rougher look, almost bitmappy," she says. "Some clients like that and some don't, so I try to find out before I start." ☞ *Use the [and] keys to cycle through the brushes in Photoshop's Brushes palette. Type Shift-[and Shift-] to jump to the first or last brush in the palette.*

Brandt went for simplicity when adding color, too, using either the paintbucket or the pencil to fill in color areas ❶. She used the burn tool with a soft brush to add shadows and the dodge tool to create highlights. Brandt finds that these tools sometimes create undesirable colors, especially when they're used on yellows. On those occasions, she chose Undo, then mixed a shadow or highlight color and applied it with the airbrush tool.

Because the paintbucket fills only pixels of the same color, and the burn tool darkens light colors but leaves blacks unchanged, her black linework was protected as she added color. When she used

1 Brandt converted her image to RGB and brought it up to her final resolution before she began adding color, using the paintbucket and pencil tools.

2 When Brandt added texture using Painter's Effects, Apply Surface Texture function, the image was darkened. "I do a fairly bright original, because I know Painter will have that effect," she says.

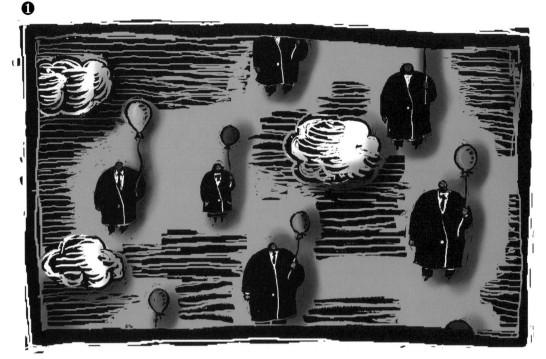

the airbrush or the dodge tool, she first used the magic wand or lasso to select an area, preventing the color from affecting the black areas. ☞ *To access Photoshop's pencil tool, type the letter* P; *for the paintbucket tool, type* K. *To select the dodge and burn tool, type the letter* O; *continue typing* O *to cycle through the tool's dodge, burn, and sponge options.*

Brandt has chosen one Painter texture effect that she uses anytime she feels an image needs to

be a step away from the computer **2**. She begins by choosing the Wheat String texture from the More Wild Textures library (accessed by clicking the Library button in the zoomed-out Art Materials:Paper palette). To roughen the texture, she drags the Paper palette's Scale slider to 284%. Then she chooses Effects, Apply Surface Texture. She doesn't like the effect of Painter's shininess, so before applying texture, she drags the Shine slider in the Surface Texture dialog box to 0. ■

Photoshop As a Layout Tool

■ *by Talitha Harper*

WHEN MCA RECORDS decided to produce *AMP,* an online magazine published on the World Wide Web, the company wanted the magazine's content rather than its interface to inspire excitement. So MCA bypassed the standard multimedia approach with its bold buttons and high-powered special effects and turned the job over to David High of Ocala, Fla., a designer with no interactive experience — and a portfolio full of print layouts that combined dramatic photography with inventive type handling.

High produces his print layouts in Quark-XPress, but *AMP'S* on-screen format called for bitmap files. For the first issue of the magazine (released in November 1994, before Photoshop 3 was available), High worked in Illustrator to arrange the type, then opened the Illustrator file in Photoshop and pasted it over the artwork. But by the time he began to design the second issue, he was working in Photoshop 3, and with the program's layering capability, High could use Photoshop as a stand-alone layout application. Now, nearly every element he creates for *AMP* is produced directly in Photoshop ❶.

Finished layouts must be provided to MCA in Indexed Color mode and CompuServe GIF format so that they can be loaded onto the web. But layering isn't available for Indexed Color files,

David High of High Design in Ocala, Fla., uses Photoshop layers to produce dynamic layouts and striking type effects for *AMP,* an online magazine published by MCA Records.

1 Almost every element in the on-line magazine is created in Photoshop. The exceptions are the scanned photos in the background of each layout and the interactive buttons on the contents screens (screens from the second and third issue are shown here). High wanted to keep the buttons simple so they wouldn't overpower other elements in the design. So he drew a circle in Illustrator, gave it a broad stroke in a contrasting color, and duplicated it to produce all the buttons he needed.

2 High set the words *Feature* and *The Murmurs* in the same shade of gold, but he placed them on different layers and adjusted the opacity of the *Feature* layer to 25 percent to create a two-tone effect. He set *Two Girls, Twelve Strings* on one layer, *And a Song Called* on a second, and *"You Suck"* on a third, then lowered the opacity on two of the layers to 50 percent.

3 Once he was satisfied with coloring, High moved the lettering, positioning it to complement the photo on the background layer. He finished the layout by adding a "button," a simple arrow (drawn with the pencil tool) and the word *Click* (rotated 90 degrees clockwise with the Image, Rotate command.)

❶

❷

❸
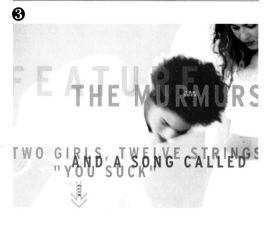

so High works in RGB mode, choosing vibrant, phosphorescent tones. Once a design is complete, he converts it to Indexed Color, selecting Adaptive as the Palette option so that his screen colors will be preserved accurately — and not replaced with the System colors or a custom Indexed Color palette. He also selects None as the Dither option in the Indexed Color dialog box to maintain the smooth coloring of the original imagery. (These reproductions were converted to CMYK mode for print, and some of the luminous tones in the original layouts were lost in the conversion process. To see the artwork on screen, you can access *AMP* at http://www.mca.com/ on the World Wide Web.)

Since Indexed Color mode doesn't support layering, the files are automatically flattened into a single layer when High makes the Indexed Color conversion. So he always saves an RGB copy of the document — with the layering intact — in case he needs to modify the design later.

CREATING SIMPLE TYPE EFFECTS

MCA supplies High with photos — more than he can use in an issue — and High occasionally uses photographs of his own (the daisy in Figure 1, for example). After selecting the images he wants for his layouts, he scans the photos, opens each scan in Photoshop, and sizes the artwork to *AMP'S* standard dimensions: 5.765 x 4.165 inches. ☞ *To crop a Photoshop image to a specific size, first select the cropping tool in the toolbox. Then choose Fixed Target Size and enter the proportions you need in the Cropping Tool Options palette. The tool will automatically size the image to those dimensions as it crops.*

Once he has sized a photo, High adds the type. When he enters text in the Type Tool dialog box and clicks OK, the type is placed on the canvas as a floating selection. High can then click on the words *Floating Selection* in the Layers palette and drag to the new layer icon to set the lettering on a new layer. Working in layers lets High position the type independently, without affecting the photograph in the background. And in addition to arranging the layout, he uses layers to produce colorful type effects.

To create two-tone lettering, High began by setting the text in several small blocks, entering a few words at a time and placing each block of type on a different layer. He could then activate a layer by clicking on its name in the Layers palette and lower the layer's opacity to soften the color. Lowering the opacity in some of the type layers and using solid-color lettering in others produced a two-tone effect ❷. High repositioned the lettering on each layer to create staggered, overlapping patterns. Although text blocks jostle into each other, the tonal distinctions keep the type easy to read **❸**. ☞ *To access Photoshop's move tool, which lets you reposition a layer's contents without selecting them, press the V key.*

Each layer High added to the layout increased the file's memory. So when he was satisfied with the position and coloring of the type, he often merged the lettering into a single layer to reduce the file size. First, he made the other layers invisible by clicking on their eye icons in the Layers palette to turn them off. Then, when he chose Merge Layers from the palette's pop-out menu, all the visible layers were combined into one.

High also used layering to apply color to hand-drawn lettering. He had doodled the word *AMP* during a conference call with MCA, and he later decided that the bold simplicity of the lettering would harmonize with the playful photo he had chosen for the "cover" of the magazine's second issue. So he scanned the doodle, opened the scan in Photoshop, selected all, and copied. Then he opened the photo in Photoshop, chose New Layer from the Layers palette menu, and pasted the scanned lettering into that new layer. Command-Option-T selected the lettering without the layer's transparent background, and High could then choose Option-delete to fill the selection with the foreground color, a vivid turquoise (see page 41).

STENCIL EFFECTS AND 3-D SHADOWS

For the third issue of the magazine (the final issue released to date), MCA gave High a set of black-and-white photos. The designer used type as a counterpoint to the understated imagery, creating "oversprayed" stencil lettering for the cover and constructing 3-D shadows for the type on other "pages." In the past, High would have used channel selections to achieve these effects. But with Photoshop 3, there was no need to create extra channels. Instead, High could work in layers and keep all the elements in view (and in color) as he designed the type.

To create the stencil lettering, High began by setting the word *AMP* in black and using Command-Option-T to select the type. When he chose New Layer from the Layers palette menu, this selection remained active. Working on the new layer, he feathered the selection and filled it with a bold orange-red. Then he activated the layer with the original black type and chose Command-Option-T again to produce a clean, unfeathered selection border around the lettering. Returning to the orange-red layer, he deleted. This removed all the color that fell inside the selection border, creating letter-shaped "holes" inside the feathered forms. Finally, High selected Delete Layer from the Layers palette to remove the black type from the layout **❹**. The opacity of the stencil-look *AMP* lettering was set to 60 percent, muting the

❹

❺

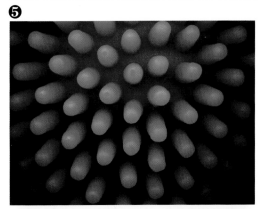

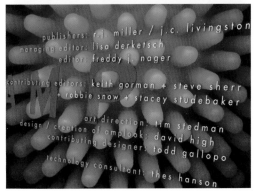

4 High set the word *AMP* in black on its own layer. He selected the lettering, then moved to a new layer and used the Select, Feather command to apply a broad feather radius to the selection border. After choosing a bright orange-red for the foreground color, he pressed Option-delete to fill the feathered selection. Repeating the Option-delete command intensified the color in the selection. To complete the effect, High selected the original black lettering again, returned to the layer with the feathered type, and deleted. This gave him transparent letters, surrounded by orange-red halos.

5 To brighten a dark photo, High created a new layer and filled it with translucent color. He finished the layout by using Image, Effects, Perspective to reshape the *AMP* lettering and applying the Skew command (also in the Image, Effects submenu) to the other type.

6 After High cropped a photo of musician Charlie Sexton to create a dramatic close-up, the image wasn't wide enough to fill the layout. So High created an abstract texture and pasted a section of the texture beside the photo.

7 After drawing an orange rectangle on one layer, High moved to a new layer and typed the word *FEATURE*. While the type selection was still active, he reactivated the layer with the rectangle and deleted. The *F* and *E* overlapped the rectangle, so deleting removed the letterforms from the rectangle. (The two letters were then deleted from the type layer). High set the orange layers to 50 percent opacity, but he wasn't satisfied with the results because the lettering that ran over the photo looked darker than the *A* on top of the white background.

8 High copied the type layer by selecting its name in the Layers palette and dragging to the new layer icon. He removed the letter *A* from one of the layers and the *TURE* from the other and adjusted the opacity of the *TURE* layer to 30 percent. Although the letter *A* is set to 50 percent opacity, it appeared to be filled with solid color when no background layer was visible; a layer's opacity and mode variations can be viewed only when an underlying layer is visible.

9 In the finished layout, the orange type seems to have an even tone, but the *A* is 20 percent darker than the rest of the lettering.

❻

❼

❽

❾

color so that it wouldn't overpower the subtle black-and-white photo (see page 41).

High used a similar technique to create 3-D shading for the lettering on the issue's contents screen (shown at the bottom of Figure 1). But this time he started with white type instead of black. He set the type on one layer, selected it, and feathered its selection border. When he moved to a new layer and filled the feathered selection with black, the outer fringes of the selection took on shadowy gray tones. He selected the original lettering again, returned to the "shadow" layer, and deleted to create transparent letterforms within the feathered shadows. As a last step, High activated the layer with the original white lettering and changed the layer's opacity to 35 percent, giving the type a milky translucence, like thick plexiglass.

APPLYING COLOR IN LAYERS

When High created a credits screen for the magazine, he started with a photograph of a nubby stress-reliever ball. He felt that the color in the RGB scan was too dark, so he used layering to brighten the tone. He created a new layer, filled it with neon green, and set the opacity to 20 percent. The sheer coloring in the new layer added a sheen to the image in the background, effectively changing its color ❺.

A variation of this color-layer technique was used to add color highlights to a black-and-white photo. The photograph wasn't wide enough to fill the canvas, so before adding color, High expanded the composition by creating an abstract texture pattern and placing it beside the image. To create this texture pattern, High opened a copy of the photo of the nubby ball, selected a small section, and pasted it into a new Photoshop document. The Scale command (in the Image, Effects submenu) was used to enlarge the selection, and the Color Halftone filter (from the Pixelate submenu) was applied to give it an exaggerated dot pattern. High changed the mode to grayscale, eliminating the color in the dots, and pasted the design into the photo file ❻.

To add color to the layout, High first converted the grayscale image to RGB. On a new layer, he drew a rectangle with the marquee tool, large enough to cover the abstract pattern on the background layer. He filled the rectangle with orange, added orange type on another layer, and lowered the opacity of the colored layers to let the black-and-white art show through ❼. When he viewed the effect, he could see that tonal variations in the background made the color in the lettering look uneven ❽. So he divided the lettering into two layers and adjusted the opacity settings independently, experimenting with different percentages until the color appeared to even out ❾. ■

Mixing Media in an Online Comic Book

■ *by Sara Booth*

WHEN NETSTAR DECIDED to use the World Wide Web to market its computer networking products, it wanted to offer something that went beyond traditional advertising. So Indianapolis illustrator Charlie Hill, along with writer and art director Emily Eaton of Prospera and copywriter Mary Ellen Amodeo of Shandwick USA, put together *The Adventures of Max Bandwidth*, a Web-based visual narrative that combined the structure of a comic book with the aesthetic of film noir.

Time was short. Hill turned out two stories — a total of 24 images — in less than six weeks. To save time, he used Photoshop's lasso, ellipse, and rectangle as drawing tools, beginning with combinations of simple shapes and then carving out the complicated selections that give his illustrations a sense of volume and light.

BUILDING COMPLEX SELECTIONS

Hill began by creating a new layer for his scanned sketch, setting the layer mode to Multiply so he could view the linework while he added color in a single layer below. He first drew the walls and other background elements that defined the setting of each piece by selecting large areas and filling them with gradients. "I take a certain artistic

"It's just like they teach you in day one of art school: Everything's built out of circles and squares," says Charlie Hill. For a comic book on the World Wide Web, the Indianapolis illustrator used Photoshop's ellipse and rectangle marquees as the starting points for his shapes, carving more complex shapes by adding to and subtracting from simple selections.
(The company that ordered the artwork has been sold, and the new owner is not using the images on its Web site, but the series will soon be available at www.charliehill.com.)

1 To add the shadow along the front of a coat, Hill drew one elliptical selection, then drew a second ellipse while pressing the Command key to subtract it from the first. The remaining shape was filled with a gradient from dark gray to transparent.

2 Once he had created the outline of a character's clothes, Hill could add back-lighting by choosing Select, Modify, Contract, feathering the resulting smaller selection, and airbrushing in a darker shade of gray.

3 A face began with a circle selection. Hill pressed the Shift key while drawing an ellipse to add the jaw, then pressed Command while he used the lasso to carve away the front of the face. Airbrushing the edges of selections added shadows and highlights to the face.

❶

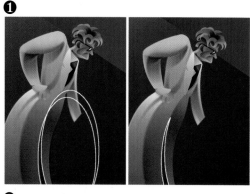

❷

❸

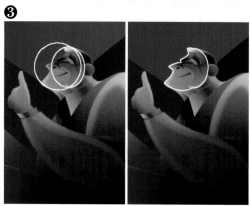

license with these perspectives," he says. "If I feel an image would have more impact with a more extreme, less realistic perspective, then I'll throw caution to the wind."

Characters' bodies and clothes were built from more complex shapes, also filled with gradients. To create these shapes, Hill first used the ellipse or lasso tool to draw a large overall shape, following his sketch, and then filled this shape with a gradient to add a light source. Next, without deselecting, he used the Command key with the ellipse and lasso tools to remove parts of the original selection, paring it down to shapes that defined creases, folds, and smaller areas such as sleeves and fingers; these were filled with new gradients (covering up the original gradient fill) or emphasized by airbrushing along the edges of the selections ❶. The Contract Selection function helped him generate a backlit effect ❷. ☞ *Press the Command key to subtract from an existing selection or the Shift key to add to it. Press the Shift and Option keys to find the intersection between an existing selection and a new one.*

A similar technique was used to draw faces: Hill began with elliptical selections, then carved out of them with the ellipse or lasso tool ❸. Clouds of steam, on the other hand, could be created by beginning with an ellipse and adding other ellipses and circles ❹.

Much of the drama of the images is provided by the lighting, and Hill has developed a variety of techniques for adding light to his images. To indicate a glow (for example, in a lamp or a computer screen), he might simply make a selection, then click once with the airbrush ❺. For beams, he used the lasso to make selections, then applied the airbrush or dodge tool slightly outside the selected area ❻. By opening the Airbrush Options palette and checking the Fade box, he could set the stroke to fade out gradually; if the effect was

too strong, he could choose the airbrush mode of the eraser, assign a fade, and brush in the other direction to remove some of the brushstroke. If he needed the airbrush to run in a straight line, he could simply press the Shift key and click once at the beginning of the effect and once at the end.

Because of the short deadlines, Hill repeated elements from one image to another whenever he could, scaling or distorting to vary effects ❼.

PUBLISHING ON THE WEB

Working for the Web, rather than for print, didn't feel restrictive to Hill. The client established fixed horizontal and vertical dimensions for all the illustrations, which were to be provided at 72 ppi, but otherwise placed no limitations on the artwork. Hill worked in RGB mode, leaving indexed color conversion to Shandwick's Web experts.

Hill's style adapted well to the small file sizes needed for Web display. Even in his print work, he usually chooses limited palettes that get their impact from vibrant colors and strong contrasts. (In fact, working for onscreen display gave him more freedom: "I could use really rich colors, as saturated as I wanted.") The final images, which displayed at about 4 inches wide, had file sizes ranging from 17K to 22K, for a download time of less than half a minute; impatient viewers could read the story while waiting for an image to load.

Hill's work relies on gradients for dimension and lighting, but the conversion from RGB to a limited indexed color palette can cause gradients to become grainy or posterized. To avoid this, Hill tried to keep down the range of hues generated by each gradient by choosing beginning and ending colors that were similar and by limiting the distance covered by each gradient. To assure color consistency, he simply kept the first illustration open as he worked on subsequent images, using the eyedropper to pick up colors. ∎

❹
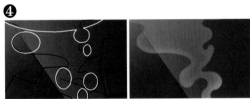

❺
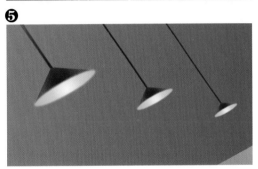

❻

❼

4 To give graceful curves to his steam, Hill used the elliptical marquee to select ellipses that followed his sketch, pressing the Shift key to make multiple selections at once. After he finished the selection using the ellipse and lasso tools and refined it in Quick Mask mode, he placed it on its own layer and filled it with a white-to-transparent gradient, adjusted the layer's opacity to make the light transparent, then airbrushed more white along the edges of the selection.

5 To make the lamps glow, he selected the lamp opening, chose a large, soft airbrush, and clicked once inside the selection.

6 On a new layer, Hill used the lasso to select the area of a light beam, then filled it with a gradient from white to transparent. After airbrushing along the edges of the beam for more emphasis, he adjusted the layer's opacity to vary the intensity of the light.

7 When elements were repeated, Hill saved time by copying and pasting. To vary the angle of the three faces on the monitors, he chose Image, Effects, Perspective. Filters (from left, Mosaic, Wave, and Pointillize) suggest a screen display breaking down.

PHOTOSHOP

Creating an Online Catalog

■ *by Lynda Weinman*

HOTHOTHOT SELLS EXOTIC hot sauces through a retail outlet in Pasadena, Calif., and a cyber mail-order outlet on the World Wide Web (http://www.hothothot.com/hot/). When the store hired Presence, a Web design service company (http://www.presence.com), to create its site, no one imagined that one year later it would account for 20 percent of HotHotHot's total sales or bring overwhelming praise from the design-starved Internet community.

Presence's goal was to limit the size of each Web page, including all its images, to 30K or less. And by restricting the palette to eight indexed colors and using aliased artwork, the designers were able to keep the size of the home page down to 19K ❶. (For more about minimizing file size in Photoshop by using an Indexed Color palette and bypassing the anti-aliasing feature, see "Controlling Online File Size," page 50.)

Presence hired Yeryeong Park, who had never designed for the Web, to create imagery for the site. Park's pen-and-ink drawings were scanned at 800 dpi as black-and-white bitmaps (though Presence has since discovered that, for Web graphics, the same quality can be obtained by scanning at 150 to 300 dpi). The scans were opened in Photoshop and converted to RGB so that Presence's production artists could add color, following tissue overlays Park supplied with the drawings.

Speed is an important goal for Mike Kuniavsky of Presence, now with *HotWired*. After experimenting with other approaches, he has decided the quickest way to color black-and-white scans in Photoshop is with the paint bucket tool, even though he often needs to fill "leaks" in the linework before coloring the imagery ❷.

Once the artwork was colored, the resolution was changed to 72 dpi and the image was cropped to size. ☞ *By using the cropping tool, selecting the Fixed Target Size option in the Cropping Tool Options palette, and entering numbers for Height, Width, and Resolution, you can size an image and reset the resolution in a single step.*

Next, the mode was changed to Indexed Color, and Exact was selected in the Indexed Color dialog box so only the eight colors used in the file were saved in the Indexed Color table.

In addition to Park's illustrations ❸, the HotHotHot site includes scanned labels from more than 50 hot sauce bottles. Each scan required individual attention, but Kuniavsky was able to limit processing time for the entire set of labels to one day by devising a clean-up system that took less than 10 minutes per image.

He began by scanning a label in RGB at 400 dpi and opening the scan in Photoshop ❹. He simplified the design by selecting and deleting small art elements and most type, which would have been unreadable when the resolution was changed to 72 dpi. Then he used the Levels command (Image, Adjust, Levels or Command-L), moving the Input Levels slider's white endpoint left to increase the contrast in the illustration and clean up the background, turning it white. ☞ *The single-click Image, Adjust, Auto Levels command is often worth a try for whitening whites, blackening blacks, and even removing a color cast.*

Some fills in the labels had to be re-created to eliminate moiré patterns that developed during scanning, when the halftone dot pattern on the printed labels was translated into a pixel pattern.

Kuniavsky chose from several methods for eliminating a moiré, depending on its color,

A World Wide Web home page designed by Presence, based in Pasadena, Calif., functions as an electronic catalog for hot sauce seller HotHotHot. In this graphic, as in all the images in the site, a small palette of bright colors creates visual cachet and minimal file sizes: The entire home page, including images, weighs in at 19K.

❶

❷
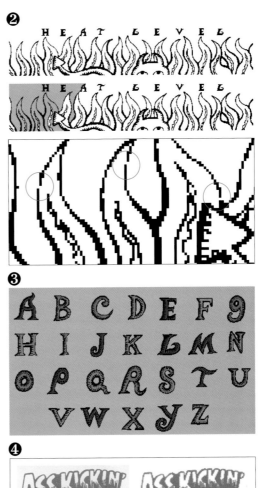

❸

❹

1 GIF images on the home page range from 3.5K to 9K. To keep the file size low, illustrator Yeryeong Park confined the palette to eight colors chosen for contrast and brightness, combining warm and cool tones.

2 There were some breaks in the bitmapped linework, so when color was poured in with Photoshop's paint bucket tool, it spilled outside the lines. For example, when the background of one graphic was filled with yellow, the color "leaked" out of the background and into some of the flames in the drawing. So the artist used the undo command (Command-Z), zoomed in to get a close-up view of the linework, and "plugged up" the leaks with the pencil tool before reapplying the fill.

3 Additional illustrations, in the same style, were used on other pages. Clicking the Name button on the home page (see Figure 1) brought up an alphabet. Each letter was linked to a list of hot sauces whose names started with that letter.

4 Sauce bottle labels were scanned at 400 dpi as a first step in making images for some of the hot buttons (left). After cleaning up a scan, production artist Mike Kuniavsky converted it to Indexed Color mode, selecting Adaptive as the Palette option and entering 8 colors for the Resolution (right). For some of the scans, the colors were adjusted by editing the Color Table (Mode, Color Table). The original red tone in this label, for example, was too maroon. So the artist opened the Color Table dialog box, clicked on the maroon-red swatch to open the Color Picker, and entered new RGB values in order to replace the original color with a brighter hue.

extent, and location. For example, he selected surrounding elements, clicking with the magic wand tool to select linework, and using the marquee to add broad sections (pressing Shift to add to the selection). As he worked, he toggled Quick Mask on and off (by pressing *Q* on the keyboard) to see the selection clearly. When the Quick Mask showed that everything but the moiré pattern was selected, Kuniavsky toggled again to select the unmasked area. Then he deleted or Option-deleted to fill the unprotected area (the moiré) with the background or foreground color. ☞ *For some selection tasks, the Select, Color Range command is quicker and easier to control than the magic wand. Clicking with the Color Range dialog box's eyedropper selects similarly colored pixels from many parts of an image at*

once (like extending a magic wand selection with the Select, Similar command). The Color Range Fuzziness slider acts like an interactive version of the magic wand's Tolerance or the Select, Grow command. Choosing Quick Mask, White Matte, or Black Matte from the dialog box's Select Preview popout menu lets you view your mask as it develops. But Color Range may not be able to make an effective selection for a moiré, which can include contrasting colors, some of which also occur elsewhere in the image — broadening the color range enough to select all the colors of the moiré may extend the selection far beyond the moiré area itself.

Finally, Kuniavsky used the cropping tool to scale each label to 122 x 144 pixels at 72 dpi, and the image was saved as an Indexed Color GIF. ∎

1 The original RGB version of this Photoshop image was created in a 500 x 400-pixel window at 72 dpi, and it took up 456K on my hard drive once I flattened the layers. That would be a tiny size for a print image — too small for high-quality reproduction — but it's big and unwieldy by Web standards. At 1K per second (that's the average downloading time), a 456K file would take more than seven minutes to appear on screen.

2 When I want to preserve the color of the original image as well as reduce the file size, I save the image in JPEG format. Choosing Low image quality (shown) for the JPEG compression cut the file size down to 33K. This is smaller than many indexed color GIFs with the same dimensions and resolution, but because a JPEG must be decompressed before it can be downloaded from the Web, it can take longer to appear on screen. (Saving the original image at Maximum, High, and Medium JPEG quality gave me file sizes of 92K, 62K, and 41K.)

3 To create a low-memory GIF file, I converted the original image to Indexed Color mode, selecting 8-bit Resolution and Adaptive Palette in Photoshop's Indexed Color dialog box. Setting the Dither to None resulted in a 72K file (top), and choosing Diffusion Dither produced an 80K image (bottom). Images saved with no dither are smaller than dithered files, but banding is sometimes glaring in an undithered indexed image, as seen here in the feathered edge.

❶

❸

❷

Controlling Online File Size

■ *by Lynda Weinman*

WHEN YOU DESIGN for print, you may not blink at large files — print images routinely range from tens to hundreds of megabytes. But file size is a serious design consideration when you create for the World Wide Web. You've heard Web graphics have to be small, but *how* small is small? Here's a rule of thumb: With a 14.4 modem (what you can expect a typical Web surfer to have), it takes about one second per kilobyte to transfer an image. At that rate, a 60K file takes one minute to download, and a 10-megger could take nearly three hours.

So how do you distill a many-megabyte image into a "timely" file? There are two basic strategies — compress the artwork or reduce the color requirements — and the file format you choose affects your options. The Web offers two format choices, JPEG and GIF. GIF images should be used whenever possible because they don't have to be decompressed before viewing (as JPEGs do), and decompression takes time. But GIF has a disadvantage of its own: The color palette is severely limited. ☞ *GIFs come in two varieties: transparent (GIF89a, in which you can designate a color to be masked out in order to make the background color disappear, for instance) and*

the original opaque format (GIF87a), which is supported by more browsers. When you save an image in Photoshop as a CompuServe GIF, it's converted to the more widely used GIF87a.

Reserve JPEG format for 24-bit files that can't be reduced to 8-bit without sacrificing integrity — generally photos and illustrations with a wide range of colors or lots of soft edges ❶. I usually save four versions of an image, using a different level of JPEG compression (Low, Medium, High, and Maximum quality) for each one. Then I open all four files, compare them to see where the image starts to fall apart, and upload the version that looks good with the least memory ❷. ☞ *The JPEG compression scheme will degrade the images — and if you open a JPEG file and then recompress it, you will degrade image quality further. You can safely open a JPEG image to view it as long as you simply close it without resaving. But if you think you may need to make some changes later, it's a good idea to save an uncompressed copy of the file, make your edits in that version, and then compress.*

GIF images must be indexed in 8-bit color (or even fewer than 8 bits per pixel). This means the maximum number of colors a GIF can contain is a whopping 256. This may not sound bad, but when

❹

❺

❻

4 Indexed Color palettes at 3 bits (8 colors, top) and 4 bits (16 colors, bottom) made feathered details murky and colors duller — but this would be acceptable for some Web graphics.

5 I can often save memory by choosing Colorize in the Hue/Saturation dialog box (Image, Adjust, Hue/Saturation) to convert a color image to monotone. This GIF file, saved as a dithered 4-bit, took up only 41K.

6 The Posterize command (Image, Map, Posterize) reduces file size further. Three-level posterization produced a 27-color image. In the Indexed Color dialog box, I could choose this 27-color palette (rather than Photoshop's 3-bit to 8-bit palettes). The resulting 28K GIF has an interesting "Web" aesthetic — and takes less than half a minute to download.

you convert a 24-bit graphic with millions of colors to Indexed Color mode, the attempt to simulate the full range of tones will either dither the image or cause banding ❸. Quality doesn't always suffer, though. Images with a limited range of colors can survive the transition beautifully, and with some artwork, you can even select an indexed palette with fewer than 256 colors. Experiment with the effect by entering a specific number of colors in Photoshop's Indexed Color dialog box. The fewer the colors, the smaller the file ❹. ☞ *To be sure specific colors don't drop out of a Photoshop image, select an area that includes those tones. Then choose Mode, Indexed Color and select Adaptive as the Palette option in the Indexed Color dialog box. An adaptive palette is compiled from the colors used most extensively in an image — and when a section is selected, the palette is compiled from the colors used most extensively within that selection.*

You can also reduce the number of colors by converting the image to a monotone ❺ or a posterization ❻ before you choose Mode, Indexed Color. Bear in mind that viewers don't expect to see print quality on the Web. To put it more positively: There's a big difference between what looks good on paper and what looks good on screen. Anti-aliased text, for example, often looks worse at small sizes on a screen than aliased text does, and you can shave a lot of memory off a file by using aliased type instead. ■

Finding the Size

Size readings on the hard drive can be deceptive. The size of the file *4-bit posterized* reads 32K on the desktop ❶. But when I open Get Info (by clicking on the file name and pressing Command-I) to find the bytes used, I can see that the true size is less than 27.9K ❷. The Size reading on the hard drive is rounded up, and the rounding depends on how the disk is partitioned. In this case, the smallest step in file size seems to be 8K, so the file was rounded up to 32K, the next highest multiple of 8K. The best way to judge size is through Get Info.

The size reading at the bottom of a Photoshop window is even more confusing. When Document Sizes is selected, the number on the right displays how much RAM the layered image occupies when it's open. The number on the left indicates the amount of RAM the image would require if it were flattened to one layer ❸. And even this "flattened" size is larger than the file size you'll find on the desktop and inside the Get Info window, because of the lossless compression schemes that are built into PICT, TIFF, GIF, and other file formats to conserve disk space without degrading the quality of the Photoshop image. ■

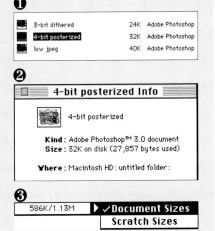

❶

3-bit dithered	24K	Adobe Photoshop
4-bit posterized	32K	Adobe Photoshop
low jpeg	40K	Adobe Photoshop

❷

4-bit posterized Info

4-bit posterized

Kind : Adobe Photoshop™ 3.0 document
Size : 32K on disk (27,857 bytes used)

Where : Macintosh HD : untitled folder :

❸

586K/1.13M ▶ ✓**Document Sizes**
                  Scratch Sizes

Removing Color Casts

■ *by Roger Hunsicker*

COLOR CAST APPEARS in images for many reasons. Photographs go yellow or green with age, Kodachrome and Fuji film have a slight magenta tint, sodium lights in factories introduce unwanted yellows, and bad chemistry in film processing shows up as browns and sepias. If these problems aren't corrected in the scanning process, what is the best way to fix them?

The real power of Photoshop is its ability to do things in more than one way. There always seems to be another tool that can produce the same results and, with it, the ability to tailor the task to the individual.

Under the Image, Adjust submenu, Photoshop has five color correcting tools that essentially do the same thing — they redefine the range of pixel values. (Each pixel in an image has a value from 0 to 255 or from darkest shadow to brightest high-

light.) The Levels, Curves, Brightness/Contrast, Color Balance, and Variations dialog boxes all perform corrections in this manner, but only Levels and Curves have the power for really high-end control. Of these last two tools, Adobe recommends the use of Curves because of its ability to zero in on a precise section of an image's overall range and adjust only that zone. Consequently, Adobe's tutorial only explores color correction within Curves.

While it's true that the Curves dialog box gives pinpoint control, a color cast affects the image's entire range, and I've found that the more operations I can complete in one step, the less the image tends to degrade. Since my first operation always is to do tonal corrections (shadows, highlights, and contrast), I prefer to do the initial phase of color correcting at the same time and within the same dialog box — Levels. And, I must admit, seeing that histogram gives me more comfort than working on a curved line.

Even if my final output will be CMYK for separations, I try to do most of my corrections in RGB. If it's critical to prevent the later CMYK conversion from dulling or altering any out-of-gamut colors, I choose Window, New Window and select Mode, CMYK Preview. Now I go back to the original window, and as I make changes, I can see a preview of what the CMYK image will look like.

The actual job of removing an overall cast is fairly straightforward. Besides the composite RGB channel where I did my tonal corrections, there are three color channels, each with its own histogram and input sliders. The middle input slider in these channels will add its color to the image when moved to the left and subtract it when moved to the right. This slider works only on the

❶

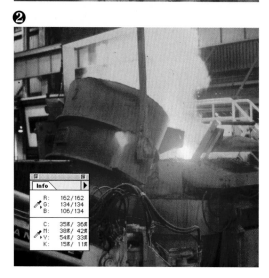

1 In the original photo, before any corrections, an orange cast lay like a fog over the entire image.

2 After I had set the shadows and highlights, there still was a cast, especially noticeable in the distant background where the brilliant foreground light should have had little impact. When I clicked the far overhead girder (which should have been a nearly neutral gray) for my reference point, I could see the cast in the RGB values in the Picker palette. These values should be much closer to one another for this color. (The Info palette shows changes already made.)

❷

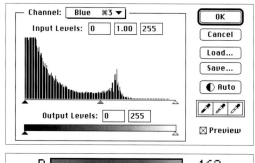

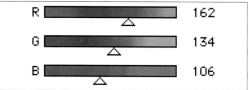

❸

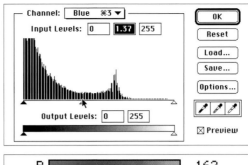

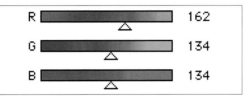

❹

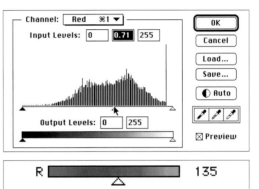

3 The Picker palette allowed me to view changes as I made them. To match my reference point values of a near-neutral gray, I needed to both raise the blue values and lower the red values. Since both were about the same distance from where I wanted to move them, it didn't matter which one I chose to correct first. Moving the blue center slider to the left brought up the blue value in the Picker to match the green value.

4 Finally, I moved the midtone slider to the right to lower the red cast and brought my reference point into a near-neutral gray. This last operation still preserved the brilliant highlight reds and yellows in the foreground.

midtones, quarter tones, and three-quarter tones, but since I've already set my whites and blacks (see "Color Correction with Levels," page 54), any cast in the highlights and shadows has been erased. The middle slider should remove whatever cast remains.

Here is where a knowledge of the color wheel (or at least a peek at the Color Balance window) helps. Remember, red's complement is cyan, green's is magenta, and blue's is yellow. One color's value increases while its complement decreases — if you lose red, cyan is pumped up.

The foundry image is a good example of color cast. The original photo ❶ had a decided orange tint caused by an improper camera filter used against the harsh glow of the molten iron. After manually setting shadows and highlights, I could see that there still was an orange cast to the gray girder in the part of the background that shouldn't have been affected by the foreground light.

Passing my eyedropper tool over a distant section of this girder and clicking my mouse to lock in an RGB value in the Picker palette (opened along with the Info palette before I began any corrections), I could see that this was not a very neutral gray ❷. (If I didn't have a neutral gray to examine, I might use a skin tone or a sky blue or green grass as a reference color.) I was much too low in blue and too high in red. Conversely, blue's complement, yellow, was too high — hence the orange tint. I decided to bump up the blue first.

In the blue channel, I moved the center slider left until the blue values matched the green values in the Picker ❸. Then I went to the red channel and moved the slider right until the red value more closely matched blue and green values in the Picker ❹. A final check with the eyedropper over various areas while monitoring the Info palette assured me that, though I had pulled out an extreme amount of color, I still had solid yellow in the foreground equipment and brilliant reds around the molten iron. Finally, I clicked OK and accepted these changes in one slick calculation.

Color cast removal is a relatively simple procedure, but by learning how colors interact with each other, you'll master the tools of color theory and lay a solid groundwork for further exploration of Photoshop's more powerful Curves palette where the next step in color correcting can take place — adjusting very narrow color ranges. ■

❶

❷

1 With software upgrades producing a dynamic range of 3.2 and the newest scanning equipment reaching 3.4, Kodak Photo CD scans can now compete with the best flatbeds and may be a viable alternative to more expensive high-end drum scans for many people. For the time being, though, many Kodak Photo CD images need some correction before they have rich, full-bodied color.

2 This scenic truck shot (not a glamorous photo, but fairly typical of what my clients bring me) has slightly burned-out highlights, so I begin by setting the white point in the Levels dialog box. (If the image were too dark, I would set the black point first.)

PHOTOSHOP

Color Correction With Levels

■ *by Roger Hunsicker*

DRUM SCANS HAVE the inherent advantage of in-process color correction, and with a flatbed, if I get a bad scan I can just scan again. But a Kodak Photo CD scan is locked in plastic. When I first open a Photo CD file, often what I see is a flat or dull image that just doesn't have the punch of a high-end drum scan of the same negative. But with a little tweaking in Photoshop, the Photo CD image can hold its own against the best flatbed or even a drum scan ❶.

After opening an image in RGB mode in Photoshop, the first step is to see if the image is washed out (overexposed) or too dark (underexposed). If the image is too light, I start correcting the color by setting the white point ❷; with a shadowy image, I set the black point first.

By default, the eyedropper tool picks up a single pixel. But for finding a black or white point, I find it easier to use an eyedropper mode that doesn't require me to be quite so precise. So I set my eyedropper tool to sample an area three pixels square (by double-clicking the tool to display the Eyedropper Options palette and choosing 3 By 3 Average from the Sample Size popout menu). Then I choose Image, Adjust, Levels (Command-L) to begin correcting the image.

If the image is so dark important shadow details are lost, as with some poorly lit interior shots, I work the shadow side of the Input Levels slider first. Otherwise, I'll work the highlight slider first. I don't want white areas to be absolutely colorless, and I don't want blacks to be fully saturated, so for a washed-out image, I define the whitest white

❸

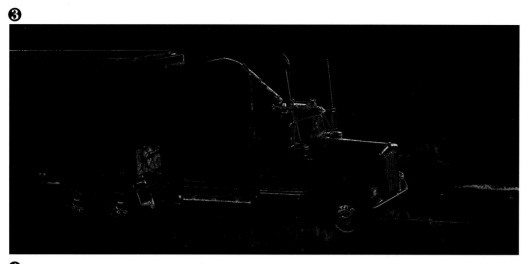

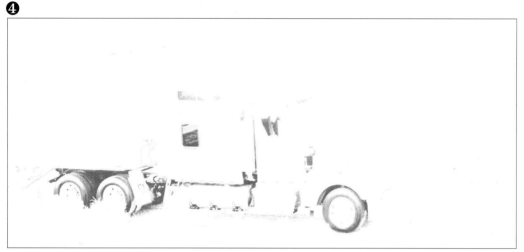

❹

3 In RGB mode, the image turns black when I press Option and click the white point eyedropper on the highlight slider in the Levels dialog box. I move the slider slowly, looking for the first area to turn white. That's where I set the white point.

4 To set the black point, I select the shadow eyedropper, press Option, and click on the shadow slider. When the image goes white, I move the slider to find the darkest shadow: the first black area to come up.

tone before I start correcting the color. I double-click the highlight eyedropper in the Levels dialog box to open the color picker, where I can set the cyan, magenta, and yellow values to about 5%, the black value at 0%, and click OK. This will specify 5% CMY white as my brightest white. (If the image is too dark, I'll define the black point instead by double-clicking the shadow eyedropper in the Levels box and specifying a black of about 13% cyan, magenta, and yellow and 0% black.)

At this point, I'm ready to begin adjusting the color. This key step only works when the image is in RGB mode and the Preview button in the Levels dialog box is turned off. To set the white point, I press the Option key as I click the highlight slider on the Input Levels bar. Instantly, the image turns black. Then I ease the slider to the left. The first cluster of pixels that turns white is the brightest highlight ❸. (Ignore the spatter of red and blue pixels and look only for the white.) I make a mental note of the precise spot (if I can't find it, I zoom in and try again), turn on the Preview, and with the highlight eyedropper click on this spot. Now I turn the preview off again and set the black point

in a similar manner by holding down the Option key while slowly moving the shadow slider to the right. As soon as I click on the slider, the image turns white, and the first area that turns black is my darkest shadow. With Preview selected, I click on this location with the shadow eyedropper, and this becomes my blackest black ❹. (Again, if the photo is too dark, I set the black point first, then the white point.)

When I set the black and white points, I always make certain that this is truly a highlight or a shadow and not a border or something else.

The next step is to adjust the midtone slider on the Input Levels scale to correct brightness or contrast, moving the slider to the left to brighten the image and to the right to bump up contrast. I use the midtone eyedropper cautiously and often not at all, because if I don't find a neutral gray, it can introduce an unwanted tint over the entire image. But if there is a good sample point, the midtone eyedropper can significantly smooth out the tonal range of some images. Color casts can often be removed by using Levels in individual color channels — but that's another story. ∎

Understanding Unsharp Mask

■ *by Janice-Marie Goett*

UNSHARP MASK takes its name from a traditional darkroom technique where a blurred negative is masked to a positive to produce a sharper image. Yes, in spite of the name Unsharp Mask, the function the filter performs is sharpening, bringing an image into clearer focus. The other choices in the Filter, Sharpen submenu (Sharpen, Sharpen Edges, and Sharpen More) act in a straightforward manner, increasing the contrast between neighboring pixels. Unsharp Mask works in roughly the same way, but unlike the other sharpening filters, it has a built-in "softening" function that keeps sharpened edges from "crystallizing." This makes the Unsharp Mask a workhorse filter. It's the best choice for bringing a scanned image into crisp focus, and it can compensate for the blurring Photoshop's anti-aliasing imposes on an image when it performs an interpolation (when an RGB image is converted to CMYK, for example, or when a selection is scaled or rotated). So it's a good idea to apply Unsharp Mask immediately after any function that calls for interpolation. And unlike the other sharpening filters, Unsharp Mask lets you control the effect precisely, through the Amount, Radius, and Threshold values you enter in the Unsharp Mask dialog box.

Amount determines the level of sharpening. Although Photoshop allows you to enter any value from one to 500 percent, the default is 50 percent — and that's a good all-purpose setting. You may want to reduce the Amount occasionally (to as low as 25 percent) for subtle sharpening. But when you need pronounced sharpening, it's better to reapply the filter (Command-F) than to set a high Amount. In fact, you should stay out of the high ranges completely unless you're experimenting with special effects.

Radius settings let you soften the effect of the sharpening by blending the sharpened pixels into their surroundings as if you were applying a feather to the sharpening function. The value you enter determines the range of pixels that will be blended, and Photoshop allows a broader range than anyone with good sense would use: 0.1 to 250 pixels. (How can you blend one-tenth of a pixel? Why would you want to blunt the sharpening effect by spreading it across 250 pixels?) It's important to note that Photoshop's default Radius is decidedly on the low end of the scale — just one pixel — and experts warn you not to stray above two pixels when you enter the Radius. Even a setting as low as five pixels can destroy the edges of the image, blurring detail.

Threshold lets you specify where the sharpening will be applied, throughout the image or only in contrasting areas. The Threshold settings range from zero to 255, representing the 256 levels of gray or color in each pixel. When you enter a Threshold of ten, for example, Unsharp Mask looks for pixels that are ten levels brighter or darker than their neighbors and sharpens them; the filter ignores areas with less contrast. At the default setting of zero, the Unsharp Mask filter acts on every pixel in an image. At 255, it effects only the edges where the contrast in brightness is extreme (black and white in a grayscale image). There's no point in sharpening high-contrast areas, so you can stay away from the high settings entirely. But with Threshold specifications, unlike Amount and Radius settings, it's difficult to establish strict rules. There are some guidelines, though. Keep the Threshold setting at zero for general-purpose sharpening, and take a careful look at the preview before increasing the value. A setting that brings out detail in the bark of a tree, for example, can etch sharp lines into other areas in a photo. If you need precise sharpening in one section of an image, select it and adjust the Threshold setting for the level of contrast you need within the selection. ■

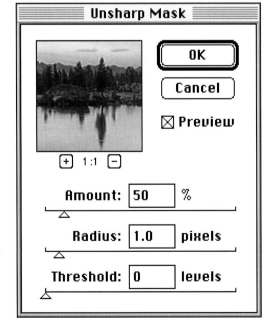

The range of settings you can enter in the Unsharp Mask dialog box varies widely, but you'll get the best results by staying close to the Photoshop defaults, shown here, and adjusting the values only when you want to fine-tune the sharpening effect.

Painless RGB to CMYK

■ *by Linnea Dayton*

ANYONE WHO'S DONE color artwork on the computer and then produced it as ink on paper has noticed some fundamental differences in the way color looks on-screen and the way it looks on the printed page. Several factors contribute to this difference, most of them probably familiar to you by now:

First of all, transmitted color (from the monitor) will look different from reflected color (from ink on paper).

Second, because the RGB gamut (the range of available colors) that you see on a monitor is bigger than the CMYK gamut used for four-color process printing, not all the colors that can be displayed on-screen can be printed. So it's possible to mix colors in RGB files that can't be reproduced on the printed page.

Third, when you make the conversion from a three-color (RGB) to a four-color (CMYK) system, black can partly substitute for mixes of the other three colors. Because the amounts of black versus the other components can vary, there are many ways to translate a particular RGB color in the CMYK system, and the results can look slightly different from one another.

Finally, variations in monitor calibration, film output, paper, ink, presses, and press operators also affect the color in the final printed product.

If you're working in a raster image program like Adobe Photoshop or Painter, any color artwork that you create on-screen and plan to print on paper will likely have to go through the RGB-to-CMYK conversion at some point. Unless your final print will be made on one of a few desktop color printers that can't handle CMYK files, the artwork will eventually need to be output as CMYK separations. But you have some choices about when to make the conversion.

WORKING IN CMYK FROM THE BEGINNING

In Photoshop, you can choose CMYK Color mode when you first create a new file. In Painter, you can limit the color gamut to Printable Colors when you start out. Likewise, some scanning services (and even some desktop scanning software) can do the conversion for you and save the scan file in CMYK mode. The quality of the result depends on the sophistication of the scanning software and the suitability of its settings for the kind of printing you want to do or on the skill of the professional scan operator.

CONVERTING DURING IMAGE EDITING

In Photoshop, at any time during the process of working with the image, you can choose Mode, CMYK Color. But once you make the conversion, you can't regain the original RGB color by choosing Mode, RGB Color. The out-of-CMYK-gamut RGB colors will have been permanently "dulled down" to CMYK-printable versions.

SEPARATING AFTER THE FACT

Another alternative is to keep the file in RGB the entire time you're working with it. Then place it in a layout and allow the page layout program or a color-separation utility to make the separation.

MAKING THE CHOICE

With all these possibilities, how do you decide when to convert? The single advantage of working in CMYK from the beginning is that it prevents last-minute color shifts, since it keeps the image within the printing gamut during its entire development. But if you're working in CMYK and your printing plans change (a different paper may be chosen for the job, for example), the conversion specifications you chose may not apply any longer. In that case you may have to start over to get the results you want.

Working in RGB and putting off the CMYK conversion until the last possible moment allows more freedom. You can get just the color you want on screen and then work with your program's color adjustments to tweak out-of-gamut colors to get CMYK alternatives that are as close as possible to your original colors. Another advantage of working in RGB in Photoshop — and a very significant one — is that some of the program's finest functions, like the Lighting Effects filter, don't work in CMYK mode.

With CMYK Preview now available in Photoshop, it makes sense to work in RGB, preview CMYK in a second window while you work, and then do the actual RGB-to-CMYK conversion at the end of the process. (To make a CMYK preview, choose Window, New Window and choose Mode, CMYK Preview for this window.)

For many jobs, you may even be able to bow out of the conversion process altogether. The conversion has to be done, but that doesn't mean *you* have to do it. Your page layout program or the separation utility used by your imagesetting service bureau may do a fine job of converting most of your RGB images to CMYK. And with today's speedy RIPs, the RGB-to-CMYK conversion often adds nothing to the cost of the job. If that's the case, you can save yourself some time and angst by using this method. Before you decide whether to take on the sizable task of making the right settings in those Separation Setup and Printing Inks Setup dialog boxes (or pay someone else to do it for you), it's usually worth the money to run an "automatically" separated file through film separation to laminate proof. You may find that you're very happy with the result. ■

Punching Holes in Photoshop

■ *by Jim Brey*

PHOTOSHOP HAS SIMPLIFIED my work as a professional photographer in some ways and expanded it in others. Take photo silhouettes, for example. Lifting an element from the background was once the responsibility of the stripping department in the print house. Now clients routinely ask me to provide silhouette images on disk.

I've found that the best way to isolate an element from its background is to magnify the photo to a size that lets me see individual pixels clearly. Then I use the pen tool to draw a clipping path exactly two pixels inside the boundaries of the object. (By working two pixels inside the outline, I can be sure I've eliminated every trace of the background.) When the photo is placed into Page-Maker or QuarkXPress, this clipping path works like a cookie cutter to cut away the background.

As I draw a path with the pen tool, Photoshop 3.0 saves it in the Paths palette under the name *Work Path.* (Photoshop 2.5 doesn't save pen paths automatically. To store the path with the file, you must select Save Path from the Paths palette pop-out menu.) ☞ *Photoshop 3.0 provides a simple shortcut for opening the Save Path dialog box (where you can give a pen path a more descriptive name than the default label Photoshop supplies). Double-clicking on the path's name in the palette opens the Save Path dialog box.*

To turn the pen path into a clipping path, I need to save the file in EPS format, then select the Clipping Path option in the EPS Format dialog box and choose the path name from the pop-out menu. ☞ *If you plan to place an EPS Photoshop image into a page layout application, you need to activate the DCS function in Photoshop 3.0 (or the Desktop Color Separation option in earlier versions) in the EPS Format dialog box. But if you want to place the image into a Post-Script draw program, turn the DCS function off. Illustrator and FreeHand can't recognize the separated color plates.*

For more complex treatments — when I want to create a drop shadow for the lift-out or flip a copy of the image to produce a reflection — I need a channel selection as well as a clipping path. So I highlight the path name in the Paths palette to activate it, choose Make Selection from the palette menu, and then use the Save Selection command (in the Select menu) to store the selection in an alpha channel. ■

❶ **1** In complex clipping paths that include an outline with inner subpaths, Photoshop recognizes the inner paths as "holes" in the image.

2 I often define multiple clipping paths so that I can produce more than one lift-out from a single photo. To create a second clipping path that included the key, I copied the original path (see Figure 1) by highlighting its name in the Paths palette and choosing Duplicate Path from the pop-out menu. While the duplicate path was selected in the palette, I traced the key with the pen tool. (For this lift-out, I chose the clipping path named *Cuffs and key* in the EPS format dialog box when I saved the image. For Figure 1, I chose another clipping path named *Cuffs.*)

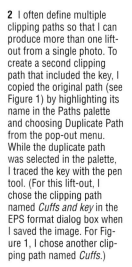

❷

Cloning a Humorous Portrait

■ *by Sara Booth*

P HOTOSHOP PROVIDES THE raw materials for Eldon Doty's portraits, but Doty uses Painter to add the traditional texture of oil paint — a witty contrast to the decidedly untraditional cartoonishness of the subjects. The Redmond, Wash., illustrator specializes in humorous artwork, but his mock portraits in oil are personal projects. He lays in each part of his illustration in Photoshop, combining the program's painting tools with scanned photos, imported textures, and other elements. After each step, he returns to Painter to brush in a hand-painted texture using the cloning function.

Doty began by sketching the character on layout paper ❶, then scanned the sketch and opened it in Photoshop. To preserve the sketch as he painted, Doty added a second layer in front of the sketch and set its mode to Darken so that he could paint into this new layer without changing the sketch below it. He first blocked in flat color using the paintbrush tool, defining a fairly large brush.

To add shadows and highlights, Doty selected a block of color with

Eldon Doty hopes one day to frame his humorous portraits and hang them in his home. To give the images a realistic oil-painting texture, Doty first paints in flat colors and adds collage elements in Photoshop, then turns to Painter's clone function to add brushstrokes.

1 Doty sketched with colored pencil, beginning with a pale blue and using darker values as he finalized the sketch. When he had made a very detailed final sketch, he scanned it to use as a guide in Photoshop.

2 On a new layer in front of the sketch, Doty blocked in the basic colors of the image with Photoshop's paintbrush tool. The burn tool gave the epaulet the appearance of separate strands of fringe and also added dimension to the collar, sleeve, and button, while stroking with the dodge tool added highlights to the sleeve and the epaulet.

❶

❷

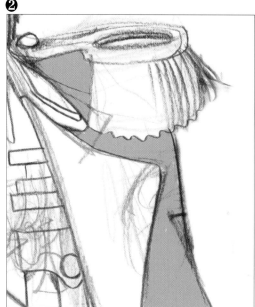

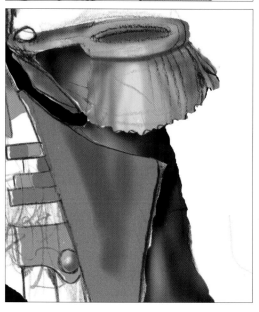

the magic wand and applied the dodge and burn tool ❷. He also added other shading (such as the blush on the cheeks and lips) by picking up the fleshtone with the eyedropper tool, then mixing a pinker version of the shade in the Color Picker before brushing it in with the airbrush ❸. When he had a shaded color image, he flattened it, saved it, and opened it in Painter. ☞ *On the Mac, when any Photoshop selection tool is active, you can access the magic wand tool by pressing the Control key.*

Doty's first step in Painter was to create a copy of the image by choosing File, Clone. He chose the Brushy variant of the Brush tool and checked Use Clone Color at the bottom of the expanded Art Materials:Colors palette so the brush would pick up the colors from his original Photoshop image. Then he began to repaint the image in oil paint.

Doty began his Painter work on the face, laying in brushstrokes to match its contours. At times, he switched to a smaller brush size (by choosing Size from the Controls popout menu of the Brushes palette) when working in detailed areas such as around the eyes. Moving outward from the face, he painted in clothes and a turban. As he worked, the black line drawing disappeared into the oil paint and became part of the shadow areas. ☞ *To resize a Painter brush interactively, Command-Option-drag. You'll see a circle that changes size as you drag.*

At this point, Doty's image had an oil-paint appearance ❹, but it was far from finished. His

❸

❺

❹

3 To add finishing touches to the face, Doty mixed a pinker version of the flesh-tone and used the airbrush to apply it to the cheeks and chin. A deeper fleshtone was used to add shadows around the eyes and under the nose, mouth, and chin. Doty didn't worry about softening the edges where two colors met, because he planned to repaint the image in Painter.

4 Doty opened the image in Painter, cloned it, and used the Brushy variant of the Brush tool in various sizes to stroke in painterly texture, picking up color from the cloned image. To define the individual hairs in the beard, he switched to the Hairy Brush variant of the brush tool, then went over the area with the Scratchboard Tool variant of the Pen tool.

5 Returning to Photoshop, Doty added color to the eyes and gave the character a fuller lower lip. He added wrinkles below the eye, detail to the ears, and rope texture to the epaulet. The patterns on the turban were created in the plug-in Terrazzo, then given sheen and shadow using the dodge and burn tool.

next step was to return to Photoshop, where he used the burn tool to define detail around the nostrils and ears and brushed in highlights around the nose, cheek, and chin with the dodge tool, in addition to adding detail to the pupils. "Painter has its own dodge and burn tools," he says, "but I feel like I have more control with the Photoshop tools." ☞ *To select Photoshop's toning tools, type the letter* O. *Keep typing* O *to toggle through the toning tools (dodge, burn, and sponge).*

For the fabrics in the turban, Doty used Xaos Tools' Photoshop plug-in Terrazzo, which creates tiling patterns. He began by creating a new layer in his Photoshop file which he could use as a palette, filling a selection with his desired background color and adding bits of other colors with

the paintbrush tool. When he opened Terrazzo, he could zero in on this area and use it to generate a variety of tiling patterns. When he chose the one he wanted, he used it to fill each selection of the turban. To make the fabric appear dimensional, he added highlights and shadows with the dodge and burn tool **❺**.

The next step was to add medals, decorations, and other elements that would give the image more variety. This involved a good deal of switching back and forth between Painter and Photoshop. As Doty added detail in Photoshop, he always repainted it in Painter so the illustration would have a consistent oil paint texture. Doty copied scanned medals into the image and sized them, then used Painter to repaint them, varying

6 The fabrics of the turban give it a luxurious look, but Doty wanted to increase that look by adding strands of pearls. He created a single pearl on its own layer, then cloned it with the rubber stamp tool. To add a sense of dimension, he used the burn tool to darken the pearls where they wrapped under the fabric or around the turban's edges.

6 Doty initially gave the figure fairly conventional proportions (top). But for comic effect, he used Photoshop's "pinch" filter to shrink the head. He also added another layer to the turban, adding to the sense that the character is overwhelmed by his clothes.

❻

❼

their colors and surfaces until they had the look he wanted. Then he returned to Photoshop and used the dodge and burn tool to emphasize the shininess of the metal.

To add richness and vary the textures, Doty wanted to create a string of pearls that looped through the turban. Returning to Photoshop, he added a new layer, then painted one pearl with the paintbrush. Then he used the rubber stamp tool, choosing Clone (Non-Aligned) from the Option popout menu of the Rubber Stamp Options palette, and Option-clicked in the center of the pearl to set it as the source point. Then he used the rubber stamp to clone a series of pearls before returning to the image layer to paint in a shadow behind them with the airbrush **❻**. ☞ *To display the Tool Options palette for the selected tool in Photoshop, press Return.* ☞ *To paint only in*

the transparent areas of the active Photoshop layer, choose Behind in the popout menu of the Airbrush Options palette.

Doty keeps a file of backgrounds created in Photoshop and Painter, but after trying several of these file backgrounds, he decided to take a simpler approach with this portrait. Creating a new layer for the background, Doty filled it with a gradient from deep red to black. Then he used the Apply Lighting filter to add two light sources.

If Photoshop had a Silly filter, Doty might have used that in his final step, in which he looked for ways to subtly play up the cartoony look of the character. After trying a variety of filters on copies of the image, he chose the Pinch filter (applied to the figure only, not the background) to make the character's head smaller and give more emphasis to the body and turban **❼**. ■

PHOTOSHOP / PAINTER

Building a Portrait

■ *by Sara Booth*

MOST ARTISTS USE electronic collage techniques when they're aiming for an obvious cut-and-paste effect. But when Westfield, N.J., illustrator Joanie Schwarz uses Photoshop to combine scanned photos, Painter elements, and bits of scanned fabric and paper, her results are fantasy images whose esthetic is closer to classic hand-painted portraits than to collages.

Schwarz began working on *Jacob With Mountain,* a portrait for a book of poetry for children, by photographing a baby in her own yard. Photoshop layer masks and layer opacity allowed her to combine the photo's background with a landscape photo, and Painter made it easy to add fantasy elements. To complete

"I like it when artwork is coming out of me and I'm not thinking too hard about it," says Joanie Schwarz. The Westfield, N.J., illustrator's collage portrait gets its dreamlike look from a very limited palette, with fleshtones and a single accent color standing out against a nature-inspired background of shades of gray-green.

1 "I take the photos pretty rapidly, so that if I have to take different parts from different shots, they'll be in close to the same position," Schwarz says. She used one shot (top) for the body and another for the head; because not much time elapsed between the two shots, the lighting and position were similar, making compositing easier. After correcting color and making other small adjustments, she applied the Median filter for a subtle smoothing effect.

❶

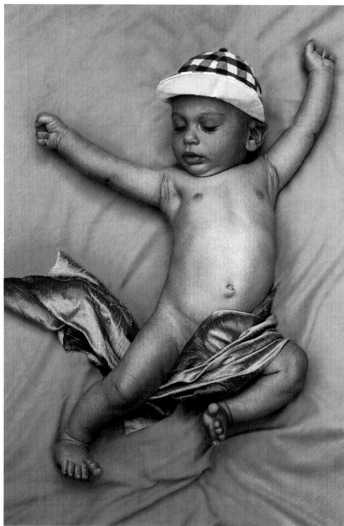

the image, she built a frame of scraps of fabric and paper from her files.

COMPOSITING A PORTRAIT

None of Schwarz's baby photos was exactly what she wanted, so she used Photoshop to combine the face from one shot and the body from another. Selecting the head with the lasso, she copied it and pasted it into the other photo. To make positioning easier, she gave the floating selection a low opacity using the slider in the Layers palette ❶. At this stage she didn't worry about making clean selections or smoothing the place where the two parts joined because she intended to smooth the entire drawing at the end of the process.

Schwarz chose the satin cloth in the photograph for its texture, but she wasn't happy with its color. She selected the cloth with the lasso and chose Image, Adjust, Hue/Saturation (Command-U), then dragged the Hue slider to the left to change its color from pink to purple. She wanted

the hat to match the cloth, but using the Hue/Saturation dialog box to change its color would have added too much color to the whites. So after using the lasso to select the hat, Schwarz chose Image, Adjust, Color Balance (Command-Y) and made adjustments in the dialog box's Midtones channel.

Though the background fabric is covered up in the final image, it shows through the partially opaque landscape, so a slight green cast in the fabric had to be corrected. Schwarz began by clicking in the fabric with the magic wand, then zoomed in close and used the magic wand and lasso until she had selected the entire background. After saving this selection as a path called *Background*, she used Hue/Saturation to adjust the color of the fabric. ☛ *To save a Photoshop selection as a path, click the selection icon at the bottom of the Paths palette or choose Make Path from the palette's popout menu.*

In creating a portrait, Schwarz sometimes finds herself needing to improve on nature. "I try to

❷

❹

❸
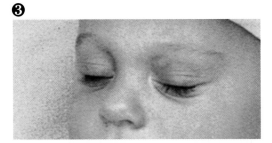

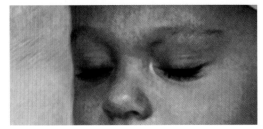

2 To add a blush to the baby's face, Schwarz used the airbrush tool, choosing a large, soft brush and setting the brush mode to Color so the hue would be changed without affecting the saturation or lightness. A low pressure setting in the Brushes palette assured the effect would be subtle.

3 To correct the baby's eyelashes, which "were going all over the place," Schwarz opened the image in Painter and used a long-bristled variant of the camel hair brush to draw new lashes.

4 To make her hillside photo fill the bottom of the background, Schwarz selected it with the rectangle marquee tool, chose Select, Float (Command-J) to float a copy, then chose Image, Reflect, Vertical. She stretched the copy by choosing Image, Effects, Scale and used the clone tool to soften the seam where the two copies met.

make a baby's skin look as babylike as possible," she says. She inversed the *Background* selection to select only the baby, then used the Command key and the lasso to remove the cloth and the hat from the selection. Then she chose Image, Adjust, Color Balance and adjusted the skin tone by removing cyan and adding yellow. She also added color to the lips by selecting them with the lasso and adjusting them in the Hue/Saturation, Color Balance, and Brightness/Contrast dialog boxes, and added rosiness to the cheeks with the airbrush ❷ before using Painter to improve the eyelashes ❸. The final step was to apply the Median filter to the face to soften contrasts.

PAINTING THE BACKGROUND

Schwarz maintains an electronic landscape portfolio, which contains both photographs she has taken and scans of her traditional oil paintings. For this portrait, she opened a scanned photo of a hillside, copied it, and pasted it onto a new layer above the baby by choosing Edit, Paste Layer. The horizontal landscape left much of the top and bottom of the image empty. Schwarz planned to use Painter for the top of the landscape, but a second copy of the image filled out the bottom ❹.

To make the landscape look like it was behind the baby, Schwarz used the *Background* path she had made earlier to add a layer mask to the landscape image. After targeting the landscape layer, she chose Add Layer Mask from the popout menu of the Layers palette. Then she loaded the path as a selection and pressed Option-Delete to fill the selection with black, masking out the part of the landscape that was in front of the baby. Schwarz liked the wrinkles in the fabric, so she set the landscape layer's opacity to 70% so some of those wrinkles would show through. "You look at it and wonder, is he lying on the background or flying through the air?" she says.

The lower part of the landscape is still fairly realistic, but Schwarz wanted the sky to be "a lit-

5 After painting the wings in Painter, Schwarz opened the image again in Photoshop. To create the moon, she zoomed in close, used the elliptical marquee to select a circle, then pressed Command while she drew a second ellipse to subtract it from the first, resulting in a crescent-shaped selection. She Option-dragged to copy this selection, then chose Image, Effects, Scale to enlarge it.

6 Schwarz wanted to unify the elements of her painting, but removing the evidence of all her cutting and pasting was labor-intensive: She zoomed in close, then used the rubber stamp, smudge, and blur tools along the edges of the image, covering obvious seams and making the baby look more connected with the background. "If anyone knows an easier way to do this, I wish they'd tell me how," she says.

7 For the frame, Schwarz began with a scanned strip of fabric. She applied the Blur and Median filters to smooth out the contrasts, then chose Image, Adjust, Desaturate to remove all the original colors. She added her own color by choosing Image, Adjust, Color Balance, trying to match the colors in the sky. When she copied the strip into the baby file, she reduced the opacity of the floating selection, so that a bit of the sky shows through, then pasted it repeatedly.

❺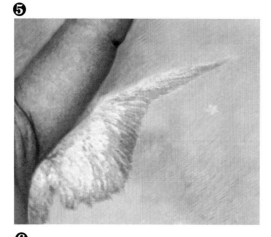

❻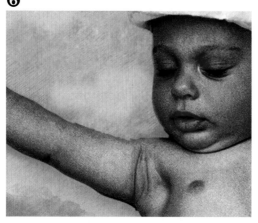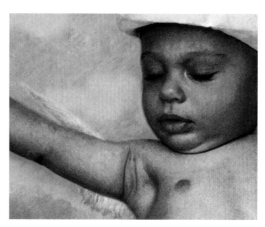

❼

tle more whimsical." So she opened the image in Painter and added the sky, using the camel hair brush as well as several variants of the brush tool that she has saved. Returning to Photoshop, she added the clouds by making selections with the lasso, adding a heavy feather, and using the dodge tool to lighten the area inside the selection.

After painting the angel wings in Painter, Schwarz brought them into her Photoshop file and applied the Median filter to smooth out the contrast within the wings, giving them a softer look. The iridescent shades of the wings also provided texture and color for other elements of the sky. Schwarz selected a star shape in the wing with the lasso tool (pressing the Option key and clicking from point to point to select straight-line segments) and pressed the Option key as she dragged a copy out into the sky. She used a similar technique to create the moon, using the elliptical marquee to select a crescent ❺. The final step was to painstakingly merge the baby with the background ❻. ☞ *To activate Photoshop's marquee, type the letter M. Continue typing M to toggle between rectangular and elliptical marquees.*

BUILDING THE FRAME

In addition to her backgrounds, Schwarz also keeps a file of scraps of fabric, wallpaper, photographs, and other images, using tiny bits of these elements to put together her trademark frames. For this portrait, she created a new layer for the border, with a low opacity to let the background show through. She constructed the outer scalloped border by scanning a fabric swatch, selecting a triangle, using the Hue/Saturation dialog box to adjust colors, and pasting repeatedly. The inner beaded border came from a bit of notepaper, while the central border with the leaf motif was taken from another bit of fabric ❼. Both were scanned, colored, and pasted repeatedly. ∎

A Garden of Color

■ *by Sara Booth*

PAINTER'S TOUCH and Photoshop's power combine to make quick work of natural-looking electronic "paintings." Salt Lake City designer Traci O'Very Covey used Painter's tools — chalk, watercolor, and even the eraser — to add tactile interest to an invitation. But Photoshop's advanced contrast controls, selection techniques, and color management tools made her work easier.

When asked to create an invitation for a garden shop's 20th anniversary celebration, Covey wanted to communicate a festive atmosphere. She began by creating a pencil sketch on vellum, which retained its texture when she created a grayscale scan ❶. She almost always adjusts her scans in Photoshop before proceeding with her images: "When you scan a sketch, the paper comes in with little dots, and the line is never black enough," she says. So she used the Levels dialog box to improve the contrast. ☞ *If you frequently touch up scans in Photoshop, it's worth the time to save your Levels settings by clicking the Save button in the Levels dialog box (Image, Adjust, Levels or Command-L). Once you have loaded the saved settings, you can still make adjustments by eye.*

Painter and Photoshop make a powerful team for Salt Lake City designer Traci O'Very Covey, who took care of contrast and color in Photoshop before adding texture in Painter.

1 Covey increased the contrast in her scanned sketch by choosing Image, Adjust, Levels (Command-L) and moving both outer sliders inward. She also moved the center slider to the right to darken the midtones, which strengthened her lightest pencil strokes.

2 To cover large areas with color efficiently, Covey used Photoshop's gradient tool. She loaded saved selections and created new ones with the magic wand tool.

3 To add a realistic sense of volume to the rocks, Covey filled them with radial gradients in Photoshop. She used Painter's watercolor brush to add texture.

After using the eraser to remove specks from the scan, Covey began doing the preparatory work that would make it easier to add color: Using the magic wand, she selected areas she planned to fill with colors or gradients — for example, the large area of grass behind the figures — and saved the selections as channels. Sometimes it was necessary to close the shapes by using the pencil to stop up gaps in the line. ☞ *Photoshop provides keyboard shortcuts to choose tools without going to the toolbox. Type the letter P to access the pencil, E for the eraser, and W for the magic wand.*

At the same time, Covey also selected the linework and saved it as a channel, allowing her to subtract it from selections when she wanted to add color without disturbing her linework. ☞ *An easy way to select linework in a grayscale sketch is to use Photoshop's Select, Color Range command. Try choosing Shadows in the Select popout menu. If this doesn't create a satisfactory selection, choose Sampled Colors in the Select popout menu and use the eyedropper to pick up a color from the image; then move the*

Fuzziness slider (which is similar to the Tolerance option of the magic wand tool) to the right to include more colors in the selection, or to the left to include fewer colors.

QUICK COLOR

When her scan was finished, Covey opened a new Photoshop document to create a palette for the invitation. She used a Pantone swatchbook to choose a set of "fresh and springlike" colors, then opened the color picker (by clicking on the foreground color swatch in the toolbox) and entered each color's CMYK percentages. When the color was displayed as the foreground color, she simply used the marquee tool to select a square, then pressed Option-Delete to fill it with the chosen color. She saved this palette document and kept it open while she worked so that she could use the eyedropper to pick up colors, then apply them to selected areas of the invitation.

Covey used Photoshop's gradient tool to rough in the basic colors of the image. She chose background and foreground colors from the palette she

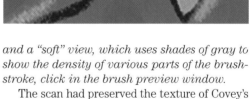

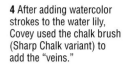

4 After adding watercolor strokes to the water lily, Covey used the chalk brush (Sharp Chalk variant) to add the "veins."

5 Using the chalk brush (Large Chalk variant), Covey traced along some of the linework, smudging the lines and adding a sense of motion to the illustration.

6 Lines (created with Large Chalk) add highlights and shadows, giving the suggestion of relief carving to the planter.

7 To add the highlights on the ripples, Covey used the eraser tool (Medium Bleach variant). This removed varying amounts of color depending on the pressure of the stroke.

had created, selected areas or loaded selections, and filled the areas with gradients ❷. Most of the gradients are linear, but in some areas — such as the sky, the rocks, and the woman's hat — she used radial gradients because they created a more realistic sense of space. ☞ *To exchange Photoshop's foreground and background colors, type the letter* X. *To return to the default black foreground and white background, type the letter* D.

ADDING TEXTURE IN PAINTER

Covey builds custom brushes for nearly all her Painter work by choosing Size from the Controls popout menu of the Brushes palette. In addition to adjusting the size of the brush, she also drags the Plus-Minus Size slider to the right. This creates a wider variation between the minimum and maximum size of each stroke. The result is a softer look. ☞ *By default, the preview window in Painter's Brush Controls: Size dialog box shows the brush as a black circle (indicating the minimum stroke size) inside a gray circle (maximum stroke size). To toggle between this view*

and a "soft" view, which uses shades of gray to show the density of various parts of the brushstroke, click in the brush preview window.

The scan had preserved the texture of Covey's original pencil drawing, and she wanted the entire illustration to have the same hand-drawn effect. Using Painter's default Basic Paper texture, she began by using the watercolor brush to add spontaneous shapes to the grass, bushes, and water. Watercolor brushstrokes also added texture to the rocks ❸ and the water lily ❹. ☞ *In Painter, you can tell which brush method subcategories will interact with the paper texture by looking for the word "grainy" in their names.*

Using the chalk brush, Covey traced along parts of her black linework, softening the lines and adding a "glow" to the shapes ❺. She also used chalk in gray and white to add a suggestion of depth to the planter ❻. To add highlights to the water ripples, though, Covey turned to an unusual tool: the eraser ❼. This lightened the underlying color unevenly, removing it completely only at the heaviest part of the stroke. ■

Electronic Overlays

■ *by John Marshall*

BEFORE PHOTOSHOP 3, electronic color often took a toll on line art — and since bold, hand-drawn lines are the foundation of comic art, I didn't like seeing them suffer. At Beckett Publications, I've used Photoshop for more than a year to color comic sections in Beckett's sports magazines. In the past, I used the magic wand tool to make selections within the scanned line art when I wanted to add color. But the tool's anti-aliasing function tended to eat into the black lines. With Photoshop 3's layering, however, the color is completely separate from the line art, so the black lines stay sharp. Of course, the magic wand is still useful for some tasks because it can be set to "see" all the visible layers. ☛ *If you select the Sample Merged function in the Magic Wand Options palette, the tool acts on all the visible layers. But the painting tools apply color only to the layer that is selected in the Layers palette.*

I begin the process by scanning the hand-drawn line art and adjusting the contrast to turn each grayscale scan into a crisp black-and-white image. Then I use the layering feature in Photoshop 3 to simulate the function of old-fashioned color overlays. First, I select Duplicate Layer from the Layers palette pop-out menu to place a copy of the art on a new layer (which I name *Line Art*) and set the mode to Darken so that the background is visible behind the *Line Art* layer.

After deleting the art on the background layer and changing the file to CMYK mode, I begin to lay in color. In general, I make selections on the background layer and use the Option-Delete shortcut to fill them. Then I go back in with the airbrush tool to add gradations, shading, and highlights. In some cases, I use filters to generate effects like speed blurs or energy bolts. Recurring colors (skin tones and uniforms, for example) are selected with the eyedropper tool and poured into the Swatches palette. By storing this palette as a separate file and loading it into other Photoshop files (with the Save Swatches and Append Swatches commands in the Swatches palette menu), I can keep the color consistent from one page to the next.

The font I use (WhizBang by Studio Daedalus) simulates traditional hand-drawn comic lettering, and it ships with a disk of indispensable word and thought balloons. I arrange the lettering and the balloons in Illustrator, then place the lettering on top of the artwork in QuarkXPress. I could set the type directly in XPress, but I prefer to work in Illustrator where I can maintain an even stroke around all the balloons, even when I scale them to different sizes. And for me, it's easier to experiment with lettering placement and word balloon styles in Illustrator — although this ability to experiment can be a curse as well as a blessing. ■

❶

❹

1 After scanning the line drawing in grayscale, the contrast is adjusted, using Photoshop's Levels controls (Image, Adjust, Levels or Command-L). I reposition the Input sliders to convert the gray tones to sharp black-and-white. There are other ways to increase contrast in Photoshop, but working through the Levels dialog box lets me control the adjustment precisely so that I don't lose the smoothness of the anti-aliased lines.

2 A copy of the scan is converted to Bitmap mode and saved in PICT format so I can use it as a template in Illustrator when I set type and arrange word balloons.

3 Once I complete the color work in Photoshop, I apply the Flatten Image command (from the Layers palette menu) and save the art in EPS format so that it can be placed in QuarkXPress. (I also keep the layered version of the file on hand in case I need to make changes later.) The Photoshop file is imported into XPress, and the Illustrator lettering is placed on top of it.

4 I try not to overdo the color because it can compete with the line art. I walk a fine line between fully painted art and the flat-color comics of the past. Although most of the coloring is done in Photoshop, I used the KPT Texture Explorer to produce the flames in this panel (from a fantasy comic for a Beckett tribute magazine honoring football superstar Emmitt Smith). The flame texture was created in a separate file and "painted" into the illustration with the rubber stamp tool.

Painting with Metallic Colors

■ *by Janet Ashford*

WHAT? There's no Apply Gold Leaf command in Adobe Photoshop? Nicole Crameri Raynard solved this dilemma and discovered a way to simulate a gold-leaf effect when she created a self-promotional illustration: She started with flat color and used Photoshop's dodge-and-burn tool to add a metallic luster to the tones. Raynard, also used Painter's Color Variability function and Photoshop's powerful channels to create the illustration, drawing on techniques she learned as an intern at Kodak's Center for Creative Imaging, as well as some she developed herself.

Raynard's imagery was inspired by the work of late-19th-century Viennese painter Gustav Klimt. Raynard was fascinated by Klimt's intricate designs and sparkling metallic tones — and by his method of depicting his favorite model, his lover Adele. In his pencil studies, Klimt often rendered Adele's face and body hastily, using only a few sketchy lines, but he drew her clothes in detail. Raynard took this combination of minimalism and embellishment a step further when she created her own pencil sketch, replacing the human figure with a clothes hanger. (She calls the illustration *Adele in Black.*)

CREATING CHANNEL IMAGES

Using her sketch as a reference, Raynard created two grayscale Photoshop images — one for the dress and another for the ornate background — that could be used as selection channels later in building the color illustration. By producing the masking channels as grayscale images, Raynard could work at a large scale (in this case, 10 x 14 inches) and still maintain a manageable file size (each of the two files filled 12MB at 300 dpi).

To create the dress, Raynard first drew an oval with the marquee tool. Then, in a process more like sculpting than drawing, she used the lasso tool to "carve" sections out of the oval until the form of a dress appeared ❶.

Raynard used the Stroke Path command and a combination of drawing and selection tools to produce the background design. She chose a small, hard-edged brush in the Brushes palette (so that the strokes would be defined with that brush) and began to draw. She used a graphics tablet when she wanted to create free-form shapes with the

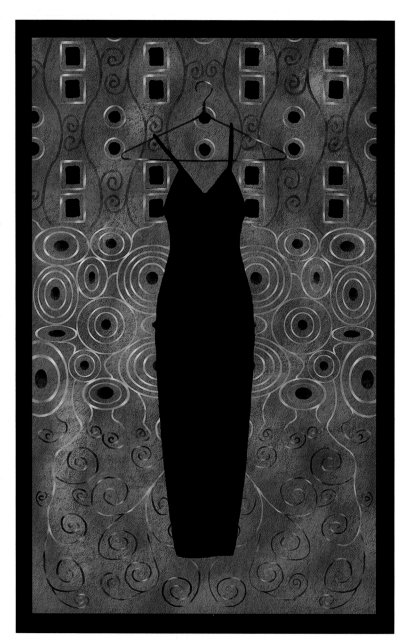

Nicole Crameri Raynard of San Francisco, used Photoshop's dodge-and-burn tool and Painter's Color Variability function to modify the colors in this illustration. Lightening tones in some areas and darkening them in others let Raynard "burnish" the background design, bringing metallic highlights to the original flat colors.

brush, the pen, or the lasso, and the mouse when she wanted to define precise forms with the oval or rectangular marquees. By pressing the Shift key, she could make several marquee selections at once and then stroke the selections as a group. She used this Shift-select technique to draw a complicated oval design. First, she defined several ovals with the elliptical marquee tool and applied strokes. Then she drew another set of ovals, centered inside the originals, by pressing the Option key as she Shift-selected so that she could draw the shapes from the center out. By repeating the select-and-stroke process, she built up a set of concentric ovals ❷. Raynard drew one half of the background, then copied it to produce a symmetrical design ❸.

CREATING A LUSTROUS CANVAS

Raynard's next step was to create a "canvas" with the look of soft, copper-colored brush strokes on a rough surface. She planned to use Painter's Apply Surface Texture function to give the canvas a rough texture, but she wanted to define a custom texture instead of choosing one of the default patterns from the Paper palette. So she scanned a piece of concrete ❹, opened the scan in Photoshop, and used the Offset filter's Wrap Around option to bring the edges of the scan together, producing a seamless pattern. (For more about creating a seamless repeating pattern in Photoshop, see "Perfecting a Pattern," page 36.)

Raynard saved the concrete texture as a PICT file and opened it in Painter. She selected all, chose Capture Texture from the Options menu, and entered a name for the new texture. Finally, she set the Crossfade value to zero in the Capture Texture dialog box (so that later, when the pattern was repeated, the edges of the texture would abut precisely, with no overlap and no space between sections). The captured texture now appeared in the Paper palette.

After opening a new Painter file (with the same dimensions and resolution she used in creating the dress and the background design), Raynard filled the entire image area with solid copper. She then chose a large, soft cover brush and selected Sponge from the Brush Looks palette. Finally, she set high Color Variability specifications for Value and Saturation in the Color palette and painted on top of the canvas with the same copper color. The variable Saturation and Value settings, in conjunction with the pressure-sensitive tablet, produced color tones ranging from deep to light and brush strokes ranging from thick to thin ❺.

Once she was satisfied with the mottled effect of her brush strokes, Raynard chose Effects, Surface Control, Apply Surface Texture. In the Paper palette, she selected the custom texture she had

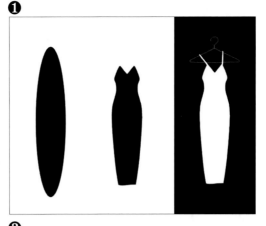

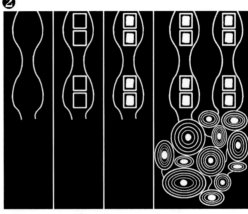

1 To create the dress, Raynard began by defining an oval with Photoshop's elliptical marquee tool. She filled the oval with black, then "carved" into it with the lasso tool, selecting curved shapes and deleting to fill the selections with white. Once she had carved out a dress shape, Raynard used the brush tool to add black straps and a gray clothes hanger. Finally, she inverted the image (Image, Map, Invert or Command-I) so that she could use it later as a masking channel.

2 Raynard drew a pair of wavy lines with the pen tool and stroked the paths by choosing Stroke Path from the Paths palette pop-out menu. She used the rectangular marquee tool to define a set of rectangles, then chose Make Path from the Paths palette to turn these marquee selections into pen paths so she could apply the Stroke Path function. The brush tool was used to draw rough-edged shapes inside the rectangles, and the wave-and-rectangle design was copied. Raynard used the elliptical marquee tool to build a set of concentric ovals, using the Paths palette option to convert the selections to paths and apply strokes.

3 The brush tool was used to add wispy tendrils to the design. Once Raynard had drawn half of the pattern, she copied it, then chose Image, Flip, Horizontal to flop the copy, producing a symmetrical design.

4 After making a grayscale scan of a piece of concrete, Raynard adjusted Photoshop's Curves settings (Image, Adjust, Curves or Command-M) to increase the contrast. Later, she used this scan to create a custom paper texture in Painter.

5 The Color Variability settings in Painter's Color palette were used to apply a mottled tone to the canvas.

6 Raynard loaded the alpha channel she had created for the background pattern (see Figure 3) and painted inside the selection borders. While the selection was still active, she used the dodge-and-burn tool to darken the color in some places and soften it in others, giving the design a metallic look.

7 When Raynard created a masking channel for the dress (see Figure 1), she used a shade of gray to draw the hanger. Once the dress-and-hanger channel was loaded into the composite image, the selection border didn't show for the gray tone — but the hanger was still an active part of the selection. When Raynard filled the selection with black, all the whites in the selection channel absorbed the black fill (so the dress became solid black, and the hanger was took on a percentage of the black fill).

❹
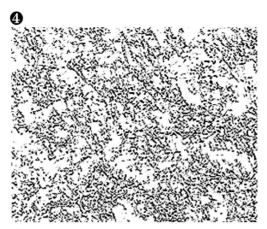

❺

❻
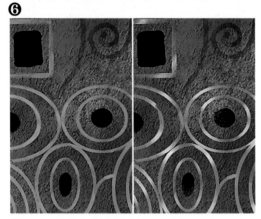

❼
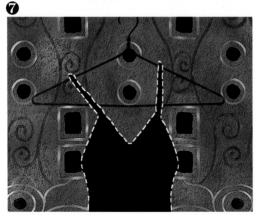

created with the concrete scan. Then she saved this Painter file in TIFF format and used it as a "painting" surface to produce the final illustration in Photoshop.

COMBINING THE FILES

Raynard launched Photoshop, then opened the copper-colored canvas, along with the grayscale background pattern she had created earlier. She planned to use the grayscale background design as a masking channel, so she loaded it into a new channel in the color image.

Raynard was working in Photoshop 2.5, so she loaded the channel by choosing Image, Calculate, Duplicate, and then setting the background pattern as the Source file and selecting a new channel in the color image as the Destination. She used the same technique to load the dress file into a masking channel. (In Photoshop 3, this process would be performed by choosing Image, Calculations, then choosing the masking file as Source 1 and 2, setting the Blending at Normal, and selecting a new channel in the color image as the Result.)
☞ *When you perform Photoshop Calculations between two or more images, the files must be open, and they must be exactly the same size and resolution.*

Next Raynard activated the mask for the background design (Select, Load Selection) and began to paint inside the selection borders with the brush tool. ☞ *You can also load a Photoshop selection channel by pressing the Option key and then clicking on the channel's name in the Channels palette.*

APPLYING 'METALLIC' PAINT

After she painted the background design, Raynard applied Photoshop's dodge-and-burn tool to "burnish" the colors, bringing a metallic shimmer to the pattern. In the Brushes palette, she set the dodge-and-burn tool's Exposure setting at about 10 percent for the Midtones. She used the dodge tool to lighten the tones, then pressed the Option key when she wanted to activate the tool's burn function in order to darken the colors. The low Exposure setting made these tonal modifications subtle enough to blend seamlessly into the surrounding colors, but Raynard could drag the tool over certain areas repeatedly for a more intense dodge-and-burn effect **❻**.

Finally, the dress and the clothes hanger were "painted" on top of this burnished background design. First, Raynard loaded the dress channel and filled the selection with black at 100 percent opacity **❼**. While the selection was still active, she used the dodge-and-burn tool to add shiny highlights to the gray tones of the hanger, giving it a silvery sheen. ■

PAINTER

Building Your Own Brushes

■ *by Cher Threinen-Pendarvis with Linnea Dayton*

SOME PEOPLE ARE CONTENT with the huge variety of brushes that ship with Painter. But if you don't rest until you get just the brushstroke you want, you've come to the right place. Like other parts of Painter's interface, the Brushes palette uses the metaphor of a drawer you can open and close. The pop-up menu below the drawer front offers a list of *variants*, different "models" of the brush you've selected from the drawer front. Besides the variants supplied with the program, you can design your own (see "Making Custom Brushes in Painter" on page 6).

THE ANATOMY OF A BRUSH

You'll have more control over customization if you understand what constitutes a brush variant. Every Painter variant has five fundamental charac-teristics — two (dab and stroke) that define the brush structure and three (brush type, method, and submethod) that control how paint applied by the brush interacts with the paper.

Dabs. Think of a *dab* as the footprint of the brush — the cross-section you'd get if you held it vertically and touched it lightly to the page ❶. To change dab type, choose Window, Brushes (Command-2) to display the Brushes palette, then choose Size from the palette's Controls menu and select a dab type from the buttons at the bottom of the zoomed-out palette:

• Circular: Most of Painter's brushes use this type. Don't be fooled by the term "circular," though. You can change a Circular brush's Squeeze setting so its footprint looks elliptical.
• 1-Pixel: Just as it sounds, this dab type makes a brush 1 pixel wide.

1 The Circular dab (top) is the footprint of the Huge Rough Out brush; the Bristle dab (center) is the Big Dry Ink brush's footprint; and the Captured dab (bottom) was made with the Square Chalk brush.

2 These brushstrokes show the three stroke types: Single (top), represented by the Square Chalk; Rake (center), demonstrated by the Big Wet Oils; and Multi (bottom), shown by the Hairy Brush.

3 These three variants have very different submethods: Huge Rough Out (Brush variant) uses Grainy Edge Flat Cover (top); Big Dry Ink (Brush variant) uses Soft Cover (center); and Oil Pastel (Chalk variant) uses Grainy Hard Cover (bottom).

❶

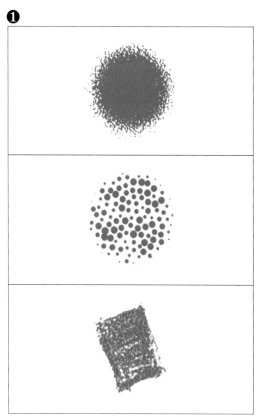

❷

❸

• Bristle: Since these brushes are made up of separate "hairs," they have a richer potential than Circular brushes. You can adjust Bristle Thickness, Clumpiness, and other settings in the Spacing and Bristles palettes (found under the Controls menu in the Brushes palette).

• Captured: Any area can be selected and turned into a Captured brush. Use the rectangular selection tool (press Shift to constrain the selection to a square) around a mark or group of marks. Then choose the Brush tool in the Tools palette and in the Brushes palette choose Brushes, Capture Brush. The footprint will appear in the Brush Controls:Size palette, where you can modify it further.

Strokes. A *stroke* is a dab applied over a distance **❷**. You can switch Stroke types in the Brush Controls:Spacing palette, accessed by choosing Spacing from the Controls menu of the Brushes palette. There are three kinds of strokes:

• Single: Because these brushes have only one path for the computer to calculate, they're fast. And in spite of their name, they're not limited to painting simple lines. If you use a Bristle or Captured dab type, you can create a fast, single-stroke brush with a lot of complexity.

• Rake: This stroke type is like a garden rake; each evenly spaced tine is a dab. Painter gives you a lot of control over dab spacing. You can make dabs overlap (by moving the Spacing/Size slider in the Brush Controls:Spacing palette to the left),

creating wonderfully complex, functional brushes. You can also change the number of *bristles* (or dabs) by choosing Controls, Spacing (keeping in mind that fewer bristles make faster brushes), and adjust the way the bristles interact by choosing Controls, Bristle and Controls, Rake.

• Multi: These computation-intensive brushes, built from randomly distributed dabs that may or may not overlap, are slowest and therefore least spontaneous. If you draw a line with a multi-stroke brush, you'll see a dotted preview of its path; the stroke itself appears a moment later. Lovely variable strokes can be made with a multi-stroke brush, but you can make faster, "real-time" brushes using a Single stroke with a Bristle dab type or a Rake stroke. ☞ *To see how stroke types operate, choose the Square Chalk variant of the Chalk (a single-stroke brush), the Big Wet Oils variant of the Brush (a rake brush), and the Hairy Brush variant of the Brush (a multi-stroke brush).*

THE PHYSIOLOGY OF PAINTING

To control how paint interacts with other paint and with the paper when you wield a brush variant to apply a stroke, Painter uses two lists of options at the bottom of the zoomed-out Brushes palette, under the variant name.

• The Method Category, or simply *method,* defines the major categories of interaction. For example, all the variants of the Pencil brush supplied with

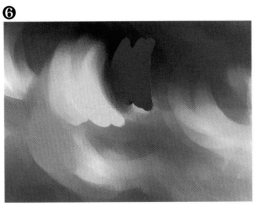

Painter use the Buildup method, which means overlapping strokes will darken to black. On the other hand, the Chalk brush variants use the Cover method, which means strokes — even light-colored ones — will cover other strokes. You can change methods at any time for any variant.

• While each method gives a markedly different effect, the Method Subcategory (or *submethod*) has a subtle result, affecting the edges of brushstrokes ❸. Submethods that include the word *flat* produce hard-edged, or aliased, strokes. Those that include the word *hard* are not quite so hard as flat brushes; they give medium-soft strokes. Strokes using *soft* submethods have feathered edges. And strokes with *grainy* in their submethod reveal the paper texture you've selected in the Paper palette (opened by choosing Window, Art Materials or Command-3 to display the Art Materials palette, then clicking the Paper icon). Adjust the Grain slider on the Controls:Brush palette (Window, Controls or Command-5) to vary the intensity of the grain shown by your brushstrokes. Surprisingly, a lower grain setting makes strokes look more grainy. That's because less of the color is allowed to penetrate the grain, so your strokes will hit only the "peaks" of the paper surface.

PUTTING BRUSHES TO USE

To begin creating *Morning View from Point Loma,* I opened a 1950 x 1350-pixel file and mod-

ified the 2B Pencil variant so I would have a pencil that could paint light color over dark. By changing the method from Buildup to Cover, and also changing the submethod, I arrived at a Grainy Soft Cover version that would show the paper grain and still cover previous strokes. I chose the Small Canvas texture from the More Paper Textures library (by clicking the Library button in the zoomed-out Art Materials:Paper palette), picked a neutral gray in the Art Materials:Color palette, and began sketching with a Wacom tablet and stylus, switching shades of gray as needed. I also used the Grainy Water variant of the Water brush to blend values in the sketch, modifying the brush by decreasing the Opacity to 40% in the Controls palette ❹. ☞ *If you make a minor change to a brush for temporary use, you may not want to bother naming and saving it as a separate variant. In that case, in the Brushes palette, choose Brushes, Variants, Save Built Variant. This saves the modified version under the original name. To recover the original, unmodified brush, choose Brushes, Variants, Restore Default Variant. This works with Painter's standard brushes as well as with brushes that you build and save with their own new names.*

To establish tonal values and bring color into the composition, I usually create a quick color study right on top of a clone of the pencil sketch. I made a clone by choosing File, Clone so that I could save an untouched copy of my sketch, and blocked in general areas of color using the Fast Flat Oil brush and the Opaque Oil Paint brush, two variants I had created and saved ❺. These two brushes are very different in character. When you paint curved strokes with Fast Flat Oil, you get graceful thick-to-thin lines with soft edges. The Opaque Oil Paint brush, on the other hand, is a fast, springy brush that feels more like traditional oil painting.

I used Painter's Grainy Water brush at 40% opacity to blend areas of the underpainting, especially in the clouds and water ❻. Then I added more colored strokes with the Opaque Oil Paint brush. To create stippled color in the water reflections to show wind activity and cloud reflections, I dabbed short horizontal strokes into light areas with a small Soft Oil brush variant. I also used a larger Soft Oil brush to modulate the color in the dark foreground tree silhouettes ❼.

By the time the painting was completed and the custom brush variants had been safely stored with Painter's originals, I had developed an almost physical memory of what it felt like to paint with each of my virtual custom brushes, so I would be able to use them when I was ready to tackle the next card in the series or put them to work on editorial art or a product illustration. ■

Making Custom Brushes in Painter

To make each of the custom brushes used in *Morning View From Point Loma*, I radically modified an existing Painter brush, then chose Brushes, Variant, Save Variant from the menu at the top of the Brushes palette to name it and save it in the current palette.

My image is 1950 pixels wide. If your file is larger or smaller, proportionally increase or decrease the Size slider settings listed here. Even if you're working on a 1950-pixel-wide image, don't worry if your slider settings don't exactly match mine — just get them as close as you can. And don't think your computer has crashed if you hit Build and nothing happens for a while. Painter is working away, building a complex brush.

In the descriptions that follow, I've used shorthand for some settings. For example, "*Well:* Resaturation, 80" means, "Choose Well from the Controls menu of the Brushes palette, set Resaturation to 80, and leave all other sliders where they are." *Color Variability* stands for the Color Variability settings in the zoomed-out Color palette.

Don't be intimidated by the seven or eight palettes used to build custom brushes. Even Painter veterans need to think carefully when building a complex brush. For a full description of the controls in each of the palettes, you can refer to Painter's user guide, although painting with the brush after you make each adjustment will teach you a lot, too. ■

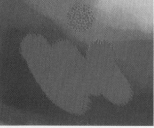

Fast Flat Oil: A Circular dab type and a Single stroke type make this a fast brush, great for painting short dabs of color with a hint of transparency at the end of the stroke. Since the brush is oval, it's great for making strokes that are narrow in the horizontal direction and wide in the vertical. Start with the Fine Brush variant of the Brush. *Submethod:* Grainy Hard Cover. *Controls:* Opacity, 100; Grain, 18. *Size:* Size, 25.3; ±Size, 1.00; Size Step, 5; Squeeze, 25; Angle, 0; Dab Type, Circular. *Sliders:* Opacity, Pressure; all others, None.

Opaque Oil: Use this springy, speedy brush for teardrop-shaped dabs with rough edges. It paints quickly for a natural feel with a stylus. Start with the Big Wet Oils variant of the Brush. *Submethod:* Grainy Hard Cover. *Controls:* Opacity, 100; Grain, 75. *Size:* Size, 14.5; ±Size, 1.80; Size Step, 5. *Spacing:* Spacing/Size, 5; Min Spacing, 1.0; Stroke Type, Single. *Bristle:* Thickness, 60; Clumpiness, 53; Hair Scale, 351; Scale/Size, 0. *Color Variability:* ±H, 1; ±V, 2. *Well:* All sliders to maximum. *Sliders:* Size, Pressure; Grain, Velocity; others, None.

Soft Oil: This brush feels like a traditional soft, flat brush with long bristles. Start with the Big Wet Oils variant of the Brush. *Submethod:* Soft Cover. *Controls:* Opacity, 50; Grain, 100. *Size:* Size, 22.1. *Spacing:* Bristles, 7. *Bristle:* Thickness, 50; Clumpiness, 70; Hair Scale, 323; Scale/Size, 0. *Color Variability:* ±H, 1; ±V, 3. *Well:* Resaturation, 70; Bleed, 40; Dryout, maximum. *Sliders:* Opacity, Pressure; Grain, Pressure; others, None. *Rake:* Contact Angle, 1.04; Brush Scale, 0; Turn Amount, 20; check Soften Bristle Edge; uncheck Spread Bristles.

Creative Collage in Painter

■ *by Cher Threinen-Pendarvis*

WHEN JIM FARMER, art director at AT&T, was looking for a designer for a set of phone cards commemorating the Atlanta Olympics, he wanted something other than the usual sports imagery. Attracted by the color sense, textures, and painterly feeling of the work of LeVan/Barbee Studio in Boston, he asked partners Susan LeVan and Ernie Barbee to create a series of collectible phone cards that would work both as stand-alone items and as a triptych. Painter's masking functions made it easy for LeVan to build up rough-edged layers of color, while floaters and patterns gave her flexibility to make the changes the client requested.

FLOATING FOR FLEXIBILITY

LeVan built the initial sketches in Painter in black and white ❶, setting up the design elements as floaters (Painter's version of layers) so she could easily add and subtract elements, realign them in her composition, and move them from one document to another by copying and pasting. To preview her design without a particular floating element, she selected it in the Floater List and clicked the eye icon shut to hide the floater. She clicked it open to show the floater. ☞ *To float an item in Painter, select it with the rectangular*

"When I was working in mixed-media collage," says Boston illustrator Susan LeVan, "I would take materials like wood, dirt, nails, and paper and attach them to canvas or a panel. I would abuse the object by scratching, burning, sanding, or scraping. I drew with sticks, cut paint bristles to the quick, and drizzled oil on things. I do exactly the same things in Painter, digitally speaking." For a set of AT&T phone cards commemorating the Atlanta Olympics, LeVan and husband-partner Ernie Barbee conceptualized together, then LeVan drew while Barbee art directed and edited.

1 Because it's often easier to resolve a design without the complexity of color and texture, LeVan built the initial sketches in Painter in black and white. So when the client requested faxed sketches, black-and-white art was already on hand for quicker, cleaner faxing.

2 After LeVan made a mask for a gray tone in the illustration, she opened the Path List (by choosing Windows, Objects or Command-3 and clicking the Path List icon at the top of the Objects palette) and clicked the center Visibility button in the bottom row of the expanded Path List palette to view her mask using the Masked Outside option.

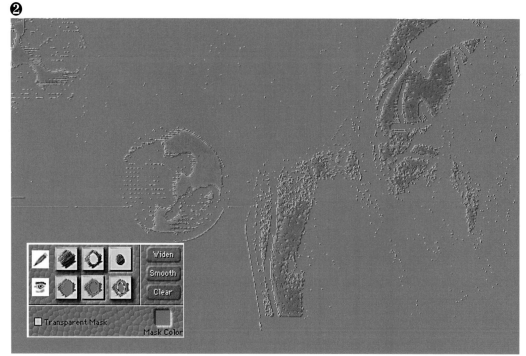

selection tool or the lasso and either click on the active selection with the floater adjuster (pointing hand) tool or choose Edit, Float. To drag a copy of a floating item within a document, Option-drag it with the floater adjuster; to duplicate it in place, Option-click with the floater adjuster.

LAYERING RICH COLOR

LeVan likes to build up multilayered color to achieve a textured, rough-edged look by repeatedly creating a color-based mask over an area, then filling or painting. Each time she made a new mask, it covered a slightly different area, creating a complex, layered edge. She continued to work the surface until she arrived at just the right amount of color and texture.

To begin the masking and coloring process, LeVan dropped the floaters in the black-and-white comp by clicking the Drop All button at the bottom of the Floater List palette, merging them with the background canvas in Painter. ☞ *Whenever a Painter technique requires you to drop your floaters, save a version of your file before you drop them, in case you need to go back to the image with live floaters to retrieve an element.*

LeVan used Painter's Auto Mask feature to make rough-edged aliased masks quickly based on color in her image. When the masked area was filled or painted into, the aliased mask left a halo of lighter color; it did not completely cover the color underneath.

To make a mask based on color, LeVan first selected a new current color by clicking the dropper tool on the color in her image that she wanted to mask. She chose Edit, Mask, Auto Mask and selected Current Color from the popout menu. She viewed the mask to be certain it covered the desired areas **2**, then activated it as a selection so she could paint inside it **3**.

Next, LeVan chose the Square Chalk variant of the Chalk brush and began painting **4**. To build

❸

❹

3 To activate the mask as a selection so she could paint inside it, LeVan went to the expanded Path List palette and clicked the right Visibility button (bottom row) and the right draw button (top row). Then she used the Square Chalk with green to paint over the gray tone.

4 The Chalk brush and pressure-sensitive stylus produced a more varied, grainy texture in the image than filling the area using the paintbucket or the Effects, Fill command, which would not have interacted with the paper texture.

up color layering, she repeated the process by sampling the color again with the dropper and making a new Current Color mask based on it, activating the mask, and then applying a new color inside it. ☛ *Painter has one 8-bit background mask that allows solid or semitransparent masking. When you make a Current Color mask, you are manipulating the background mask. Each time you make a new Current Color mask, your previous mask is erased.*

PAINTING A BACKGROUND TEXTURE

LeVan began the background patterns using brushstrokes made with a large brush over a smooth paper texture. After covering the area with the first color, she chose the Line 0 paper texture from the Simple Patterns library (by clicking the Library button at the bottom of the expanded Art Materials:Paper palette) and applied another color. She repeatedly used her masking and coloring technique to isolate and fill areas of her image

until she had arrived at the richly layered color surface that she liked.

LeVan selected Cotton Paper from the Grains library, chose the Square Chalk variant of the Chalk brush, picked a dark orange in the Colors palette, and stroked in a layer of orange. To overlay the repeating linear texture, she chose a yellow in the Colors palette and accessed the Line 0 texture. Using her stylus, she carefully laid in thick yellow strokes with the Square Chalk brush, using the pressure sensitivity to aid in subtly bringing out the paper texture.

Next, she picked up the orange color with the dropper tool and used it to make a Current Color mask, activated the mask as a selection, and used the Square Chalk brush to paint white strokes over the selected area.

LeVan took the background design for the medalist card one step further: She turned the selection into a floater (by clicking on it with the floater adjuster tool) and gave it a soft, black drop

5 When the client asked LeVan to remove the torch and other elements from a card (top), she used the pattern function to fill an area with the striped background, then cloned portions of that background into other parts of her image to cover unwanted shapes before adding the new figures (bottom).

❺

shadow using Painter's automatic shadow command (Effects, Objects, Create Drop Shadow).

USING PATTERNS TO RESTORE

When the client wanted to change a card, LeVan used Painter's cloning and pattern features to remove a torch and other items without having to reconstruct the layered background texture, saving time and retaining the established character of the background.

To restore the background, LeVan selected a piece of the background texture using the rectangular selection tool. She chose Capture Pattern from the Patterns popout menu of the Art Materials:Patterns palette to save the selected area into the pattern library. She made a quick selection of the area that needed to change using the rectangular selection tool, then chose the paintbucket tool and clicked Fill With Clone Source in the Controls:Paintbucket palette, then clicked in the selected area with the paintbucket tool to fill the selection with her pattern.

Next, LeVan chose the Scratchboard Tool variant of the Pen brush. In the expanded Brushes palette, she selected Cloning and Soft Cover Cloning from the Methods popout menus. With her background pattern still selected as a clone source, she used her stylus to draw around the shape of the figure and cover the rest of the image that needed to change ❺. ☞ *If no other clone source is designated under the File, Clone Source menu, Painter will use the pattern currently chosen in the Pattern palette as the clone source.* ☞ *You can also use the Cloner brush's Soft Cloner variant to restore areas.*

The restoration gave LeVan a starting point for the new card design that retained the head and background texture. She had saved the black bars and globes in source files; she pasted them back in as floaters and resolved the new card design. ■

Painting an Intricate Pattern

■ *by Talitha Harper*

NANCY STAHL'S VIEW is always dramatic. The New York City illustrator combines daring composition with haunting color. And because she places her figures in unique poses, she often takes photographs of herself and uses them as reference when she needs to work out perspective or foreshortening. This elegant self-promotional illustration, for example, had a humble beginning: a photo of Stahl bending backward over an ironing board.

Stahl wanted to drape the figure over a chair, and she planned to cover the chair with an upholstery pattern. So she used MetaCreations Painter's Capture Texture command to build a custom paper texture and used this paper to "print" the upholstery.

GENERATING TRACING PAPER

After opening the photograph in Painter, Stahl cloned it (File, Clone) so that she could activate the tracing paper function. Working in the clone window, she selected all, deleted, and chose Options, Tracing Paper (Command-T). This gave her a non-printing ghost of the photo. As Stahl traced the figure, the color was sheer, so the ghosted image remained visible as she worked. But Stahl could see the

When New York illustrator Nancy Stahl wanted to create a fabric print, she defined a custom paper texture in Painter and "rubbed" color over the paper grain. To capture the dramatic pose, Stahl took a photograph of herself, opened the photo in tracing paper mode, and drew on top of it.

1 Stahl worked in a separate PainterX2 file to build a paper texture. She started with a single leaf, copied it three times, and rotated the copies (Effects, Orientation, Rotate). She selected the leaves and applied the Capture Texture command, choosing a high Crossfade setting (75 percent) in the Save Texture dialog box so that the leaf clusters would overlap in the finished pattern. (A low Crossfade value retains space around the captured element to produce a step-and-repeat pattern.)

2 A frisket (shown in blue) was drawn around the woman's arms and hair to define the back of the chair. The Apply Surface Texture command filled the frisket with the leaf pattern.

3 When Stahl used the Chalk brush to "rub" a rosy brown color over the green leaf pattern, the high points in the pattern took on the color (top). Choosing Invert Grain in the Paper palette reversed the grain, so the indentations in the pattern were filled with color (bottom). Stahl used the two methods to create contrasting prints on the chair (see page 1).

4 Before adding highlights and facial details, Stahl defined a set of friskets so that the changes she applied could not run outside the frisketed shapes.

❶

❷
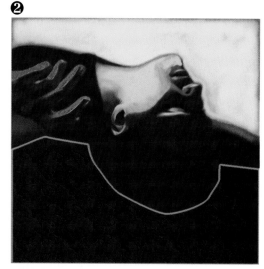

❸

❹
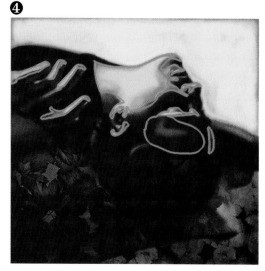

color at 100 percent opacity (without the ghosted image) by pressing Command-T to toggle between tracing paper mode and the standard view (with 100 percent color and no ghosted image). ☞ *To produce a non-printing tracing image, you must delete the original image (or a selection of it) before applying the Tracing Paper command. If you choose tracing paper mode without deleting first, you will see a ghosted image, but this image will revert to 100 percent opacity when you return to standard view.*

Stahl began blocking in the background elements, using the Large Chalk brush set to Soft Cover. Then she roughed in the figure, turned off the tracing paper function, and set to work creating a custom paper texture. ☞ *Closing a cloned image breaks its link to the source file. So if you reopen the clone later in order to continue working on it, you won't have access to the Tracing Paper command. To re-establish the clone-source link, open both files, make the source image active, and choose Options, Set*

Clone Source. Or open the source file first, apply the Open command again, and then locate the clone file and press the Option key when you click on the Open button.

CAPTURING A TEXTURE

With the PainterX2 extension, Stahl could isolate a scanned leaf from its background to create a floating selection. (See "Silhouetting a Painter X2 Selection," page 3.) After copying this selection to produce a cluster of leaves ❶, Stahl used the rectangular marquee tool to select all the leaves and chose Capture Texture from the Options menu. This turned the leaves into a paper texture and added the texture to the Paper palette. ☞ *Before turning a floating selection (or a group of floating selections) into a paper texture, you must defloat them by choosing Drop All in the Floating Selections palette.*

Next Stahl used the frisket knife to make a selection in the shape she needed for the chair. Although she planned to use the leaf pattern to

Silhouetting a Painter Selection

Painter's magic wand selects by color values. So with grayscale and color images, where there's a range of tonality, you can usually select only a small portion of the artwork with the magic wand. But when you've scanned an image on a white field — as Nancy Stahl did when she placed a leaf directly on the scanner bed — you can work through the Magic Wand dialog box to make a silhouette selection quickly.

First, choose Edit, Magic Wand to open the Magic Wand dialog box and activate the magic wand tool. Once you click the tool on the image, the selected tones will be highlighted in red ❶. Click on the Value (V) slider and drag to the left, all the way to 0 (zero) percent. This will expand the red selection slightly ❷. Then bring the settings on the right side of all three slider bars up to 100 percent (you can do this by simply clicking on the numerals). Resetting the Hue (H) and Saturation (S) values to 100 percent won't produce any changes in the selection area. But setting the Value to 100 percent will select all, filling the window with red ❸. Click on the right end of the Value slider and "back off" 100 percent saturation until the background is deselected ❹. When only the image is selected, click OK in the Magic Wand dialog box.

Zoom in and take a close look at the edges of the selection. A magic wand selection is antialiased, so you will have captured a few white pixels from the background along with the image. If you see only a tiny bit of white, you can reduce it by applying a slight feather in the Frisket palette. But if you see a white outline between the image and the selection border, undo the selection and try again, setting the Value percentage a little lower in the Magic Wand dialog box to remove more of the white pixels from the selection. ■

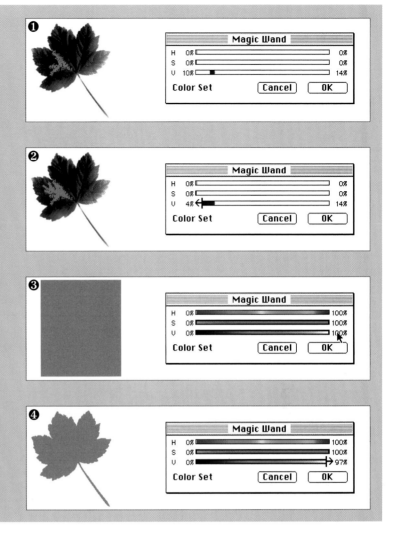

print the fabric, she applied another texture first (Medium from Painter's default Paper palette) to simulate the rough weave of the fabric. To produce the texture, Stahl clicked on the Medium icon in the palette and chose Effects, Surface Control, Apply Surface Texture. This filled the frisket with the selected paper texture. Then she selected the leaf pattern icon in the Paper palette and used the Apply Surface Texture command to add its texture to the frisketed selection ❷. Finally, she "rubbed" over the pattern with the Large Chalk brush, set to Grainy Flat Cover ❸. ☞ If you want your brushwork to react to the texture of the paper, choose a Brush palette Method setting that has the word Grainy in the name. ☞ Although you can save a Painter document in several formats, only RIFF format retains textural information like the paper grain or the wet layer. So if an illustration is created with these effects, it's a good idea to save a RIFF version of the file in case you need to modify the image later.

ADDING FINE DETAILS

Once she had completed the leaf texture, Stahl chose Soft Cover as the Method setting so that she could use the chalk tool to draw smooth shadows on top of the leaf pattern, shadows that didn't show the paper grain. Then she drew a new set of friskets and used them to define details in the hand and face ❹. To activate an individual frisket, she clicked on the frisket selection icon (the arrow) in the toolbox, which made the entire set of friskets visible. Then she returned to the image and used the selection tool to click on the frisket she wanted. When she chose the brush icon in the toolbox, the other frisket borders disappeared, but the selected frisket remained active.

As she worked, Stahl used the Large Chalk brush, but she changed the Method setting in the Brush palette to Soft Cover when she wanted to produce a smooth stroke with a soft, diffused edge and to Grainy Edge Flat Cover when she wanted the edges of her strokes to take on a ragged, stippled texture. ■

PAINTER

Electrifying a Hand Painting

■ *by Janet Ashford*

Triska Seeger combined delicate hand-drawn lines with bold, electronic color to create the illustrations in a children's book. Working in Painter, she applied smooth strokes of color, then changed the brush style to add a translucent bubble texture.

DESIGNER TRISKA SEEGER started with a set of hand-drawn, black-and-white illustrations and added splashes of bold electronic color to create *La Gallinita Roja*, a Spanish-language version of the classic children's story, *The Little Red Hen.* Seeger worked in pen and ink, then used Painter's Water Color brush to add layers of sheer color that didn't obscure the delicate linework of the original ink drawing.

Seeger, who created the illustration while working as a staff artist at Josten's Learning Corp. in San Diego, Calif., designed the book as part of a language arts curriculum for children who are learning English as a second language. The assignment called for one layout printed at two sizes: a 16 x 16-inch format for teachers to read

aloud while showing the pictures to the children and an 8 x 8-inch version of the book for the children to read on their own.

ROUGHING OUT THE BOOK

Although Josten's beginning-reader books are usually 32 pages long, Seeger opted to produce a 16-page book. Reducing the page count cut film and printing costs, and Seeger used the savings to upgrade the paper. She chose a soft-textured 80-lb. stock in a warm beige tone with multicolor flecks to complement the rustic style she planned to use for the illustrations.

Seeger began by producing a dummy layout and rough pencil sketches of her illustrations at the 8 x 8-inch size. Once the sketches were approved, she created pen-and-ink drawings, using a

❶

❷

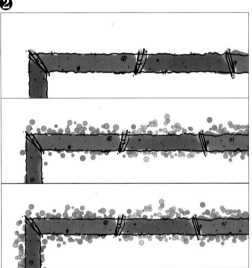

❸

❹

1 Each 8 x 8-inch illustration was drawn in pen and ink, then scanned at 300 dpi and used as a canvas in Painter.

2 Seeger added color to the border, using the Simple Water brush (a variant of the Water Color brush) to paint transparent color over the scan (top). While the paint was still wet, she used the Spatter Water brush (another Water Color variant) to create "bubbles" (center). After drying the paint, she added more spatters to the design (bottom).

3 Once the border was complete, Seeger began to paint the figures. First she used the Simple Water brush to apply a layer of smooth color in the hen's scarf and apron.

4 While the paint in the apron was still wet, Seeger gave it a mottled texture by applying darker color with the Spatter Water brush. Then she returned to the Simple Water brush to paint the beak and define yellow highlights on the hen's body. While the paint in the beak was still wet, Seeger flowed a layer of orange on top of it. The orange paint blended with the yellow to shade the underside of the beak.

technique she calls her "loose scribble style." For the cover art, Seeger used the same scribble technique to create the title lettering . But in her other illustrations, she left some open space in the art so that type could be added later in QuarkXPress. She scanned the drawings at full size and opened one of the scans in Painter ❶.

ADDING COLOR

Color applied with Painter's Water Color brush is translucent, so Seeger could keep her linework crisp and clear as she added an overlay of bright color. By changing the Variant option in the Brush palette, she changed the behavior of the brush to produce different textures. She chose the Simple Water variant to lay down a base coat of smooth color and the Spatter Water variant to add a bubble texture to the design. To keep the look consistent from one illustration to the next, she selected colors from a custom paint palette. ☞ *To create a custom palette in Painter, first select a tone in the Color palette, then Option-click on one of*

the color swatches in the pad to fill the swatch with the selected color. You can save custom colors (in order to reload them later) by clicking the Palette button in the Color palette and then choosing Save. ☞ *Unsaved custom colors disappear from Painter's paint pad when you turn a page.*

With each scan, Seeger began by painting the border, filling in the lines with smooth strokes and then adding bubbles. As long as the paint was wet, the colors pooled at the edges and ran together where they touched. Once the border was complete, Seeger dried the paint (Options, Dry or Command-Y) before moving on to the foreground figures ❷. ☞ *Painter's Water Color brush works in a "wet" layer, accessed by choosing Options, Wet Paint. This extra layer increases the file size of a Painter document, so it's a good idea to turn off the Wet Paint option when you finish using the Water Color brush. (Using the Dry command sets the paint, but it doesn't deactivate the wet layer.)*

5 As she painted the hen's body red, Seeger overran the yellow paint in some places and worked around it in others to leave some of the highlights intact.

6 The Pure Water variant of Painter's Water Color brush is colorless. Seeger used it to blend colors together, smoothing the transition between the red body and the yellow highlights.

7 The Pure Water brush was also used to shade the rat's eyelids. After applying light pink paint, Seeger placed a bright pink dot in the corner of each eye (top). Then she used the Pure Water brush to blend the colors (bottom).

8 To finish the illustration, Seeger filled elements with the Pure Water brush and added texture with the Spatter Water brush.

⑤

⑥

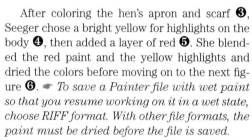

⑦

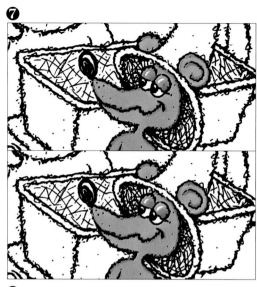

⑧

After coloring the hen's apron and scarf **❸**, Seeger chose a bright yellow for highlights on the body **❹**, then added a layer of red **❺**. She blended the red paint and the yellow highlights and dried the colors before moving on to the next figure **❻**. ☞ *To save a Painter file with wet paint so that you resume working on it in a wet state, choose RIFF format. With other file formats, the paint must be dried before the file is saved.*

Using the Simple Water brush, Seeger filled the rat's body with a soft pink tone and added bright pink highlights **❼**. Finally, she painted a layer of pink spatters on top of the rat's body. She used the same technique to paint the other animals and to fill in background details, applying smooth color and then adding darker spots **❽**.

Seeger worked quickly as she painted the illustration, overrunning the black lines in some places and letting the colors merge together in others. "I could have used friskets," she says, "but I wanted a spontaneous look."

PRODUCTION AND PRINTING

When Seeger tried to convert one of the RGB files to CMYK, the bright colors shifted to dull, cloudy tones. Seeger didn't feel confident about her color correction abilities, so she undid the conversion and turned the RGB files over to her service bureau. After experimenting with several conversion programs, the service bureau settled on Xerox's Color Access to maintain the bold tones in the art. ☞ *To minimize color shift between RGB and CMYK in a Painter file, activate the Printable Colors Only option in the Color palette before selecting colors and choose Enforce Printable Colors in the Effects, Tonal Control submenu.*

Once film was output for the 8 x 8-inch pages, it was enlarged 200 percent to produce the film needed for the 16 x 16-inch book. In effect, this enlargement reduced the resolution from 300 dpi to 150 dpi, but because of the forgiving style of the linework, the illustrations in the oversize book retain their hand-drawn quality. ∎

POSTSCRIPT STRATEGIES

To soften the hard-edged shapes of his FreeHand artwork, Peter Alsberg chooses palettes of muted, closely related colors, most of which use a percentage of all four process inks. "Even my purples will have a little yellow," he says. "It helps ease the transitions between colors" — as well as helping to eliminate trapping problems. Alsberg intensifies the soft effects of his color choices by using blues, rather than blacks or grays, to define shadows.

Alsberg often uses the same colors in many illustrations. To reuse colors, he could define custom color libraries (by choosing Export from the popout menu of the Color List, selecting the desired colors, and naming the library), but he finds it easier to open an image with an appropriate palette and save it with a new name, then delete all the contours. This also saves him the trouble of re-creating his styles.

To illustrate an in-house magazine article on dealing with adversity (below), Alsberg wanted his colors to be "ominous, like a storm coming." His main colors were muted purples and red-browns. For more on Alsberg's work, see "Simulating Marker Lines" on page 150.

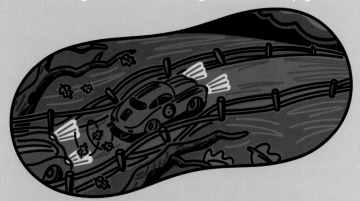

Some artists avoid Illustrator's filters, plug-in tools, and other advanced functions because the results are too predictable, too obviously computer-generated. But for Ron Chan, these functions are a starting point — an easy way to generate the skeleton of an effect which he can flesh out.

For *Winter Sports*, an illustration created for *Macworld* magazine, Chan created the pattern on the seated figure's sweater by drawing overlapping bands, then choosing Filter, Pathfinder, Soft to divide the bands. This gave the overlaps a new fill color, making it easy to select all the shapes (using the Select Same Fill Color filter) and fill them with the desired color.

To generate the snow, Chan turned to the Ink Pen. Choosing Filter, Ink Pen, Effects, he set the Hatch to Dots, the Dispersion and Rotation to Random, and the Scale to Constant. Then he experimented with the Settings menu and the Density and Dispersion Range sliders to get the look he wanted. Once he had a good scatter of snow, he didn't want to try to repeat his success, so he simply copied and pasted the snowflakes into other areas, moving flakes around to make the snow follow the edges of the shapes. For more on how Chan gets the most out of Illustrator, see "Planning for Reliable Color" on page 91.

We've all been advised to use Illustrator's gradient fills sparingly if we want our files to make it through the image-setter. But Clark Tate ignores the warnings. This design is made up of more than 800 PostScript paths, and all but four of them are filled with gradients. Tate has developed several tactics for working efficiently with gradient fills (see "The Pen Tool as a Brush," page 95).

Although he's relatively new to the computer, Tate has never hesitated to experiment. He began working electronically in 1993, and within six months, Adobe technicians had spotted his Illustrator work and asked him to become a beta tester. They knew Tate would give the program a thorough workout and uncover all its flaws.

Tate exploits technology in every aspect of his work. Two of the tools he relies on most often are a modem and a toll-free phone line. With them, he's always accessible to his clients — and free to divide his time between studios in Gridley, Ill., and Solec Kujawski, Poland.

Planning For Reliable Color

■ *by Sara Booth*

G RADIENTS AND BLENDS add a painterly touch to the PostScript art of Ron Chan, and reliable color is a priority. The Mill Valley, Calif., illustrator puts his printing experience to work choosing process colors that will perform well on press, then mixes a palette of tints and places them in Illustrator's Paint Style palette to keep them accessible as he works.

When he was asked to design a paper carton, part of a campaign he illustrated for Designframe (New York city) for Strathmore Paper Co., Chan began with a detailed sketch, which he scanned and used as a template in Illustrator. He generally worked in three stages. First, in Artwork mode, he redrew the sketch. Then he added flat-color fills, adjusting color until the balance pleased him. Finally, he added the blends and gradients.

DEFINING COLORS AND GRADIENTS

Using a swatchbook and a list of colors suggested by the client, Chan (working with his wife, designer Nancy Yee-Chan) chose six colors

Mill Valley, Calif., illustrator Ron Chan gave familiar office supplies a fresh look with a cubist approach and a rich color palette. For a carton for Strathmore Paper Co., Chan ensured that his colors would print reliably by choosing process colors without black ink, and he carefully defined gradients to assure that no muddy colors were generated in the ramp.

1 After choosing a shade of each color, Chan generated lighter and darker shades by pressing Command and Shift as he dragged one of the Paint Style palette's process color sliders. For example, to mix a lighter brown, he pressed Command and Shift as he dragged the slider of the color with the highest percentage (in this case, yellow) down about 20%.

2 To organize his Paint Style palette, Chan began by using a swatchbook to select process colors. Once the major colors were defined, he placed them in the large swatches of the palette, then added the lighter and darker shades in the smaller swatches.

3 Using a standard process black in a gradient often produces muddy colors in the middle of the gradient (top). Chan has discovered he can create a more gradual range of tones by defining a custom black that adds 100K to the original color (bottom).

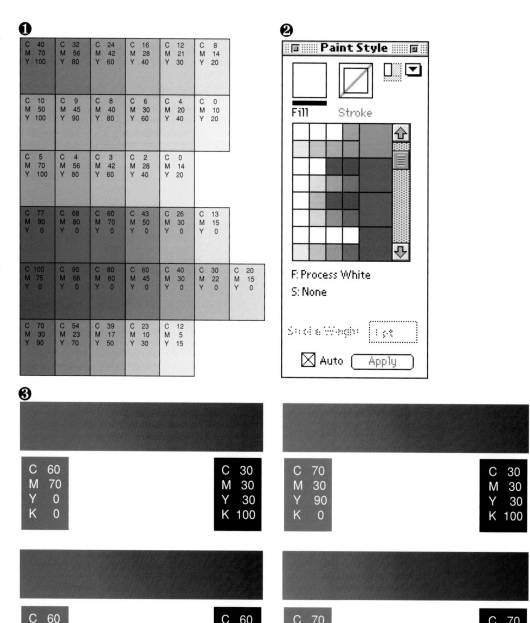

and generated a range of shades for each ❶, then added them to his Paint Style palette ❷. ☞ *To add a color to the swatches in the Paint Style palette, display it in the Fill or Stroke swatch at the top of the palette, then drag and drop onto the desired swatch. To remove a swatch, Command-click it.*

Chan prefers to mix process colors with a minimum of black ink. "Black tends to get unpredictable on the press, and it can turn muddy," he says. So as he chooses colors from the swatchbook, he examines their CMYK percentages. If a color has more than about 15% black, he tries to

see if he can get similar results using cyan, magenta, and yellow without black. Chan is also cautious about blending to black, creating a custom black just for a particular gradient to avoid generating murky colors ❸. "I try to be judicious about not having two different blacks sitting too close together," he says, "but even that can be less jarring than an ugly ramp."

Chan uses many gradients, and he often has several files open at the same time. To prevent Illustrator from replacing a gradient in one illustration with a gradient from another, he must be certain no two gradients have the same name. So

❹

❺

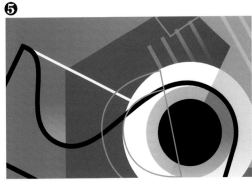

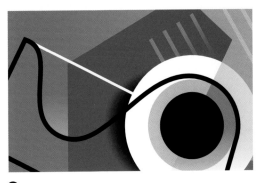

❻

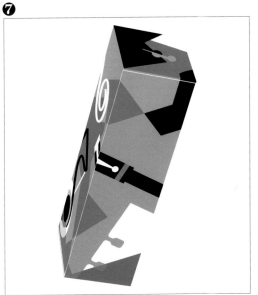

❼

4 One way Chan added softness to his artwork was to fill contours with gradients, matching one end color of the gradient to the background color to make the grad-filled shapes appear to fade into the background.

5 Chan dislikes radial gradients because he doesn't find it easy to control the results. In places where he wants a curved ramp (for example, to echo the circle of the tape dispenser or contrast with the flat edge of the paper), he uses a blend instead.

6 Chan used the spiral tool as a starting point (shown in black), but adjusted the curves to create his final spirals (shown in blue). After extending both ends of the spiral to give it a more graceful shape, Chan converted the stroke to a contour by choosing Object, Offset Path. He cut the spiral into two parts so he could fill the end curve with a gradient, making it fade away into the background.

7 To be certain the composition worked from all angles and the color relationships on all sides of the box were pleasing, Chan took an early version of the image (before gradients and blends were added) into Dimensions, where he mapped it onto a rectangle using Appearance, Map Artwork (Command-Option-M). This allowed him to look at his design from all angles.

---

he chooses a two- to three-letter abbreviation for each job and uses it at the start of each gradient name. This has the added advantage of keeping all his custom gradients together in the Paint Style and Gradient palettes. ☞ *Illustrator's Paint Style and Gradient palettes display all gradients in all open documents. If two open documents have gradients with the same name, Illustrator will use the specifications of the most recently opened document. Existing filled objects are not changed, but the gradient is replaced in the document that was opened first — even after the later-opened document is closed.*

SHAPE SHORTCUTS

One thing that sets Chan's work apart from other PostScript illustration is touches of softness. He used gradients ending in the background color to make shapes seem to fade into transparency ❹. But gradients couldn't always serve his purpose. When he needed a color ramp to follow a certain shape, or when he wanted a rounder shape to contrast with a corner, he used blends ❺.

Unlike many artists, Chan doesn't shun Illustrator's spiral tool. Instead, he gives spirals his own twist ❻. "The spiral tool is OK," he says. "I just like to add a segment to the end to make it

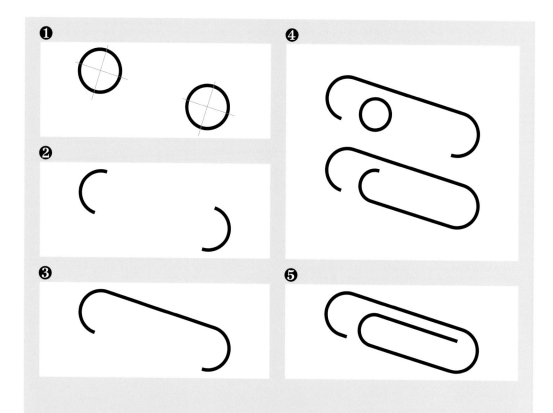

To make it easier to draw elements such as the paper clip following the angle of his sketch, Ron Chan took advantage of Illustrator's ability to constrain lines and generate shapes at a pre-determined angle.

By default, Illustrator's angle of constraint is 0. This means the bottom side of a rectangle is exactly horizontal; the curve points on a circle or ellipse are perfectly vertical and horizontal; and lines drawn with the pen while pressing the Shift key are drawn at 0°, 45°, 90°, and 135°.

However, the angle can be changed by opening the General Preferences dialog box (Command-K) and entering a new number in the Constrain Angle box. Before he began drawing the paper clip, Chan measured its angle and used that as the angle of constraint.

Chan began by drawing a circle, then Shift-Option-dragged a copy. Because the constraint angle was changed, the original circle was drawn at a slant, and the copy was positioned at the same slanted angle ❶. Chan cut the circles in half at the top and bottom points ❷, then selected and joined the top points on the two semicircles ❸. A smaller circle in the center was treated the same way to create the inner loop of the clip ❹. Then Chan clicked an end-point with the pen tool and Shift-clicked to lengthen the line with a segment parallel to the other lines ❺. ■

gracefully swirl off." When he had perfected a spiral, he assigned it a heavy 4- or 5-point stroke, then choose Object, Offset Path to transform it into a contour so that he could add a gradient fill.

BUILDING A BOX
When he sketched the design, Chan knew each of the box's sides would have to function on its own, but the image would also have to have continuity as it wrapped around each of the box's corners. As he worked on his sketch, he often photocopied it, cut it apart, and used it to build a small model of the box, allowing him to check the composition of each side and to be certain that lines matched up at the corners. Once he began working on color, he used Dimensions to map the art to a rectangle so that he could check the color balance ❼.

The client provided an Illustrator template showing diecut lines and bleed lines. Chan used the diecut outline as a mask, and he placed the fold lines on their own layer in Illustrator so he could turn them on and off easily as he worked. ■

ILLUSTRATOR

The Pen Tool as a Brush

■ *by Talitha Harper*

CLARK TATE WIELDS Illustrator's gradient tool like a paintbrush, flicking color into his PostScript drawings and giving his imagery the luminous tonality of oil paintings. The key to Tate's style is simple, but the results are complex. He begins by breaking a drawing into tiny fragments with the Divide and Minus Front filters. When he fills those fragments with gradients and fans the gradients in different directions, each shape takes on the look of an individual brushstroke. The finished design is an intricate mosaic of interlocking elements, and Tate uses several tactics to speed up the drawing process and to keep screen refresh time to a minimum as he builds his imagery.

LARGE FILE STRATEGY

Tate's illustrations often include thousands of tiny elements, all filled with gradients — and with a Quadra 900 and 72MB of RAM, he's equipped to handle complex files. He also works with two monitors. As he creates an image, he uses the Window, New Window command to keep two copies of the file open, one on each monitor. He sets the active window to Artwork view (View, Artwork or Command-E) so that he can draw quickly and selects Preview mode (View, Preview or Command-Y) for the other window so that he can see the full-color drawing as it progresses.

But even with this sophisticated configuration, Tate has to rely on other techniques to keep his work moving at top speed. In addition to using the Layers palette to organize his illustrations — and turning off a layer when he's not working on it by clicking the bullet under the palette's eye icon to make the layer invisible — Tate often uses the

PostScript draw programs are known for their crisp line-work, not for painterly color. But Clark Tate uses those clean PostScript paths in conjunction with Illustrator's gradient tool to give his drawings a hand-painted look. And he relies on the Duplicate function in the Gradient palette to build related fills that bring subtle color variations to his imagery.

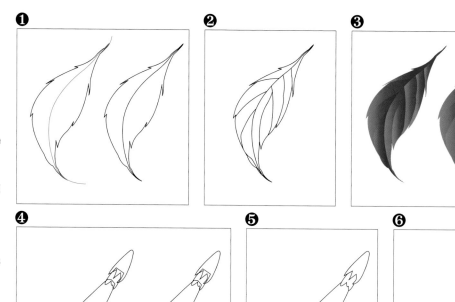

1 Tate drew the outline of a leaf, then added a line to define a "vein" through its center. He Shift-clicked to select the leaf and the line and applied the Divide filter.

2 Additional vein lines were drawn, and the Divide filter was applied to each line, one at a time, to break the leaf into smaller shapes. (As he continued to divide the leaf, Tate typed Command-Shift-E to reapply the filter.)

3 After filling all the segments of the leaf with a green-to-blue gradient, Tate selected individual segments and used the gradient tool to adjust the fill angles, making the color fan out from the center of the leaf.

4 Rough outlines were drawn to define the trumpet flower; only one petal (shown in blue) was created precisely. After placing this perfectly shaped petal in front (Command-=), Tate Shift-clicked to add an intersecting petal (shown in red) to the selection. The Minus Front filter clipped off the underlying leaf where the front leaf covered it.

5 Tate continued to apply Minus Front (using the Command-Shift-E shortcut to reapply the filter) to overlapping sections of the trumpet flower, reshaping the elements to make them fit together as snugly as a jigsaw puzzle.

6 The petals were filled with a gradient, and the fill angles were adjusted.

Preview Selection command (View, Preview Selection or Command-Option-Y) so that only the selected element or elements are shown in preview. This is especially useful when Tate applies gradient fills to adjacent contours. He can adjust the angles of side-by-side fills to hone the "brushwork" while all the unselected elements remain in keyline view. ☞ *When you apply the Preview Selection command, every element you select will be displayed in Preview until you deactivate the function by choosing Artwork or Preview mode.*

Tate also counts on meticulous rendering to make every element in an illustration recognizable, even in Artwork view where only the outlines are visible. There are no overlapping shapes or hidden elements in his drawings. All the contours fit together like pieces of a jigsaw puzzle.

DEFINING PRECISE SHAPES

When he created this bird-and-flower illustration for the cover of *Cosmetics and Toiletries,* a trade magazine, Tate began by drawing a detailed pencil sketch. After opening a scan of the sketch as a template in Illustrator, Tate used the pen tool to outline the basic shapes and then applied the Divide or Minus Front filter (from the Filter, Pathfinder submenu) to break these basic outlines into smaller components.

To create a leaf, for example, Tate first drew a simple leaf shape, then added a line running through its center and selected the Divide filter to cut the leaf in two ❶. He repeated the process to break the leaf into tiny facets ❷ that could be filled separately ❸. ☞ *The Divide filter removes any stroke values that were specified for a element. So if you want to retain the stroke, you must redefine it after dividing.*

For more complicated designs like the trumpet flowers, Tate couldn't draw a single outline and divide it into sections as he had done with the leaf. So he drew individual outlines for each petal and the base of the flower and used the Minus Front filter to make the separate shapes fit together perfectly ❹. Each time Tate applied Minus Front, the front shape was eliminated. Tate didn't want to lose the contour when he applied the filter, so he copied each shape first and used the Paste In Front command (Command-F) later to place a copy into the position the original contour had occupied ❺.

After filling the petals of the trumpet flower with a gradient ❻, Tate used the Minus Front filter to create delicate veins on top of each of the petals ❼. Once the veins were complete ❽, they were filled with a darker gradient, created by duplicating the original fill and modifying the CMYK values slightly ❾.

DEFINING RELATED GRADIENTS

As Tate colored the illustration, he used related but slightly different gradients to bring subtle

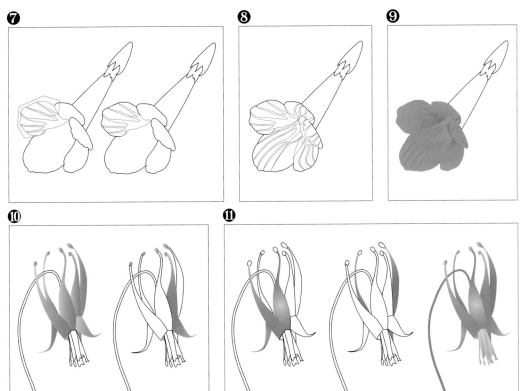

❼ ❽ ❾

❿ ⓫

7 To create veins on the petals, Tate began by copying one petal and pasting the copy in front (shown in blue). A shape defining the outside of the veins (shown in red) was drawn on top of the duplicate petal. When Tate selected the petal and the outline and applied the Minus Front filter, the resulting vein shape fit the petal precisely.

8 Tate repeated the process to produce veins for each of the petals.

9 To create a gradient for the veins, Tate opened the Gradient palette, selected the fill he had used for the petals, and clicked the Duplicate button. Then he adjusted the CMYK values of the colors in the duplicate fill, darkening them slightly.

10 Tate also used duplicate gradients to paint a columbine blossom. He began by defining a basic gradient and applying it to all the petals (left). By the end of the coloring process, only a few elements retained this original fill (right).

11 A radial fill, created by duplicating the original linear gradient and clicking the Radial button in the Gradient palette, was used to add highlights to the foreground petals (left). Tate duplicated the linear gradient again and adjusted the colors slightly to make a darker gradient that was used to fill the shadowy, background petals (center). The different fills brought painterly color variations to the finished flower (right).

tonal distinctions to the image. The petals of the columbine flowers, for example, are filled with three gradients, two of them created from duplicates of the original linear fill **❿**. For the first duplicate, Tate adjusted the CMYK specifications of the starting and ending colors to produce a darker version of the same linear gradient. For the second duplicate, he kept the original CMYK values, but selected the Radial option in the Gradient palette when he duplicated the fill.

Tate uses radial fills to create three-step gradients that flow from a deep tone to a highlight and back to the deep tone (when the light tone is the first color in the gradient) or from highlight to shadow to highlight (when the deep color is the first tone), and he uses the gradient tool to adjust the effect precisely. Clicking the tool defines the center point of the fill, and dragging the tool establishes the length of the graduation — so Tate can stretch out the radius to disguise the "roundness" of the fill **⓫**.

By the time Tate built all the fills he needed for the illustration — one for the leaves, another for the background, and a set of six related gradients for the flowers and the birds — he had a total of 34 gradients. The feathers alone called for 19 different fills. (Only three elements in the design have solid fills: a stack of rectangles in the center of the illustration that form a mortise and its border.) As Tate creates each gradient, he names it systematically, identifying the color and the object the gradient was created to fill so that he can find the fill he wants in the Paint Style palette. The first gradient created for the columbines, for example, was named *Red Columbine Flower*. Related gradients, based on duplicates of that fill, were given related names: *Red Columbine Dark* and *Red Columbine Rad* (for *radial*).

When Tate creates his fills, he mixes the colors by eye. "When I started working on the computer, I sat there with a Pantone book and drove myself crazy," he says. "Now I work with a calibrated monitor and mix colors like paint."

HANDLING THE RIP

In the past, output was often a problem with artwork as complicated as Tate's. But imagesetters have improved, and Tate rarely has trouble processing his images now. Even so, he often uses T-Script, a Mac-based raster image processing application, to RIP the files himself before sending them to the service bureau. At other times, he sends the original Illustrator image for output but runs a test copy of the document through T-Script first to make sure it can be processed. And Tate has developed definite hardware preferences. "Linos [Linotronic imagesetters] don't like my PostScript work. My files choke the older ones, and the newer models don't handle my work as well as Agfa machines do," he says. "If I have a choice, I go to Agfa imagesetters. They greatly cut down on the output time for my work." ▪

Fleshing Out Silhouettes

■ *by Sara Booth*

To create convincing people, illustrator Albert Kiefer of Belfeld, Netherlands, starts with simple outlines and applies color to suggest highlights and shadows. He used an assortment of Post-Script techniques — from layered shapes to gradient fills — to add dimension to the silhouette figures in this crowd scene.

SIMPLE FIGURES COMMUNICATE a convincing level of detail in a crowd scene designed by Albert Kiefer of Belfeld, Netherlands. Kiefer created the illustration for a brochure launching Digital Video, a plug-in cartridge that enables compact disc players to display interactive CDs on a television screen, and he used a variety of PostScript techniques — from adding highlights in a single color to sculpting with gradient fills — to add realism to the stylized figures.

"The client asked for a movie premier look," Kiefer says. "So I used a kind of theatrical layering — the foreground elements, the masses of people, the background building, the backdrop sky and spotlights." The popular arts influenced the piece in other ways, too: Kiefer's atmospheric color palette was inspired by his fondness for the Batman comic books.

ROUNDING OUT THE FIGURES

Kiefer began by creating detailed pencil sketches of the people in the crowd. He drew each figure individually, then scanned the sketches separately, opened the scans as templates in Illustrator, and traced them with the pen tool. Although each figure in the illustration was carefully planned, the placement of those figures was spontaneous and changed continuously as Kiefer arranged and rearranged the crowd scene.

Most of the people in the crowd are silhouettes, simple outlines filled with a solid color and surrounded with a yellow highlight. "They're drawn very simplistically," Kiefer says, "so they needed that edge of light to flesh them out a little. It gives a bit of depth even to very flat people." Many of the figures were copied, then reflected or skewed slightly, rather than completely redrawn, "so you feel there are more people than there actually are," Kiefer says.

When he wanted to direct attention to a figure, Kiefer increased the detail in the drawing ❶ or applied bright colors ❷. The woman in the doorway is the focal point of the design, and Kiefer used color to model the figure. Her body is constructed with a few simple shapes, but she got a three-dimensional look when Kiefer applied gradient fills, using the gradients to mimic dramatic lighting ❸.

❶

❸

❷

❹

He finished the figure by defining the crook of one arm ❹, drawing a crescent to create a shadow under the coat collar, and adding a gradient-filled shape to sculpt the crown of the hat. (He drew the shoes and their spike heels as separate contours in order to apply gradient fills, but he later decided to simplify the effect and filled all the shoe shapes with a single color.)

SIMPLIFYING COLOR CHOICES

As Kiefer created each new fill, he specified it as a custom color by choosing Object, Custom Color and entering CMYK values in the Custom Color dialog box. And he gave it an easy-to-recognize name (like *coat green* or *highlight*) so that he could quickly choose the color name he wanted from the Paint Style palette as he created and filled new elements. Kiefer also used the custom colors to define gradient fills. When he selected New in the Gradient palette and chose the custom color icon, his entire selection of colors was listed in the palette. Clicking on one of the color names defined the first color in the gradient. To create a fade-away fill for bathed-in-light effects, Kiefer specified a tint of the color as the second value in the gradient. And he selected a darker tone for the second value in the gradient when he wanted the color to deepen into shadow. Here again, as he created the custom gradients, he gave them easy-to-recognize names so that he could find the fill he needed quickly in the Paint Style palette.

To create the overlapping searchlights, Kiefer used gradient fills in conjunction with Illustrator's Mix Soft filter. He drew two beams of light with the pen tool, filled each one with a different color, and shift-clicked to select them both. He chose Filter, Pathfinder, Mix Soft to create new contours wherever the two beams overlapped. But he ignored the colors the filter produced and replaced them with custom gradients, dragging the gradient tool at a different angle in each of the contours to make the color fade in different directions ❺.

The theater building was rendered in the 3-D program Form-Z and saved in Illustrator format. But Kiefer wanted to avoid the distinctive surface texture that characterizes images created in 3-D programs, so he used the Form-Z shading only as a rough draft for his Illustrator design. "I was able to check the lighting and see how it had to fall, and then use Illustrator gradients for the colors," he says. However, applying gradients to the fireworks proved to be more complicated (see "Explosive Color" on page 100).

STAYING ORGANIZED

As the illustration became more complex, Kiefer made extensive use of Illustrator's Layers palette so that he could work on one section of the design and leave other elements undisturbed. He defined four layers to manage the people in the crowd, for example, one layer for the pointing man, another for the colorful couple, a third for the two photo-

1 Kiefer drew the figure with the pen tool and filled the shape with yellow. When he traced the shadows (shown in blue), the yellow fill on the bottom layer formed a halo around the figure.

2 The same basic technique was used to produce the pointing couple, but Kiefer gave himself more color options by drawing each figure in several sections (rather than one continuous outline) and drawing shapes for the darker fills on top.

3 After drawing an outline for the woman's coat, Kiefer specified a gradient fill. He dragged the gradient tool so that most of the coat was filled with the bright color that faded quickly to a pale tone. Then he drew additional shapes and applied the same fill, dragging the gradient tool in a different direction.

4 To create the negative space in the crook of the arm, Kiefer drew a "hole" shape, shift-clicked to select the coat and the hole, and selected Object, Compound Paths, Make (Command-8).

5 Kiefer used bright colors to direct attention to the center of the illustration and subdued tones to make peripheral elements recede. The soft-colored search-lights served as a backdrop for type in the printed piece, a brochure launching a plug-in cartridge enabling CD players to display inter-active CDs on the TV.

graphers, and a fourth for the simple silhouette figures. (The woman in the doorway is on a fifth layer, with the building.) By working in layers, Kiefer could freely rearrange the silhouettes to work out the composition of the crowd scene without disturbing the more important figures, isolated on other layers.

To create a new layer, Kiefer first chose Layers from the Window menu to display the Layers palette. He selected New Layer from the palette's pop-out menu. This opened the New Layer dialog box where he could name the layer and use the Selection Color pop-out menu to assign a different selection color to each layer so that he could eas-ily identify the layer he was working on, even in Artwork view. ☛ *A layer's selection color is dis-played beside its name in the Layers palette.*

Because he created layers as he went along, Kiefer often needed to change their characteris-tics later. Double-clicking a layer name in the palette displayed the Layer Options dialog box where Kiefer could rename the layer, change its selection color, or lock it. He also used the Layers palette to hide layers by clicking on the bullets under the eye icon to turn layers off. In an illus-tration of this complexity, he could speed up screen redraws considerably by hiding contours he wasn't currently working on. And at times, he kept a layer visible but protected it from changes by turning off the bullet under the pencil icon to make the layer uneditable. ■

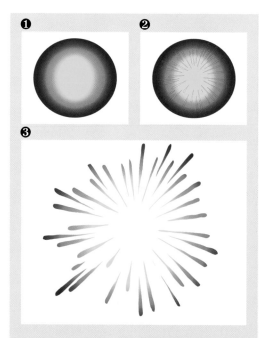

Explosive Color

Albert Kiefer's struggle to create realistic — and reproducible — fireworks will be all too familiar to Illustrator 5.0 users. He experimented with three different methods before he found one he could confidently send to his output bureau.

Initially, Kiefer created the fills the easy way, applying gradients to the sparks in the fireworks. But then he had second thoughts. Illustrator 5.0 gradients "are notorious for not printing," he says.

When Kiefer moved on to Plan B — saving the file in Illustrator 3 format — his 752K file became a 39MB monster. He opened it to see why and found that Illustrator "had made a separate blend for every little sparkle," he says. "I thought, 'This is impossible. I'm asking for trouble.' So I went back into Illustrator 5.0 and did it the old-fash-ioned way."

First he created a pair of concentric ovals, pressing the Option key to draw the ovals from the center out. He applied a yellow-to-red blend between the two, then drew a second set of ovals, blending from red to purple ❶. He ungrouped the two blends and placed them behind the set of sparks ❷, then created a marquee selection to se-lect the sparks and the blends, and chose Object, Masks, Make ❸. ☛ *Some Level 1 imagesetters have trouble outputting Illustrator gradient fills, and Illustrator 5.5 includes a setting that makes the fills compatible with these machines: the Compatible Gradient Printing option, ac-cessed by choosing File, Document Setup (Command-Shift-D). This setting may slow down output time on an imagesetter that han-dles gradient fills well, so consult your output bureau before applying the Compatible Gradi-ent Printing function.* ■

Subtle Lines with Illustrator Filters

■ *by Janet Ashford*

LLUSTRATOR FILTERS make it easier than ever to create sophisticated electronic linework that mimics the thick-thin look of hand-drawn strokes, and Mill Valley, Calif., illustrator Jeffrey Pelo used those filters to good advantage in an illustration he created in response to a call for entries from the Japanese postal service. The postal service wanted a stamp to commemorate the 45th anniversary of the Universal Declaration of Human Rights, and Pelo's entry features a Third World figure cradling the earth from violence. The finished piece didn't win the competition, but Pelo put it to use in self-promotional mailers, and in an ad in *American Showcase*.

When Pelo starts a project, he typically begins by choosing colors from a Pantone swatch book, then opening the Pantone Process Color System document provided with Illustrator (located inside the Color Systems folder). This adds the PMS color names to the custom color menu in the Paint Style palette — and the color values have already been converted to CMYK.

Pelo sometimes uses the Custom Color dialog box (accessed by choosing Object, Custom Color) to modify the CMYK values in a color he's chosen from the Color System file. When he does, he's careful to change the color name. ☞ *When you edit the CMYK specifications in a color chosen from one of Illustrator's color system files you need to change its name, so that you don't have two colors sharing the same name. Then the next time you open both a color system document and an illustration containing an edited color from that system, the specifications of the file that was opened most recently will prevail.* ☞ *You can protect the Illustrator color system*

Jeffrey Pelo uses a combination of techniques to give his PostScript linework a hand-drawn look, from specifying round end caps to using Illustrator's Outline Path filter and Average command to create tapering lines.

1 Using Illustrator's pen tool, Pelo drew an open contour to define the man's arms and shoulders. Filling this open contour left an unfilled gap across the man's chest. A shape was drawn in to fill the open area, and lines were added to articulate the man's face, hands, and feet. When Pelo added the globe, it obscured the arms. He hid the globe (Command-3) in order to work on the arms.

2 Pelo cut the arm away from the body, then cut the arm in two places to turn the hand into a separate path. Finally, he changed the stroke value of the line around the hand, creating a thinner outline.

3 After converting the strokes to outlines, Pelo selected points where the thick and thin lines met and used the Average command (Object, Average or Command-L) to bring the points together. He repeated the process to align all the contours in the man's arm.

4 Pelo drew two small lines to add definition to the arm (shown in blue), converted them to outlines, and united them with the rest of the arm. A copy of the arm was pasted in back (Command-B), and the Offset Path filter (in the Objects submenu) was applied to thicken the copied contour. This copy was filled with purple.

5 Pelo drew a masking path (shown in blue) on top of the arm, then selected the masking shape, the black outline, and the dark purple shadow line, and chose Object, Masks, Make. He copied the torso again, cut away the arm, and filled the cut contour with purple. The mask clipped off the dark purple shadow beyond the thumb and outside the arm.

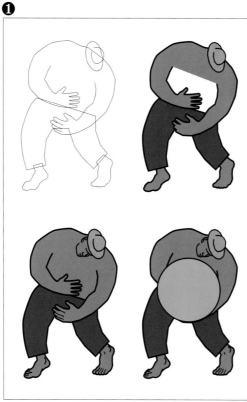

❶

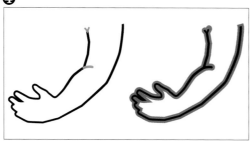

❷   **❸**

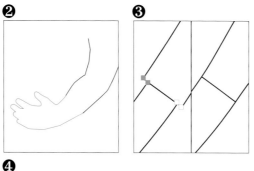

❹

❺

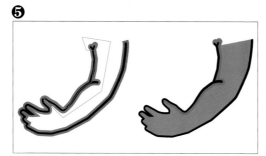

documents from being overwritten by locking the files. Select each document on the desktop, open the Get Info dialog box (Command-I), and click inside the Lock box.

TAPERING A STROKED PATH

Pelo started by making rough pencil sketches. He scanned his final sketch, opened it in Illustrator as a template, and traced it with the pen tool, specifying different stroke weights (3.75 to 5.25 points) to define the man holding the globe **❶**. In order to give the stroked lines a blunt-end, hand-drawn look, Pelo selected round end points in the Paint Style palette before drawing the lines.

Pelo wanted to adjust the line weights of the arms to make them taper from the shoulders to the fingers. So he copied the shape defining the torso and used the Paste In Front command (Command-F) to place a duplicate shape on top of the original. Working on the duplicate, Pelo cut the left arm away from the body with the knife tool, then cut the limb at the forearm and decreased the line weight around the hand **❷**. The Outline Stroked Path filter in the Filter, Objects submenu converted all the lines defining the arm to closed contours, and Pelo used the Average command to make the wide contours in the forearm meet the thin contour around the wrist precisely **❸**.

After selecting all the shapes forming the arm Pelo applied the Unite filter (Filter, Pathfinder, Unite) to combine them into a single thick-and-thin outline. To shade the arm, he copied this outline and applied a broad stroke in a dark shade of purple **❹**. Then he copied the original outline defining the arm, pasted the copy in back, and specified no stroke and a lighter shade of purple for the fill **❺**. The lines forming the fingers were placed in front (Command-=).

Pelo used the same techniques to taper the outline around the right arm before positioning both of the modified arms on top of the figure **❻**.

BUILDING THE BACKGROUND IMAGERY

After drawing a background rectangle at specified postage-stamp proportions, Pelo copied the rectangle. He deleted a corner point in the copy to turn it into a triangle, effectively dividing the background in two **❼**. Pelo filled one section with images of violence and the other with a paper-doll pattern symbolizing unity.

To create the paper-doll pattern, Pelo drew one half of a simplified female figure, reflected a copy across the vertical axis, and joined the end points (Command-J) to create a symmetrical figure. He repeated the process to draw a male paper doll. He placed the figures side by side, selected them, and created copies by pressing the Option key as he dragged the pair of figures into a new position.

The Repeat Transform command (Command-D) produced a row of duplicates. Pelo copied the row, staggering the copies to create a grid of paper dolls. He masked the grid into the background **❽**.
☞ *You can also use Illustrator's Crop Fill and Crop Stroke filters — rather than creating a masking path — to crop a design to fit into a background shape.*

After drawing simple shapes to define symbols of death and violence **❾**, Pelo copied the background rectangle (with no fill or stroke) and used the copy to mask these symbols. He added a barbed wire design, drawn with black-stroked shapes, to form a border between the symbols of violence and the paper-doll pattern.

A halo was used to separate the man holding the globe from the complex design in the background. To create the halo effect, Pelo began by hiding everything in the illustration except the man. ☞ *Illustrator's Hide command (Command-3) hides a selected element or elements. To hide everything in an illustration except for the element (or elements) that's selected, use the Option key in conjunction with the Hide command (Option-Command-3).*

Pelo selected the large shapes defining the man's body, copied them all, pasted in back (Command-B), and applied the Unite filter to combine the copied shapes into one contour. He gave this contour no fill and a yellow stroke, 14 points wide. He used a broad-stroked duplicate of the globe, placed at a slight offset behind the original, to create a purple shadow.

CREATING SPINNING STARS

Pelo felt that a final decorative touch was needed, so he created a swirling star design and placed a copy into two corners of the illustration.

First, Pelo drew a circle. Since he wanted a 12-point star, he divided 360 by 12 to determine the width, in degrees, he needed for the first ray: 30. After drawing a pair of guidelines at the edge of the circle 30 degrees apart, he drew a wavy ray as wide as the guidelines. He copied the ray, rotated the copy 30 degrees around the center of the circle to produce another ray, and used the Repeat Transform command (Command-D) to complete the star shape **❿**. Finally, Pelo combined the shapes with the Unite filter.

Once the star was filled with yellow, a copy was pasted in back and given a wide black stroke to create an outline. Pelo made a duplicate star with a red fill, masked the stars into squares drawn with no stroke or fill, and placed the masked stars in opposite corners of the illustration. Then, with all the elements in place, Pelo drew a large, zig-zag red star, gave it a red fill and a rusty red stroke, and placed it behind the man with the globe. ∎

❻

❼ **❽**

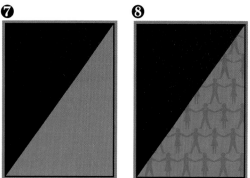

❾

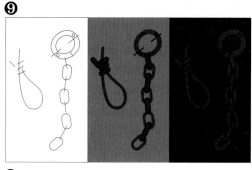

❿

6 The modified arms were placed on top of the figure so that they covered the original arms and the globe. Pelo used the pen tool to add details to the pants and to draw highlights on the shoulders, feet, and hat.

7 To create the background, Pelo drew a black-stroked, black-filled rectangle. A copy of the rectangle was pasted in back and given a broad purple stroke. After a third copy was pasted in front, Pelo deleted the top left point to turn the shape into a triangle. He filled the triangle with green.

8 After creating a paper-doll design, the green triangle was copied, and a duplicate was pasted in front (Command-F) and given no stroke and no fill. Pelo selected the copied triangle, along with the paper-doll grid, and chose Object, Masks, Make.

9 A view in Artwork mode shows the simple shapes Pelo used to draw a noose and a chain. The lines were defined as thick strokes with round end caps. To create outlines around the shapes that overlapped others, Pelo gave them black strokes and pasted unstroked copies in front. The black outlines are visible against a red backdrop, but they disappear on a black background.

10 To create a star, Pelo started with a circle and drew a vertical line through its center. He selected the line, then Option-clicked on the *x* in the center of the circle with the rotation tool and chose 30 degrees and Copy in the Rotate dialog box. He used the two lines as guides to determine the width of the first ray. Copies of the ray were rotated 30 degrees around the circle's center to produce additional rays.

Dashing Patterns

■ *by Laurie Wigham*

WHEN DESIGNERS Maryanne Ackerman and Linda Lane came to me to illustrate a corporate identity system for a newly formed public relations agency specializing in internet-related companies, the client asked for an illustration with an Art Deco or Bauhaus feel, bold and architectural but without the hard mechanical feel of much computer-generated art. At the client's suggestion, I used the Chrysler building as an inspiration for the style of the antenna, but I decided to draw radio waves in a way that would soften the antenna and bring some magic and delicacy to the illustration.

It seemed to me that an easy way to do this would be to use Adobe Illustrator's dashed-line capabilities to draw lines of dots, varying the sizes and spacing of the dots to create a feel of shimmering motion. Unfortunately, rather than being a quick, elegant solution, this turned out to be the source of all my problems.

I first drew the starburst of the radio waves so they radiated from a common center. But the dots all clumped together randomly in the center, looking like a pile of scrambled eggs. So I rotated all the lines so that their point of origin was in the center of the starburst, then moved the lines away from the center. After I pulled all the lines back, I

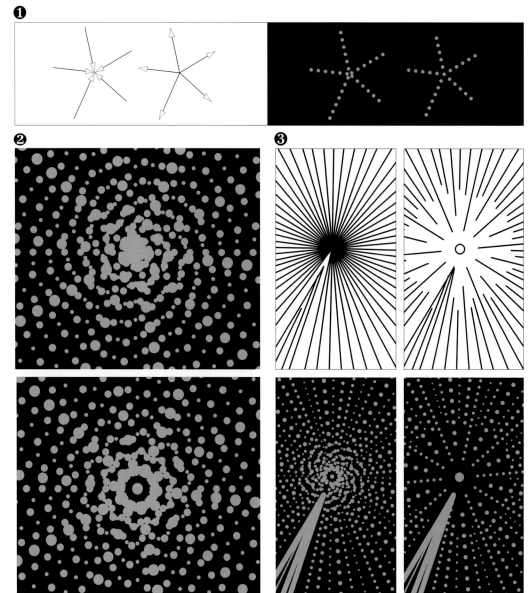

❶

❷

❸

1 When I began working on art for a corporate identity system, I drew a line from the outside in, then rotated it around its endpoint. This is a problem because when Illustrator draws a dotted line, it starts the dots at the point where you first click. So the beginning of the line was the only place where I could be sure exactly where a dot would fall.

2 The dots clumped in the middle of the starburst, so I used Arrange, Transform Each to rotate each line 180° around its own center.

3 Rotating the lines produced a more regular pattern, but it still was too cluttered. I needed to pull most of the lines away from the center so I could carefully control placement of the remaining dots. So I used Transform Each to scale each cluster of five or ten lines. This reduced the size of each line individually, moving the end away from the center — more efficient than the scale tool.

added a single large dot in the center. The next challenge was getting the dot size right when the design was scaled to fit the different elements in the identity system — especially tricky because the dots were reversed out of black, and at very small sizes there was a risk that they might close up. It was necessary to run numerous proofs on an imagesetter because my laser printer's 300 dpi output was just not accurate enough. And every time the art was resized for a different application, the look and feel of the emanations changed. I would usually turn on the Scale Line Weight option in the General Preferences dialog box (File, Preferences, General or Command-K) before I scaled the image in order to maintain the overall dot spacing. But when I enlarged the illustration, this often produced dots that were too large and clumsy. And when I reduced it, the dots often

became so fine they disappeared entirely. So I had to select each group of lines and adjust the line width and gap settings until they looked good in the new configuration.

I did do three smart things when I first constructed the image which made it easier to make all these changes. First, I grouped each cluster of five to ten lines with the same characteristics (line weight, dot spacing) so that I could quickly select them. Second, I put each element (the waves, the crescents, the border, the type, and different parts of the building) on its own layer so I could lock or hide anything I wasn't working with at the moment. And third, I made the dotted lines longer and the building larger than I actually needed and put a mask around the edges to crop the illustration. This gave me extra flexibility in adjusting sizes and angles. ■

❹

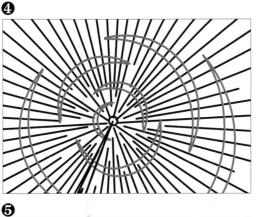

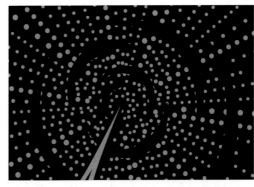

4 To get a look suggesting stylized radio waves, I added black crescents cutting across the dotted lines. But these introduced a whole host of new problems. Being negative shapes, they were defined by the dotted lines that crossed them, and tended to bulge out, like lumpy slugs, wherever the dots were too widely spaced to define the edge of the crescent. I had to keep redefining the rhythm of the dotted lines each time I resized the image until the crescents held their shape. I also had to alter the shapes of the crescents slightly to pick up the best dots placement.

❺

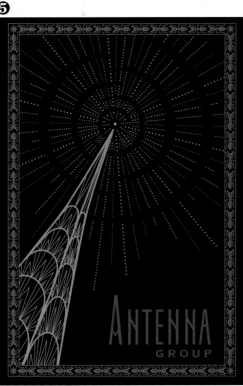

❻

5 For a postcard and a press kit, the client wanted to add a border of marching ants. The border needed to read as decorative at first glance, with ants visible only on closer inspection — as subtle as the pun on the company name, Antenna Group.

6 On the business card and stationery I used a bolder, simplified building, composed of solid shapes rather than lines, without the extra radiating lines between the triangles. I drew the building as a flat plane in Illustrator, then slanted and rotated it in Adobe Dimensions before bringing it back into Illustrator and nudging the lines around until they looked right to me.

Where Stylus Meets Mouse

■ *by Talitha Harper*

Another designer might have clipped the rough edges off this Illustrator image or used the ellipse tool to draw the sun, but Marina Thompson of Nahant, Md., strives for the same freeform energy that characterized her gouache and cut-paper work. "I try not to clean things up too much," she says. She draws most of the shapes with a pressure-sensitive stylus and uses the mouse to make minute adjustments like repositioning handles to bring graceful curves to the ships and rotating the cars to follow bends in the road.

A PRESSURE-SENSITIVE STYLUS invites spontaneity, but a mouse offers pinpoint accuracy. So Marina Thompson relies on both tools to create her PostScript imagery, using the stylus to draw the primary shapes that make up an illustration and turning to the mouse when she wants to reposition individual points — to smooth out a curve, for example, or to reshape elements she's copied so that she can keep the duplicates from looking like clones. "Unprocessed" is the effect she strives for. "I really try to stay away from a computer-generated look."

Even the simplest shapes, like circles and squares, are often drawn with the stylus and the pen tool. "I resist using the rectangle and circle tools," says Thompson. "I think about shapes, not geometry." So when she created a tropical harbor scene in Adobe Illustrator, she began by drawing a background rectangle (with slightly out-of-square sides) and filling it with a three-part gradient to define the blue-green water in the harbor, the crystal clear look of the shallows, and the rich,

clear blue of a tropical sky.

On top of the rectangle, Thompson drew a set of rolling hills, filled the hill shapes with a two-tone green gradient ❶, and sprinkled palm trees across the landscape. First, she created three trees ❷, selected all of them, Option-clicked with the reflect tool to open the Reflect dialog box, and chose the Copy option in the dialog box to produce a set of six trees. She selected two of the trees, Option-clicked with the scale tool, entered 80 percent in the Scale dialog box, and selected Copy. Two other trees were copied and scaled to 70 percent. This gave Thompson a cluster of ten trees, and she used the mouse to Option-drag them, creating copies of the trees and scattering them across the hillside.

BUILDING A BOISTEROUS PALETTE

Thompson counts on color to add vitality to her imagery, and she usually has a color palette in mind before she begins the design. In the early stages of an illustration, she defines the palette by drawing a set of small squares off to the side of the

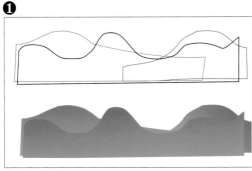

❶

❷

❸

❹

1 Thompson drew three hill shapes, gave them the same graduated fill, and then used Illustrator's gradient tool to adjust the depth of the graduation in each shape to vary the density of the color where the hills overlap.

2 After drawing a palm tree with the pressure-sensitive tablet, Thompson repositioned points on a duplicate to create a second tree. She drew a third palm and used copies of the three trees to fill out the landscape.

3 Thompson used complementary colors for the palm trees and the roofs. "I like the contrast, but too much can be off-putting," she says. So she softened the effect of the complements by coloring the houses in a tone that harmonizes with the background and filling some of the larger shapes (like the sun) with tones that don't clash with the surrounding color.

4 After selecting dominant colors — orange, yellow, red, several bright blues, and two shades of green — Thompson rounded out her color palette by creating lighter and darker versions of several of those dominant colors and introduced a bright pink accent color.

Illustrator page and filling the squares with the tones she plans to use most often. Then she can use the Option key to toggle between the eyedropper and paint bucket tools, selecting colors from the squares and pouring them into the shapes she creates.

"I like to limit my palette," Thompson says. "It keeps a piece cleaner." And she also likes to work with complementary colors. "They have impact." But even Thompson admits that the effect of bright blue against orange and pure red against green can be jarring. So she confines the complementary "clashes" to small shapes and adds a bright "neutral" or two to the palette (in this case, a warm yellow to fill the lopsided sun) **❸**.

As the image progressed, Thompson needed additional colors to bring more tonality to the design. So she used the colors in her basic palette to produce lighter and darker variants by selecting one of the color squares she had created and then pressing the Shift key in order to adjust all the color-value sliders in the Paint Style palette in unison **❹**. "You can really stretch the range of color

that way," says Thompson. ☞ *To lighten or darken a CMYK color in Illustrator — and maintain the proportions of the original CMYK mix — press the Shift key and drag one of the color sliders in the Paint Style palette. The other sliders will move correspondingly.*

DISGUISING DUPLICATION

Throughout the design, Thompson used copies of elements she had drawn, but she was careful to keep the copies from looking identical (as she had been when she created the palm trees). For example, Thompson drew a single bus, then altered copies to produce two more vehicles.

When she drew the bus, Thompson deviated from her usual drawing technique, choosing the ellipse tool to create the wheels (although she usually favors irregular, hand-drawn circles and ovals). In this case, she knew that the vehicles would be used as tiny elements in the finished scene. And if she made individual segments of the vehicles too irregular, they wouldn't appear to fit together cohesively at a minuscule size.

5 To make the bus windows transparent so the background could show through, Thompson selected the bus shape and the windows and chose Object, Compound Paths, Make (Command-8).

6 A second bus was created by copying the first, repositioning some of the anchor points, and drawing new windows and wheels.

7 Another copy of the bus was used to create a Land Rover. Thompson moved the top points down to lower the roof, drew a shape to define the open interior, and turned this interior path and the body of the vehicle into a compound path. A set of rectangles in alternating shades of blue and white form a canopy roof.

8 After drawing a wave shape on top of each ship, Thompson selected the wave and the ship's body and chose Filter, Pathfinder, Minus Front. She added a wake by drawing a scalloped shape at the bottom of the ship and pasting a copy of the scalloped shape in back (Command-B).

9 Thompson added some irregularities to even the smallest details to avoid a computer-generated look. Portholes and windows on each ship were arranged with intentional imprecision, and the rectangular windows were drawn individually. (The blue guides were added to show the lack of alignment.)

10 Thompson drew the pennants separately, then filled them by sampling color from other elements with the eyedropper tool and pressing the Option key to turn the eyedropper into the paint bucket. Some pennants were created as open shapes, but because they are filled, they appear to be closed.

❺

❻
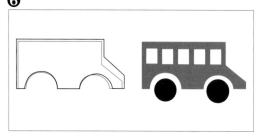

❼

❽
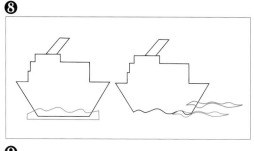

❾
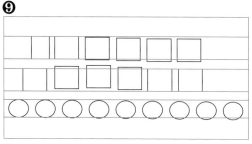

❿

Thompson worked in the pasteboard, outside of the Illustrator page, as she drew the first bus. (She wanted to create it at a comfortably large size and then scale it to fit into the illustration. And since she wasn't drawing the bus in proportion to the rest of the imagery, she didn't want to be distracted by other elements as she worked.) Once the bus was complete ❺, she grouped it and duplicated it by copying and pasting (rather than Option-dragging) so that she could later recolor the copy and scale and position it independently.

☞ *When you use the Option-drag function in Illustrator to copy a group (or a contour within a group), the copied element will be grouped to the original — and this can cause problems later. For example, if you try to reposition the duplicate, the original will move with it. And if you change the color of one element, the fill in the rest of the group can be affected. But when you use the copy-paste function to produce a duplicate, the copy will be recognized as a separate element and not part of the group.*

After repositioning points in the copied bus to modify its shape slightly, Thompson changed the color in the body and grouped the body and the wheels ❻. Then she pasted in another copy of the original bus, and turned this second duplicate into a Land Rover by drawing a new window shape and adding a striped roof ❼. After grouping the Land Rover elements, Thompson selected each vehicle and dragged it onto the illustration, scaling it and rotating to correspond to the curves in a broad-stroked line she had drawn with the stylus to define a winding road. She also drew a taxi and a Jeep to add traffic all along the road.

To finish the design, Thompson placed several ships in the harbor. She drew the ships in the pasteboard at a larger size than she needed, using the stylus to give them irregular, wavy bottoms that suggested waves along the bow ❽ and the mouse to draw the tiny rectangles and circles that form windows and portholes ❾. To create multicolor stripes on the smokestacks and the sides of some of the ships, Thompson drew straight lines on top of each ship, then selected the straight lines and the underlying contour and chose Filter, Pathfinder, Divide. This broke the outlines defining the ships and the smokestacks into separate shapes that could be filled with different colors.

Thompson brought a final splash of color to the illustration by adding simple triangular pennants, drawn with the stylus, to the ships and filling the pennants with random color, sampled from other elements in the design ❿. Each ship was grouped before Thompson dragged it into the foreground of the illustration so that she could experiment with the size and placement of each one until she was satisfied with the composition. ■

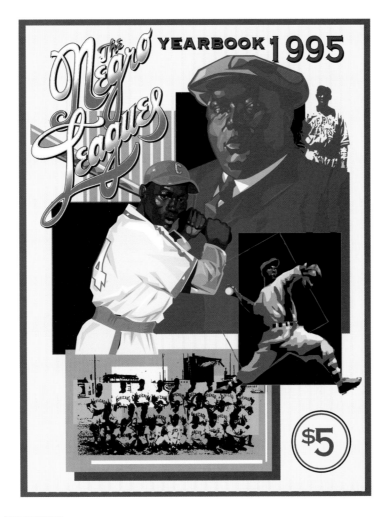

ILLUSTRATOR / STREAMLINE

Posterizing in PostScript

■ *by Sara Booth*

CHARLY PALMER likes his art to be a visual paradox — both stylized and realistic. The Stone Mountain, Ga., illustrator uses PostScript contours as though they were paint, building up layer upon layer of color in a technique similar to painting with gouache. For a self-promotional Negro League design, he worked with scanned photographs and sketches, using a variety of methods to give the imagery a posterized look, from hand-tracing the scans in Adobe Illustrator to converting them to PostScript contours with Adobe Streamline or Illustrator's autotrace tool.

Palmer began by roughing out the composition in a thumbnail pencil sketch. Then he created each figure in a separate Illustrator document and grouped all the elements before copying the figures into the final file. This made it easier for him to make small adjustments to their placement when he arranged the composition.

ADDING DIMENSION WITH COLOR

In Palmer's design, each figure has a different level of detail. To achieve this effect, he used several methods to turn his photo reference into illustrations. For the sepia figure, he used a detailed sketch as an Illustrator template, tracing it by hand and adding detail as he went. The figure is one of the most prominent elements of the design and is correspondingly more detailed than most of the other figures. Palmer began by making a tight sketch based on photo reference. He scanned this and opened it as a template in Illustrator, then traced it with the pen tool, using hard-edged shapes as though they were layers of opaque paint. ☞ *Be aware of copyright law when you*

Charly Palmer created the posterized look in this self-promotional illustration by stacking PostScript contours as though they were layers of opaque paint. He used a variety of techniques to create the posterized effects, from drawing chunky shapes with Illustrator's pen tool to using Streamline's Color/Grayscale Setup options.

1 In his initial pencil sketch (left), Palmer had carefully rendered the shapes that would define the sepia-tone figure. But as he traced the template, he added details in the lips and around the eyes to produce a more realistic look. He began by defining the outline of the figure and filling it with 100 percent of his custom brown. Next, he added the midtones, then the highlights (right).

copy or scan other people's work. In general, copyright-protected artwork, including photography, cannot be legally copied or scanned without the creator's permission. But most illustrations and photos printed before 1919 are copyright-free.

Palmer calls the sepia figure "a study in one-color variation." He defined a single custom brown, then used the Tint slider in the Paint Style dialog box to assign a tint of this brown to each contour. ☞ *When you plan to use a tint throughout an image, it's a good idea to specify it as a custom color. To add a tint to Illustrator's Custom Color list, you must first drag it from the Fill swatch onto the process color icon in the Paint Style palette. Then, once the tint has been defined in CMYK values, drag the color from the Fill swatch to the custom color icon.*

He began by drawing around the edges of his template, creating a large background shape, which he filled with 100 percent of his custom brown. Then he continued to add shapes in lighter shades, following his template and going from dark tones to highlights. In the process, he added a great deal of detail, especially in the facial features, to create the planes of light and shadow that define the shape of the figure ❶.

For the batter, Palmer scanned an old photograph and opened the scan in Streamline. He wanted Streamline to posterize the image, so he

opened the Color/Grayscale Setup dialog box (Options, Color/Grayscale Setup or Command-B), set the Maximum Number of Colors to five, and checked the Generate Custom Color List function. When the Streamline file was opened in Illustrator, the Custom Color list included five shades of gray. Palmer opened the Custom Color dialog box by choosing Object, Custom Color and changed each shade of gray to a process color, then adjusted CMYK values until he had a palette of custom neutrals and reds for the uniform and bat.

For the batter's face and hands, Palmer wanted a very different color palette ❷. So he selected hues from an Illustrator file containing about 50 colors, which he keeps on his computer and uses in nearly all his illustrations. ☞ *If you have a set of colors you use often — and you don't mind sacrificing a bit of speed — you can add your colors to Illustrator's startup file. Open Adobe Illustrator Startup, found in the Plug-Ins folder. (You might want to save a copy in a different folder before you make changes.) Create your desired custom colors, or pick them up from another document by choosing File, Import Styles. Then either add swatches to the custom color swatches at the lower right of the startup document or replace existing custom colors with your own. (You can also add custom patterns and gradients to the startup file.) Save the file as Adobe Illustrator Startup and*

❷

❹

❸

place it in the Plug-Ins folder. Keep in mind that if your startup file is large, Illustrator may take longer to launch.

Palmer wanted the pitcher to be rougher than the other figures, so he scanned a photo and used Illustrator's autotrace tool. "It's by no means as refined as Streamline," he says, "but what I wanted was a looser look." ☞ *For more efficient autotracing, click the tool in a place where you would place a point if you were tracing the art with the pen tool.*

One of the Illustrator features that Palmer is most enthusiastic about is the eyedropper tool; he used it to pick up colors from other parts of the art and apply them to the pitcher, ensuring color continuity. ☞ *To fill multiple contours with the same attributes, select them, then double-click the eyedropper tool on the desired color.*

FINE-TUNING THE COMPOSITION

Using his thumbnail for reference, Palmer combined the finished figures and added a striped background in "nostalgic" colors, reminiscent of old-fashioned baseball uniforms.

Minor elements in the design were given simple treatments. For the team photograph at the bottom of the illustration ❸, Palmer used a photocopier, which is one of his favorite tools, to copy a photo repeatedly until he had created a high-contrast image. He scanned it and opened it in

Photoshop, where he saved it as an EPS image. After he placed the photo in Illustrator, he added rectangles of color behind the image, which show through the transparent areas.

The standing figure in the upper right corner was taken from another team photograph. Palmer photocopied it, cut out a single figure with scissors, then photocopied the figure repeatedly until he had achieved a high-contrast look. "I know you could do the same thing in Photoshop, but this way was just faster for me," he says. But because he needed to manipulate the figure further in Illustrator, he used Streamline, with Maximum Number of Colors set to two, to convert it to Post-Script contours.

To integrate the standing figure into the rest of the design, Palmer used Illustrator's Divide filter to split the contours where they touched the sepia figure and the rectangle behind the pitcher. Then he filled the split contours with new colors ❹.

Palmer's wife and business partner, Dorothea Taylor-Palmer, is the computer expert in the family and "the best teacher I had," Palmer says. Most of the illustrations that bear either partner's name are actually joint projects. In addition to giving technical advice to her husband, who is still exploring Illustrator, Taylor-Palmer produced the *Negro Leagues* lettering in this image, drawing it freehand in pencil, then scanning it and redrawing it in Illustrator. ■

2 Palmer wants his illustrations to be realistic, but not photographic. He experiments to see how far his palette can diverge from nature and still deliver a natural effect. Though the colors are extreme, the tonality is realistic. "I'm conscious of all the colors having the correct value," Palmer says, "the right contrast of dark to light."

3 After scanning a high-contrast photocopy of a team photo, Palmer opened the scan in Photoshop, chose Mode, Bitmap, and saved it in EPS format, checking the Transparent Whites box in the EPS Format dialog box.

4 Where the standing figure overlapped other elements, Palmer wanted a change of colors. He selected intersecting shapes and chose Filter, Pathfinder, Divide to create a new shape everywhere two contours met. Then he filled these shapes with new colors.

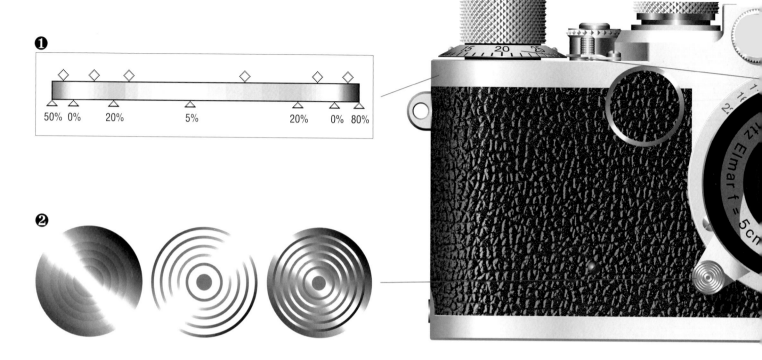

❶

50% 0% 20% 5% 20% 0% 80%

❷

ILLUSTRATOR/DIMENSIONS

Photorealism in Black-and-White

■ *by Sara Booth*

1 Blakeley kept the Gradient palette open as he worked so that he could change the gray values and adjust the sliders to hone the effect of the gradients as he applied them. This seven-step gradient, used to fill the body of the camera, adds multi-tone shading and highlights.

2 Blakeley filled a set of nested circles with a linear gradient, setting the angle to 45 degrees in the Paint Style dialog box (left). Next, he created rings by drawing stroked circles and selecting Filter, Objects, Outline Path. These rings were filled with the same gradient, with the angle set at –45 degrees (center). Together, the circles and the rings mimic the look of machined metal.

WHEN VANCOUVER DESIGNER Gary Blakeley began teaching one day a week at the Emily Carr Institute of Art and Design, he noticed that his students tended to turn to Photoshop no matter what effect they were after. So Blakeley embarked on a project to showcase Illustrator's capabilities, using Photoshop and Dimensions only as helpers: to create a photorealistic, black-and-white illustration of one of the cameras in his collection.

As a collector, Blakeley values his 1954 Leica IIF. As a designer, he's fond of its industrial design. It also offers many challenges for the illustrator — leather wrapped around a curved surface, a complex three-dimensional diamond pattern on the winding knobs, and a variety of reflective surfaces. Blakeley drew no sketches for this project. Instead, he made a series of detailed measurements, then used guides to be sure his drawing matched the dimensions of the camera.

APPLYING GRADIENTS INTERACTIVELY

Blakeley built the camera with simple geometric shapes, most of them drawn with the rectangle and ellipse tool, and used gradients to add dimen-

sion. To make the process of creating and modifying gradients easier, he has two monitors attached to his computer: One displays the drawing while the other provides an area where he can keep all his palettes open.

Once a gradient was applied to a shape, Blakeley could modify it interactively in the Gradient palette until he produced the sense of depth and light that he wanted. He created 35 custom gradients to simulate a range of surfaces — from the subtle shading of the brushed steel body ❶ to the sharply defined reflections on some of the chrome knobs, as well as the glass of the lenses. ☞ *To copy a color or tint from your illustration into a gradient, first select a color pointer in the Gradient palette and then use the eyedropper tool to Control-click on the desired color. To copy a color pointer in the Gradient palette, Option-drag it. And to swap two colors, drag one pointer on top of the other.*

For one camera knob, Blakeley applied gradients in layers to simulate a fan-shaped reflection. First, he used the Shift and Option keys to draw a series of circles from the same center point. He filled these concentric circles with a gradient, then applied the same gradient, at the opposite

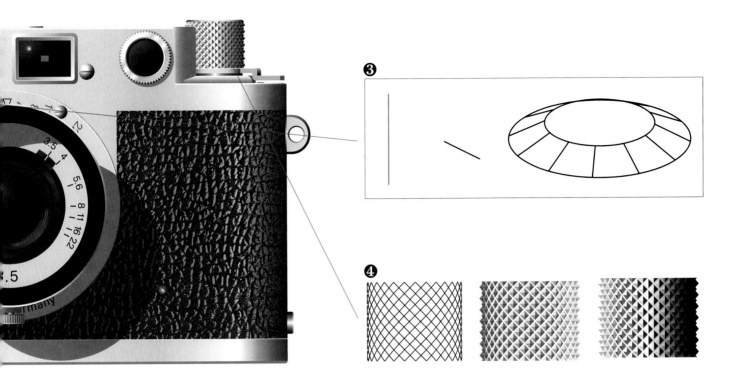

angle, to a set of rings which were placed in front of the circles ❷.

BUILDING 3-D SHAPES IN DIMENSIONS

For the illustration's most involved three-dimensional effects, Blakeley relied on Dimensions. He used the Revolve function (Operations, Revolve or Command-Shift-R) to create a frame counter. In the Revolve dialog box, he selected No Caps so the resulting shape would be hollow and entered 360 degrees in the Angle box ❸. Then he worked in the Mapped Artwork window (Appearance, Map Artwork or Command-Option-M) to wrap numerals and tic marks around the form. ☞ *Dimensions can import elements to be mapped onto three-dimensional shapes. But simple textures can also be drawn in the Mapped Artwork window, where most of the tools are similar to those in Illustrator. Several Illustrator keyboard shortcuts are also available in the Mapped Artwork window, including Command-D to repeat a transformation and Command-I to display the Surface Properties palette, where you can change colors and gradients.*

After measuring the circumference of the winding knob, Blakeley used Dimensions to draw

a cylinder that size by double-clicking on the cylinder icon in the toolbox and then entering the radius and height in the Cylinder dialog box. To add a complex diamond pattern to the knob, he began by drawing a set of diagonal lines and mapping them to the cylinder in Dimensions. He used the mapped lines as guides to draw the diamond pattern in Illustrator ❹. "Dimensions could give me a structure, but not the final effect — it's too complex," he says.

MODELING A SCANNED TEXTURE

Blakeley had already filled the surface of the camera with a gradient that mimicked the shadows on either edge of the camera and the highlight on the left side. He used this gradient to add shading to a scanned texture that was wrapped around the body of the camera.

Blakeley first scanned a photograph of leather, opened the scan in Photoshop, and converted it to a dithered bitmap. Then he saved the scan in EPS format, checking the Transparent Whites option in the EPS Format dialog box. When he placed the leather texture in Illustrator and set it in front of the gradient fill, the gradient showed through the white areas in the scan. ■

3 To create a frame counter, Blakeley drew a guide and a short diagonal line in Illustrator (left). When he revolved the line in Dimensions, the guide worked as the axis for the rotation (right, shown in wireframe).

4 After using Dimensions to map a grid to a cylinder (left), Blakeley opened the art in Illustrator and drew four triangles in each grid shape, assigning colors to the triangles (center) because "it was easier to work with contrasting colors." The Select, Same Fill Color filter let him select all the triangles of a particular color in order to fill them with a gradient. Dragging the gradient tool across the cylinder while the triangles were still selected made the gradient flow through all the triangles as though they were a single shape (right).

❶

❷

❸

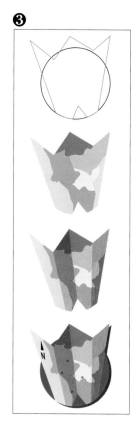

❹

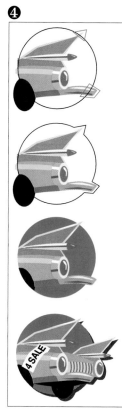

Breaking the Boundary

■ *by Sara Booth*

1 Yahoo asked Canary Studios for "something trendy" for its Los Angeles site, says Ken Roberts. "But L.A. is like London: Trendy changes every 15 minutes."

2 The skyline and ground contours were masked in the background circle (shown in red) for the Business/Stocks icon.

3 The bottom of the map in the Maps/Views icon seems to be masked in the background circle, but English simply traced the circle as she drew the lower edge of the map (shown in blue). Masking creates the illusion of folds: After shapes were masked in the map shape, shapes with darker shades of the same colors were drawn in front in the folded area to simulate shadows.

4 To let the fin and bumper in the Classified icon break out of the background, English drew shapes (shown in red) and used the Unite filter to join them to the mask contour.

W HEN CANARY STUDIOS was asked to design a series of icons for the Internet search firm Yahoo, the challenge was to make images that were appealing and clear when displayed at less than an inch across. Canary's principals, Ken Roberts and Carrie English, wanted to produce images that were lively and lighthearted, and Illustrator's layers and masking functions allowed them to create icons that seem to burst out of their circular boundaries.

In addition to Yahoo's original site, which allows World Wide Web users to search the Web by keywords and then link directly to the locations they find, the firm is also developing a series of sites which provide the same search functions within a local area. English and Roberts were hired to design icons for the Los Angeles site (la.yahoo.com), and they chose a cheerful look and a palette of bright colors to tie into the city's visual identity. After Roberts and English worked with the clients on initial sketches, English had the task of translating these sketches into the final Illustrator files.

For many of the icons, English added depth by masking background elements inside a circle, then allowing foreground shapes to extend beyond that boundary. In other cases, however, she wanted part of an object to be contained inside the circle, while other parts extended beyond the edges. Sometimes she solved this problem by trimming the shapes that fell outside the circle. Other times, she used the Pathfinder filter to alter the shape of the mask itself.

To stay organized, English usually began each piece with two layers, one for masked elements and another for contours that sat in front of the mask. "I just kept moving things from one layer to the next as I saw what needed to be masked," she says. ☞ *To move a contour from one Illustrator layer to another, select it to display a colored dot to the right of its layer in the Layers palette, then drag that dot to the desired layer.*

The final touch was to add a drop shadow by copying each icon, deleting foreground elements, choosing Filter, Pathfinder, Unite to combine the remaining parts into a single contour, then filling it with gray and sending it behind the icon. ■

Designing Gradients by Eye

■ *by Sara Booth*

CHRISTOPHER SPOLLEN is only half joking when he says his favorite Illustrator function is the Undo command. The Ocean Breeze, New York, illustrator has a free-flowing, serendipitous approach to his work, and the ability to undo gives him the freedom to experiment with different techniques — colors, blends, gradients, filters — to find the liveliest effect.

When Spollen was asked to illustrate an article about the World Wide Web in *Net-Guide* magazine, his design was driven by the abundance found on the Web. "The art director kept saying, 'More, more, more!'" he says. The final design uses icons orbiting a globe to illustrate the variety of options on the Web — and, incidentally, the variety of effects Spollen can achieve in Illustrator.

Spollen hates to waste time drawing the same thing twice. He often reuses palettes, gradients, and even figures from past illustrations. He also borrows freely from his own line of clip art, Moonlightpress Studio Stock. The globe, for example, was taken from a clip art illustration. But gradients transformed the familiar shapes of the continents, creating the illusion of oceans floating above the surface of the globe.

USING A SINGLE ANGLE

Spollen created the original globe illustration by scanning a hand-drawn sketch, then

"I sit down at a computer in summer, and I look around and it's winter," laments Christopher Spollen, who can spend hours at the keyboard exploring Illustrator's functions. To illustrate an article about the World Wide Web, Spollen achieved a surprising variety of effects by experimenting with gradient fills.

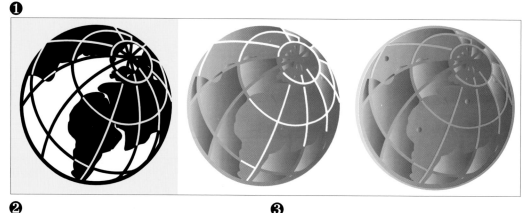

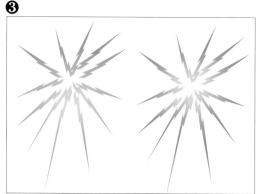

1 Spollen began the image with a black-and-white globe illustration. Auto-tracing in Streamline had produced one large and several small black-filled contours. Breaks in the shapes defined some of the latitude and longitude lines, and white contours layered on top defined the oceans. (We've placed the illustration on a tinted background to show which longitude and latitude lines are negative space and which are fillable contours.) Spollen filled all the contours with the same gradient, creating a spatial illusion. A circle behind the globe, filled with a red-to-yellow gradient, shows through the negative space which defines the remainder of the latitude and longitude lines.

2 All the contours that make up the batter are filled with the same gradient at the same custom angle: about 128 degrees.

3 Spollen tried selecting the lightning bolts, filling them with a radial gradient, then dragging with the gradient tool to fill them as if they were a single shape (left). But he wanted each bolt to have a red point, and the radial fill didn't give him that effect. So he filled each bolt with its own linear gradient.

converting it to PostScript contours using Adobe Streamline. With its default Outline setting, Streamline rendered the oceans as contours in front of the basic globe shape and used negative space for some of the latitude and longitude lines. For the Web illustration, Spollen selected all the black and white contours and filled them with a custom blue-to-purple gradient. When he placed a circle behind the globe, its gradient showed through the gaps between contours ❶.

Spollen used a similar technique for the base-ball player, which also began life as an illustration from one of his clip art collections. This time, Spollen wasn't happy with the effect of applying the light-green-to-dark-green gradient at the default angle of 0. Instead, he used the gradient fill tool to experiment with different angles ❷. "If I angle the gradient another way, it looks like a completely different piece of art," he says. "I'll try it several ways and Undo until it looks right." *☞ If you drag the gradient tool while several contours are selected, Illustrator will fill those contours as though they were a single shape. To apply a gradient separately to multiple contours, but still use the same custom angle for all of them, select all the contours and enter a number in the Angle box of the Paint Style palette. To determine the custom angle you want, experiment with the gradient tool by filling a single contour. When you have an angle you like, note the Angle setting in the Paint*

Style palette, and use this number when you select and fill all the contours.

RADIATING GRADIENTS
The lightning bolts are also the result of Spollen's experiments. He tried a radial gradient first, but he wasn't happy with the effect: "It didn't give me the hot red points I wanted." So he filled each lightning bolt with a linear gradient, dragging the gradient fill tool to set a different angle for each one ❸. *☞ To constrain the angle of the gradient fill to 45-degree increments, press the Shift key as you drag the gradient fill tool.*

USING TIGHT TRACINGS
Spollen wanted to add a hint of roughness to contrast with the smooth PostScript contours that made up most of the image. So for two of the icons — the musicians and the rocket — he used Streamline to convert scans. Spollen began with royalty-free images from his collection of antique books on radio and other "modern" technologies. After photocopying the images repeatedly until their lines began to break down, he used white and black pencils to make small adjustments on the photocopies. Then he scanned the images and opened them in Streamline for conversion. He wanted Streamline to faithfully reproduce the rough edges, speckles, and broken lines created by his multi-generation photocopying process (and he has the RAM and hard drive space to han-

❹

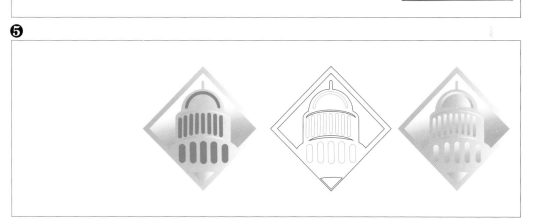

❺

4 Spollen opened a Stream-line conversion of a scan and used the gradient tool to fill all the contours with his blue-to-purple gradient. When he selected some contours and changed their fill by clicking on a red-to-yellow gradient in the Paint Style palette, the angle stayed the same. A blue-filled rectangle was placed behind the image, and some of the contours were filled with flat colors.

5 To create gaps between the columns in the Capitol icon, Spollen drew lines (shown in blue) with round end caps and heavy stroke weights (from 5 points for the top row to 8 points at the bottom). The Objects, Outline Path filter transformed these lines into contours that could then be filled with gradients.

dle the complex files this creates). So he chose Options, Conversion Setup (Command-J) and moved the Tolerance slider all the way to the left for maximum tightness. ☛ *When using Streamline to convert images like these with very small parts, you'll get the best results if you either enlarge the image before scanning or scan at a resolution of 300 dpi or above. File size will increase, but the extra information captured by the scanner will help Streamline create a more accurate conversion.*

To add a shimmer to the rocket icon, Spollen applied two gradient fills, both at the same angle. To achieve this effect, he first filled all the contours with one gradient at a custom angle (using the same technique he had used on the baseball player). Then he selected some contours and chose another gradient in the Paint Style palette, which changed the fill without changing the angle ❹.

OUTLINING IN ILLUSTRATOR

A different gradient approach adds dimension to the Capitol dome: Most of the shapes are filled with a gradient applied at a custom angle, but the background and some of the details are filled with the same gradient at the default angle. To create the rounded areas between the columns, Spollen drew a series of vertical lines, then chose Filter, Objects, Outline Path to transform the lines into shapes that could be filled with gradients ❺. The Outline Path filter was also used to create the

smoke and reflections in the chemistry icon at the top of the illustration (see page 1). ☛ *When you apply the Outline Path filter to a path that includes corner points or crosses over itself, it often creates oddly shaped overlaps and extraneous points. To remove overlaps, choose Filter, Pathfinder, Unite. To remove points, click on them with the delete-anchor-point tool, accessed from the scissors tool's popout menu.*

COMPLETING THE ARTWORK

The jagged shape behind the globe and lightning bolts is simply a circle, broken up with the Distort, Roughen filter. As a background for the entire image, Spollen used a favorite gradient that he had created for an earlier illustration. ☛ *If you want access to a gradient fill used in another document, simply open the second document, and all its custom gradients will be displayed in the gradient palette for the new document as well. These gradients will disappear from the new document's palette when you quit Illustrator, though, unless you add them permanently to the new document's palette by using them to fill contours in the new document. Or if you want to add all the gradients, custom colors, and other fill options from another document to the palette of your new document, choose File, Import Styles. This way, all of the additional fill options remain with the file, even if you don't use them in your artwork.* ∎

ILLUSTRATOR

Desktop Silkscreening

■ *by Sara Booth*

LIKE MANY ELECTRONIC artists, Ted Wright sometimes misses the tactile element of more traditional media. So the Hillsboro, Mo., illustrator combined the computer with his other art tools, using Illustrator to draw an image and output spot color separations, then using these separations to make screens for a limited-edition serigraph. And since he was creating an edition of only 100 copies, he was able to do the silkscreening himself.

For *Wild Ride,* part of a series of Western prints, Wright began by traveling to a rodeo and taking a photo, which he projected onto a wall and used as the basis for a marker sketch. Because his end result would be stylized, he aimed for a high-contrast photo, "but of course, with rodeo, you're not always in control of the lighting," he says. So to get the dramatic lighting he wanted, he made adjustments in his sketch — for example, leaving much of the rider's face in shadow, while picking up bits of color in his clothing.

Wright scanned his sketch at 600 dpi, converted it to contours in Streamline, and reworked it in Illustrator, still in black and white, smoothing out rough lines and redrawing shapes. To take the image a step further from realism, he used the scale tool to reduce it horizontally.

When he was happy with the linework, Wright began to add color. He has no set number of colors for his prints — he may use as few as two colors or as many as 27, but generally he chooses eight to 12 match colors from a swatchbook for each illustration. (*Wild Ride* uses 11 colors.) "Sometimes the client will decide for me," he says. "Otherwise I choose based on the time and cost involved. If I have time to do a lot of colors, I will."

Because these are handmade prints, registration can be problematic, so Wright does a sort of large-scale trapping by adding a heavy stroke to each color shape. He created the image at about 5 inches wide, and applied a .382-point stroke to each color shape. When the illustration was scaled up to its final width of 18.5 inches, these lines were roughly 1.5 points — wide enough to assure good registration even in a hard-to-register medium.

When the electronic illustration was finished, Wright was ready to make separations. After considering how inks would be applied, he decided he

1 Wright used the same screen to apply all colors to his serigraph, blocking out all but one color at a time with a removable screen filler. He started with the most prominent color and worked his way to the least prominent one.

2 After all the colors were applied, Wright added the black. Heavy strokes on the color shapes acted as traps, assuring complete coverage even if the paper or screen got stretched or distorted in the printing process.

could use two plates: one for all the colors ❶ and a second one for the black linework ❷. He added registration marks to the image, then made two duplicates of it. For the color plate, he opened a duplicate and changed black contours to white; for the black plate, he changed color contours to white. The white areas of each one would "disappear" in the output files, creating negative space.

Wright loaded his 1600 dpi laser printer with stat paper and printed the separations. His output bureau reproduced them in black on acetate film. Wright used these films to make screens for silkscreening: After coating a tightly stretched mesh screen with photo emulsion and allowing it to dry, he placed one of the acetate films on the screen and exposed it to light, hardening the exposed emulsion. The emulsion that was not exposed to light — in areas that would be inked — could be washed off. For the color screen, which was used to print a variety of colors, he began each color pass by painting a removable screen filler onto all the shapes that wouldn't be filled on that pass.

The next step was to mix the inks, which Wright does by hand, using a swatchbook for reference. "If they had silkscreen inks all mixed up in Pantone colors, I would surely use them," he says, "but silkscreen inks only come in about 25 colors." He uses Rising's Stonehenge paper (chosen for its durability and fade resistance) to create his limited-edition prints. ■

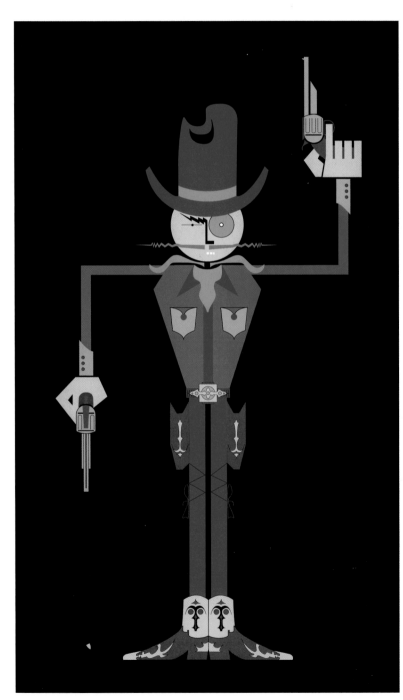

Exploring Symmetry

■ *by Sara Booth*

SMOOTH GEOMETRY and perfect symmetry may be staples of PostScript drawing, but it takes creativity to make them whimsical. That's what Dino Paul does, adding vibrant colors and unexpected asymmetrical touches to his geometric illustrations so that each of his creations has a personality of its own. The Phoenix-based illustrator begins by drawing simple shapes with the ellipse and rectangle tools, then uses Illustrator shortcuts such as the Join and Average commands and the Pathfinder filters to combine the shapes into more complex contours.

Paul's characters are loosely — very loosely — based on cowboys and Indians of the Southwest. He calls them "Dino's Kachinos" and describes them as "sort of an Italian's view of Hopi kachina dolls." In Paul's irreverent take on tradition, the boots worn by the dolls become waffle-soled Dr. Martens look-alikes, and wranglers are given facial features that seem to hang like mobiles. The illustrations are silk-screened on T-shirts, and Paul plans to put the designs on a variety of other items, from dinnerware to salsa and spaghetti sauce packaging. Each character is accompanied by its own story, written by Paul and writer Sarah Harrell, detailing how ordinary denizens of the Southwest were transformed into "kachinos."

Before Paul discovered that his style was tailor-made for the computer, he created similar figures

Dino Paul made extensive use of Illustrator's ellipse and rectangle tools to create this cowboy, one of the "Dino's Kachinos" series of T-shirt illustrations. "Any imperfection really shows up in my work," he says. So he uses the Join and Average commands to align contours precisely.

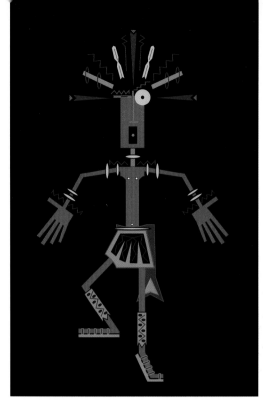

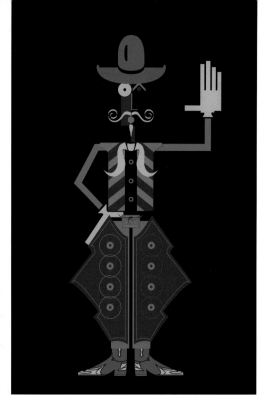

in a variety of traditional and not-so-traditional media, from acrylic paint to ink to back-painted mylar. Working in PostScript, "they were reborn," he says. "I can draw them, change them, get the colors I want without oodles of time and money."

Paul uses the same vibrant colors over and over with only small variations. When he wants to re-use an entire palette, he chooses File, Import Styles, which brings all the custom colors, patterns, and gradients from one document into another. At other times, he copies objects with custom fills and pastes them into a new file to add their colors to the document. His palette always includes a custom black which contains a percentage of each of the other process colors. "I want that black to be as rich as I can get it," he says. This technique also reduces trapping problems, because the process inks that make up the rich black abut the color fills.

BUILDING SYMMETRY

Symmetry is one of the most recognizable features of Paul's style, and he gives Illustrator's guides a workout to make creating perfect symmetry easier. "I'll have sometimes as many as 50 guides in one illustration," he says.

After pulling a vertical guide from the rulers to define the center of the illustration, Paul draws some elements symmetrically — by clicking on the guide with the rectangle or ellipse tool, then pressing the Option key to draw the shape from the center out. He reflects other elements across the guide to produce two identical halves ❶. And he uses the center guide in conjunction with the rotation tool to create symmetrical headdresses

❶
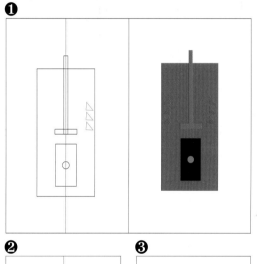

❷ ❸
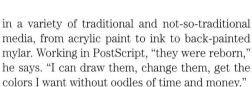
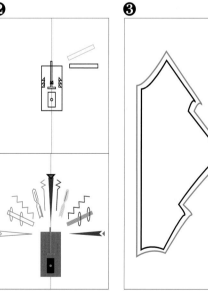

1 Paul drew a triangle in Illustrator, Option-dragged to create a duplicate, and used the Repeat Transform command (Command-D) to produce a third. To copy the triangles and reflect them across the guide, he Option-clicked on the guide with the reflect tool. Option-clicking set the axis for the reflection and opened the Reflect dialog box where Paul chose Vertical and Copy.

2 After drawing a rectangle, Paul clicked on the guide with the rotation tool. This made the guide the center of the rotation, and Paul could then drag the rectangle in a circular path. He used the same technique to rotate other elements and create half of the headdress, then selected the headdress elements and reflected copies across the guide.

3 To create a double outline for a pair of chaps, Paul used the pen tool to draw the inner contour. He made a copy, enlarged it slightly, and converted it into a guide (Object, Guides, Make or Command-5). Finally, he redrew the outer contour, roughly following the guide but making changes to keep the lines parallel.

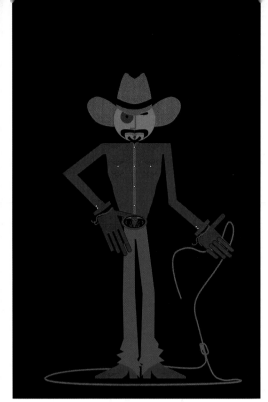

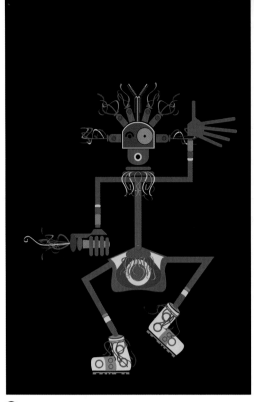

❹

4 To create ribbons for a kachina, Paul drew three or four strands, then rotated, reflected, and scaled them, occasionally repositioning points to produce a variety of shapes.

5 To produce a design for a cowboy's belt buckle, Paul started with a pair of curves and joined them, using the Average command to bring the end points together precisely (top). He created another set of curves, then averaged and joined the end points for that set (bottom).

6 Paul selected one end point from each set of arcs, averaged and joined them, then did the same to connect the final set of end points.

7 To create a candy-cane shape for the belt buckle, Paul drew a set of arcs and joined two end points. Joining produced a short line between the arcs (top). Paul Option-dragged a copy of that line to the spot where he wanted the shape to end (center) and joined its end points, one at a time, to the ends of the arcs (bottom).

❺ ❼

❻

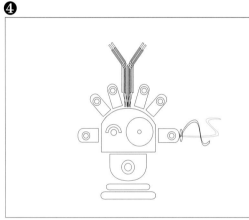

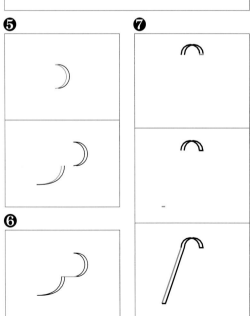

for the kachina figures ❷. ☞ *New guides are automatically locked in Illustrator. To unlock all guides, choose Object, Guides, Unlock or Command-7.* ☞ *To move a locked guide, press the Control and Shift keys as you drag it.*

Illustrator will also make a guide out of any contour — a feature Paul finds especially useful when he wants to be sure a figure's arms and legs are the same thickness or when he wants two shapes to have the same angle. Paul also used custom guides to draw a set a parallel lines around a pair of cowboy's chaps ❸.

Because Paul's art is so strongly symmetrical, the rare areas of asymmetry — a winking eye here, a raised foot there — give the figures humor and personality. When he added ribbons to a dancing kachina ❹, he made the ribbons on the figure's head and neck symmetrical, while those on his waist and feet are more random. "I figured the head and neck would be more stagnant while he was dancing," Paul says. "The feet and hands would have a different motion, so I drew them in loose pieces."

ALTERING BASIC SHAPES

Often, rather than use Illustrator's pen tool to draw curves, Paul creates a circle or oval with the ellipse tool, then deletes the unwanted parts. To create a set of double-arc designs on a cowboy's belt buckle, for example, he first drew a pair of concentric ovals, using the Option key with the ellipse tool to draw the ovals outward from the same center point. After cutting away half of each oval with the scissors tool, he selected two end-points and chose Object, Average (Command-L).

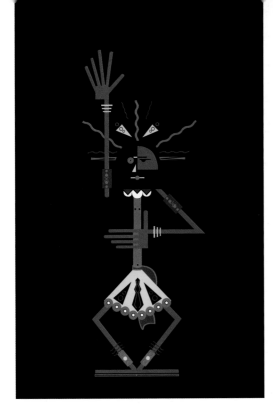

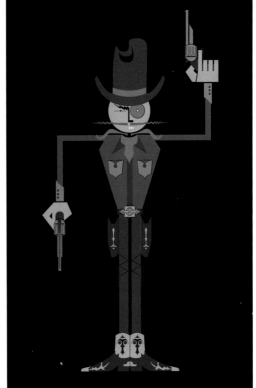

This brought the points together at the midway point, placing them in exactly the same location. Next, he joined the two points (Command-J) to produce a crescent. ☞ *To average and join two selected points at the same time, press Command-Option-J.*

Paul repeated the process to create another crescent ❺, then joined the two ❻. He used a similar technique to add a candy-cane shape to the belt buckle. He began by drawing a circle, then pressed the Shift and Option keys as he dragged it to produce a copy, offset slightly from the original. He cut away half of each circle with the scissors tool and used the Join command to combine the arcs into a single shape ❼.

Paul also uses basic shapes (usually rectangles) to draw hands, then applies the Pathfinder, Unite filter to join them into a single contour ❽. The hands are generally the last features he draws. "They're so grotesque and oversized," he says, "that if I start putting them into position right away, they'll throw everything off."

CREATING A PERSONAL CLIP FILE

Working on the computer lets Paul save and re-use bits of his illustrations. If a figure doesn't work out, all his work isn't lost. He stores the elements he likes in a folder named *Body Parts* so that he can use them in future drawings ❾. For example, the cowboy at the top of this page wears boots that were originally drawn for another figure. And Paul got extra mileage out of the barbed shape that decorates the boots, reflecting a copy across the horizontal axis and lengthening it slightly to produce a design for the holsters. ■

❽

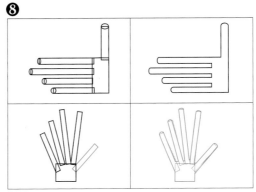

❾

8 To create hands for some of the figures, Paul drew the palm and fingers as separate rectangles, added ellipses to form the fingertips (top left), then Shift-clicked to select all the shapes and chose Filter, Pathfinder, Unite to combine them into a single contour (top right). In other cases, he rotated rectangles to define the fingers (bottom left) and turned the hand shapes into guides (bottom right) in order to draw the hand with the pen tool. This way, he could draw graceful junctures between the fingers, rather than settle for the deep V-shapes the Unite filter would have produced.

9 Paul creates his figures spontaneously, so occasionally a drawing doesn't work out. But Paul salvages the elements he likes, storing them in a "clip" file so that he can use them later. For example, he lifted the boot (shown in blue) from one of his clip art files when he created the cowboy at the top of this page.

Four of the five dancing waffles in this illustration for a political magazine were created by skewing, rotating, or recoloring a single set of shapes.

1 The palette included six browns. Subtle variations in hue give a feeling of life and depth that simple light-to-dark changes (like the straight blend shown behind the actual color swatches) would not convey.

2 The first waffle was assembled from rounded rectangles with graduated fills and contrasting outlines. The bottom layer would be the light highlighted crust; the next one, with a blend from dark top to light bottom, the face of the waffle. Fills are applied in alternating directions.

3 The waffle was rotated and scaled horizontally to make an angled version. The back rectangle, with its light outline, was copied to add thickness to the edge-on view. The inside boxes of the grid were offset a bit to the left, and fills were re-angled to match the new perspective.

4 A twisted transition waffle was drawn by eye in four parts. Distorted boxes (ellipses on the left) were colored and aligned with the surfaces by blending sequences and trial and error, then pasted inside.

❶

❷

❸

❹

FREEHAND

Waffling

■ *by Tom Gould*

AN ILLUSTRATION FOR a column of political comment regarding the tendency of some politicians to waffle suggested a visual of real waffles. I thought they might be prancing and twisting to convey the flip-flop of public statements. I would start with a simple face-front waffle. I defined six toasty colors from light brown to dark, alternating roughly between warmer and cooler variations (red-browns and yellow-browns) ❶.

At last, a legitimate use for the round-corner box tool: waffle-making. I drew two of these boxes and filled them with graduated tints. Now a grid of smaller round-corner boxes made the sides of the holes. A strong graduated tint contrast in each "hole" creates a shadow (top) and a highlight (bottom). A grid of still smaller rounded squares was joined as one element so that a single dark blend across all of them would follow the graduation on the face of the waffle, creating the flat areas at the bottom of the "holes" ❷. These alternating tints create the illusion that the identical middle boxes aren't so identical, since the background is constantly changing. Simple outlines on the large rectangles give a little texture to the edge of the waffle.

For the second waffle, a copy of the first was tilted and scaled horizontally, then the box layers were offset horizontally to convey depth ❸. Number four was a reflected, rotated copy of number two. Number five was number one, rotated.

Number three had to be drawn; then skewed copies of the holes were pasted inside the faces. I removed and repasted them a time or two to adjust individual fills ❹.

To define the ground plane as the waffles bounce gently across the page, gray ellipses were blended to fade into the white background. ■

Creative Repetition

■ *by Sara Booth*

THE SIMPLEST tools can yield the best results, and San Francisco designer Paul Woods knows how to get maximum impact out of basic Illustrator functions. When asked to design a joint promotion for Adobe software and output bureau Star Graphics, Woods created a poster that shows the variety of effects that can be achieved using Illustrator's ability to build patterns by blending shapes and repeating transformations.

Because the poster was to promote Star Graphics' output capabilities, it communicated its message through quality rather than content. So Woods had an unusual amount of freedom to choose his subject. "I picked the fish because they were a fun excuse to do something colorful," he says.

Using a pencil sketch as reference, Woods began by drawing a background of abstract color areas, using wavy curves to suggest water, then roughed in three large fish. When he was satisfied with the positions of the major shapes, the next step was to make each one interact

"Man against white space" is how Paul Woods describes his work process. The San Francisco designer put Illustrator through its paces for a poster promoting both Adobe and Star Graphics, an output bureau.

FINAL FILM FOR THIS POSTER WAS PRODUCED ON THE AGFA SELECTSET 7000 22" X 26" POSTSCRIPT IMAGESETTER WITH 300 LPI AGFA BALANCED SCREENS EXPOSED AT AN OUTPUT RESOLUTION OF 3,600 LINES PER INCH.

1 To make one fish interact with its background, Woods divided its shape along the background contours, then recolored each new shape.

2 To make one fish's eye (top), Woods rotated a triangle repeatedly, using its point as the axis of rotation, then masked it inside a circle (shown in blue) whose center falls on the axis of rotation. Other circles drawn from the same center complete the effect. For another eye, he rotated a diamond (shown in red) around a center point before adding concentric circles.

3 Woods rotated a copy of a triangle 24 degrees, repeated the rotation twice, then masked the shapes inside a larger triangle (shown in blue) to create a fin. Pink triangles, drawn with the pen tool and the Shift key and rotated into position, complete the fin.

❶

❷

❸
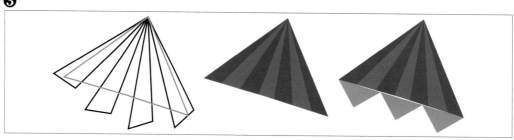

with those it crossed — by dividing one contour along the line of another, for example, or adding a shape in front of another shape ❶. ☞ *In Illustrator 6, you can cut shapes along a selected contour by choosing Object, Apply Knife. This command cuts all underlying contours, even those that aren't selected. To protect an object from being cut, hide it (Arrange, Hide or Command-3) before choosing Apply Knife.*

After drawing four smaller fish, Woods began adding details. He achieved two different radial patterns on the eyes of the two large fish by rotating shapes around a central point, then adding layers of filled or stroked circles ❷. ☞ *To rotate copies of a shape around a full circle, first generate an angle of rotation by dividing 360 by the number of copies. For example, for 10 copies, the angle should be 36 degrees. ☞ Illustrator 6's Control palette (Window, Show Control Palette) provides a shortcut for choosing some common rotation axes. Click the desired point on the icon, then enter an angle of rotation in the rotation area of the palette and type Return to rotate the object or Option-Return to*

❹

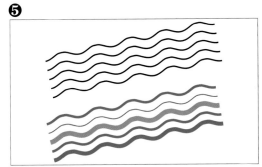

❺

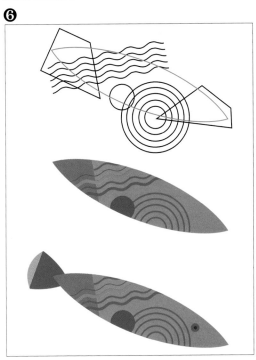

❻

❼

4 Woods knew what shape he wanted for another fin, but he didn't have the colors established. He drew one square, pressed the Option key as he dragged out a copy, and chose Arrange, Repeat Transform (Command-D) to copy it repeatedly. Then he copied the entire row of squares, deleting the ones he didn't need. When the final grid was complete, he could experiment with different color combinations.

5 After drawing a wavy line, Woods copied it repeatedly. Then he changed the color and stroke weight of the lines to vary the effect.

6 A variety of lines and filled shapes were masked inside a single contour (shown in blue) to create one of the smaller fish.

7 To make a blend that followed the shape of a tail, Woods drew two chevron shapes and filled them with contrasting colors, then blended between them. Then he masked the blend inside the tail.

---

copy it. Note that the icon represents the object's bounding rectangle, not the object itself.

For one fin, Woods rotated triangles to build a set of wedge-shaped stripes ❸. For another, he drew a square, then used Arrange, Repeat Transform (Command-D) to produce a checkerboard pyramid ❹. He also used Repeat Transform to generate a series of concentric circles and wavy stripes ❺, masking them inside a fish shape ❻.

The final step was to add shading. Because Woods wanted shadows and color changes to follow the curves of his shape, he used blends rather than gradients ❼. Where the two largest fish overlap, blends create a confusion of dimension, making each fish appear to pass both behind and in front of the other. ☞ *When you create a blend, Illustrator requires you to select at least one point on each contour. Clicking more than one pair of points can give smoother results, especially if the shapes are not similar.* ☞ *For a smooth blend, make sure the two shapes have the same number of points. Sometimes you may need to use the add-point tool to add a few anchor points to one or both shapes.* ■

Designed for Recycling

■ *by Janet Ashford*

Richard Puder was asked to create a poster promoting recycling, and he exceeded the assignment with a layout that made recycling all but irresistible. The die-cut poster, produced in Free-Hand and Illustrator, can be folded into a box and used to grow flowers.

FOR THE PAST 12 YEARS Richard Puder of Richard Puder Design in Dover, N.J., has created a poster for an annual summer concert series sponsored by the Morris County Park Commission. For the 1993 poster, illustrator Geoffrey Moss suggested a design that humorously reinforced the theme of the concert series (Reduce, Reuse, Recycle), a poster that could be folded into a hat. Puder was delighted with the idea of a piece that begged to be recycled, and he wanted to continue the trend with the 1994 design. So he and staff designer Lee Grabarczyk developed a die-cut poster that could be folded into a box, filled with soil, and used to grow flowers. (Flower seeds were donated by the Burpee Seed Company.)

The design itself cycled between Puder's firm (where the program of choice was FreeHand 4) and artist Mike Quon of Mike Quon Design Office in New York City (who prefers Illustrator 5). The first step was to work out production requirements. Puder talked to his service bureau, printer, and die-cutter to find the maximum size they could handle. Based on the information he received, he decided on an 18 x 24-inch poster and asked Grabarczyk to rough out the design in a pencil sketch ❶. Puder took Grabarczyk's sketch to the die-cutter, Cut-Outs Inc. of New York City, and worked with the technicians there to develop a template for the cut lines, folds, tabs, and slots required for the box. Cut-Outs supplied Puder with a *vinyl,* an inked template on acetate. Grabarczyk redrew the template in FreeHand, using measurements taken from the vinyl (he thought he could produce a more accurate template by recreating it than he could by scanning the large vinyl in sections and piecing the sections together) ❷.

SETTING THE TYPE

Puder wanted to be sure that important information would be visible once the design was folded into a box. So even before the art was developed, he had Grabarczyk set to work composing the type. Puder had decided that some of the lettering would be arranged on curved paths, roughly following the shapes in the sketch, and that other type would be placed on top of the illustration. He opted to use only two typefaces: Adobe Frutiger, a simple font that would maintain its legibility when bound to a curve, and Child's Play from The FontShop, a rough-drawn face that would complement the hand-drawn look Puder wanted for the art.

When Grabarczyk set the Frutiger type, he took advantage of FreeHand's orientation options to keep the lettering in an upright position, even though it flowed along a curve ❸. Concert times and dates were to be placed on top of three large flowers, one flower for each of the summer months. Grabarczyk typed the information for each concert in a separate text block that could be rotated to follow the angle of an individual flower petal. There were to be four concerts in June, six in July, and five in August — and this determined how many petals the flowers would have in the finished illustration ❹.

The FreeHand text and template files were exported in Illustrator format and sent to Quon, along with Grabarczyk's sketches.

DEVELOPING THE IMAGERY

Although Grabarczyk had already sketched out the composition, Quon began his illustration work by developing sketches of his own to hone the style of the imagery, using felt-tip pens to create thick-and-thin outlines that look as if they were drawn with a brush.

After scanning the drawings, Quon autotraced the scans in Streamline and opened the autotracings in Illustrator. He selected all, copied, and pasted the art onto a new layer in the text-and-template file so that he could adjust the shape and position of some of the elements to correspond to the placement of the type. He colored the flowers and leaves ❺ and added a blue background ❻. Once the illustration was complete, the type layer was deleted, and the file was saved in Illustrator 3

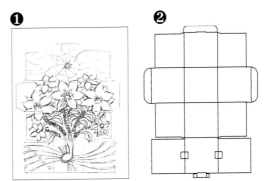

1 Puder wanted the composition to be equally effective when hung as a poster or folded into a box. So he worked with the designer to hone the image, arranging art and type carefully so that important information would be visible when the piece was folded.

2 After consulting with their die-cutting service, the designers used FreeHand to create a template.

3 To set type on a curve, the designer drew a curved line, selected the type and the line, and chose Bind To Path (Type, Bind To Path or Command-Shift-Y). He stretched the lettering 130 percent horizontally and increased the Range Kerning in the Text Inspector palette to add space between characters (top). Then he clicked the object icon in the Inspector palette to access the Orientation submenu and selected Skew Vertical so that the downstrokes of all the letterforms would be vertical (bottom).

4 Concert information was set in Child's Play, a font that mimics a child's handwriting. Concert descriptions were rotated around a circle so that each month's concert series was arranged like the petals of a flower.

5 The autotraced art was opened in Illustrator, and the black shapes defining the outlines were filled with color. To add color inside the petals and leaves, new shapes (shown in blue) were drawn on top of the artwork, then filled and placed behind the outlines.

6 To make the flowers stand out from the background, the designer copied the inside shapes (in this case, the light pink fill in the flower and the light green in the leaf), filled the copies with white, and sandwiched them between the flowers and the background.

7 When the Illustrator 5 art was saved in Illustrator 3 format (so that it could be opened in FreeHand), the gradient fills were converted to masked blends.

8 A white-filled compound path, created in FreeHand by joining the template outline to a white rectangle (Command-J), was placed on top of the art to show how it would look when die-cut. This image was used for television promotions, but for the printed piece, the white border was deleted before the file was output so that the art would bleed beyond the die-cut edges.

9 The back of the poster, printed in black-and-white, includes a map, production notes, and instructions for folding the poster into a box.

❼

❽

❾

so that Puder's staff could open it in FreeHand to finish the design ❼.

Saving the art in Illustrator 3 format converted all the gradient fills to masked blends — which were interpreted as blends pasted inside clipping paths when the file was opened in FreeHand. The designers could have replaced the blends with graduated fills by ungrouping the blend-filled elements and using the Cut Contents command (Edit, Cut Contents or Command-Shift-X) to release each blend from its clipping path, then deleting the blend and reapplying color. But they decided to leave the blends alone. The blends added a little more than 300K to the document, boosting the file size from 148K to 464K, and the designers felt the increase wasn't dramatic enough to cause problems. More important, they felt that blends often print more smoothly than graduated fills, which sometimes band. ☞ *Banding will show when a blend is calculated at low resolution, then output from a high-resolution imagesetter. To be sure that the blend is smooth, set Illustrator's Output Resolution (accessed by choosing File, Document Setup or Command-Shift-D) or FreeHand's Printer Resolution (accessed by clicking on the measurements icon in the Inspector palette) to match the resolution you want for the final output before defining the blend.*

Grabarczyk pasted the lettering he had already created into the illustration and set additional type for the poster. The original type had influenced the composition of the art. But at this point, Grabarczyk used the forms in the underlying image to determine the arrangement of the type, drawing paths that followed curves in the illustration — for example, ray shapes at the top of the image and a treble clef at the bottom of the design — and bound text to these paths ❽.

CREATING A POSTER BACK

To produce artwork for the back of the poster, Grabarczyk copied a flower and several leaves from Quon's illustration, enlarged them, and rearranged the pieces. The poster back was to be printed in black-and-white, so Grabarczyk selected the filled shapes and changed the colors to tints of black.

A map to the concert site was placed in the center of the flower. The map was created by scanning a reference map, autotracing the scan in FreeHand with the tracing tool, and then editing the paths to refine the curves and eliminate unnecessary points. At the bottom of the design, Grabarczyk added diagrams showing how to construct the flower box. To produce these diagrams, he used the die-cut template as a starting point, then skewed and repositioned the shapes by eye, using a model of the box which had been supplied by the die-cutter as a visual reference ❾. ■

FREEHAND

A Mosaic in PostScript

■ *by Janet Ashford*

AUGUST STEIN wanted to demonstrate his versatility when he created a self-promotional design for his ad in *The Creative Illustration Book.* So the San Diego freelancer produced a mosaic of realistic and improbable images, including a centaur archer, a stylized ladybug, quilt-like geometric tiles, rows of three-dimensional buttons, and a set of grayscale gears.

Though the imagery varies dramatically, Stein used the same basic drawing technique throughout the illustration. He drew simple PostScript shapes — often squares and circles — then broke these shapes into segments with FreeHand's knife tool to build a complex, mosaic-like design.

BUILDING A COGGED GEAR

When Stein drew the fragmented gear, he rendered one half in shades of gray and the other half in bright, bold colors to create a transition between the realistic elements and the fanciful sections of the design. He began by drawing a circle and ungrouping it. Once the circle was ungrouped, Stein could use the selection points as guides to divide the circle into perfect halves and quarters. After cutting through the top and bottom points of the circle, he selected each half circle and closed the shape. (In

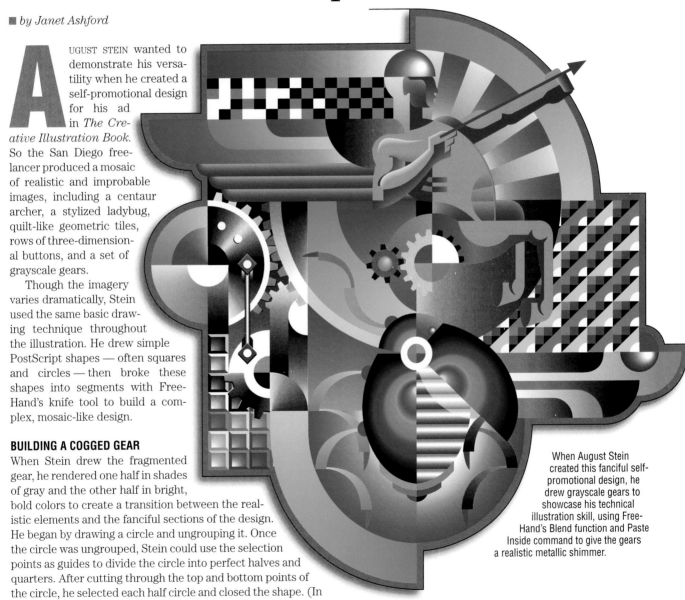

When August Stein created this fanciful self-promotional design, he drew grayscale gears to showcase his technical illustration skill, using FreeHand's Blend function and Paste Inside command to give the gears a realistic metallic shimmer.

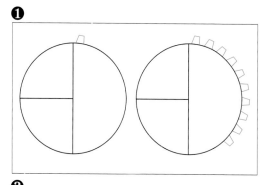

1 Stein wanted to create a fragmented gear, so he drew a circle and cut it into sections. Then he added gear teeth by drawing a single tooth and rotating clones of the tooth about one-third of the way around the circle.

2 After joining the gear teeth into a single path, Stein drew a circle (centered inside the original fragmented circle) and cut away an arc. He turned the arc and the gear teeth into a closed shape by selecting the two paths, applying the Join command, and then clicking the Closed option in the Object Inspector palette.

3 Stein used three black-to-white blends to produce the metallic surface of the gear wheel. He positioned these blends next to each other so that they appear to be a single fan-shaped gradation.

4 The gradation was pasted inside a half circle.

5 In order to create a white break between the center of the gear and the teeth, Stein selected the half circle he had created when he cut the original circle into segments (see Figure 1). He filled this with white and sandwiched it between the gear teeth and the gradient shape.

6 Using the center of the fragmented circle as the anchor point, Stein scaled the original quarter-round shapes (shown in blue), reducing the outside perimeter to match the size of the grayscale half of the gear. The scaled contours (shown in red) were used as clipping paths, and multicolored blends were pasted inside them.

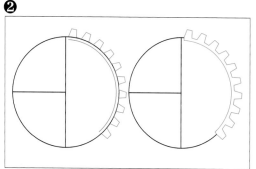

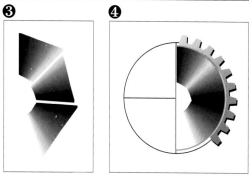

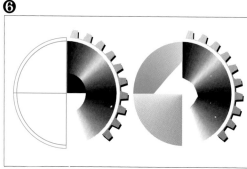

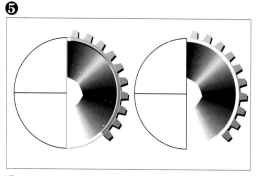

FreeHand 4, open paths can be turned into closed shapes by clicking Closed in the Object Inspector. In earlier versions, the Closed option is accessed by choosing Element, Element Info or Command-I). He cut one of the half circles again to produce two quarter-round shapes. These quarter-round elements were closed.

To create teeth for the gear, Stein used the fragmented circle as a guide so that he could arrange the teeth along a curved path. First, he drew a single tooth at the top of the circle. He cloned the tooth (Command-=) and clicked the rotation tool on the center of the circle to define that point as the center of the rotation. Then he dragged the cloned gear tooth to a new position. The Duplicate command (Command-D) repeated the clone-and-rotate functions, copying the tooth and moving the copies around the circle ❶.

Once Stein had created a set of gear teeth, he selected all the teeth and chose Arrange, Join Objects (Command-J) to combine them into a single path. (The command inserted "legs" in the spaces between the individual teeth to connect them.) Stein then cut an arc from a circle and joined it to the teeth, forming a closed, cogged shape ❷. ☞ *In order to join non-touching elements in Free-Hand 4, you must select the Join Non-Touching Paths function in the Editing Preferences dialog box, accessed by choosing File, Preferences and then selecting Editing from the pop-out menu. Unless this option is selected, the end points must align perfectly before two paths can be joined.*

Stein planned to fill the gear-teeth shape with a gradient, but he wanted the graduation to follow a circular path — and FreeHand's default gradient fills couldn't provide the effect he wanted. So he used the blend function instead to build the curved graduation. First, he drew a light gray line and a dark gray line, both at slight angles. Next he selected the two lines and typed the keyboard shortcut for the Blend command: Command-Shift-E. The gear-teeth shape was positioned on top of this blend, and the blend was cut to the clipboard (Command-X). Stein then selected the cogs and pasted the blend inside them by typing Command-Shift-V. "I get a lot of use out of the keyboard shortcuts in FreeHand 4," says Stein. "I used to have to go to the menu every time I wanted Paste Inside or Blend."

A clone of the cog shape was used to shade the edges of the teeth, giving the grayscale portion of the gear a three-dimensional appearance. After cloning the cog shape, Stein used the Cut Contents command (Edit, Cut Contents or Command-Shift-X) to remove the circular blend from the clone. Then he filled the cloned shape with black and placed it behind the original, offsetting it slightly so that it formed an irregular shadow around the teeth of the gear.

Stein finished the black-and-white half of the gear by building a three-part blend to simulate the look of a polished metal surface ❸. He drew a circle on top of the gear design, slightly smaller than the original, fragmented circle. After cutting this smaller circle in two, he deleted one of the arcs and closed the remaining shape to produce a half circle. The three-part blend was pasted inside the half circle ❹, and a white shape was used to create a gap between the gear teeth and the grayscale gear ❺. The other half of the gear was filled with multi-colored blends ❻, and a small circle was placed to the center of the design ❼.

CREATING A REALISTIC CONNECTING ROD

Additional fragmented gears — in combinations of gray tones and color — were drawn in to extend the background design ❽, and Stein used the blend function to build a shiny metal rod connecting two of the gears.

First, Stein drew a 4-point black line. When he cloned this line, the clone was placed directly on top of the original. Stein selected the clone and changed the line weight to .5-point and the color to white. He then selected the end points of both the lines and executed a blend between them to create the look of a rounded rod ❾. A gray square, rotated 45 degrees, was used as the basis to build a set of bolts at the top and bottom of the rod ❿.

DEFINING 3-D BUTTONS

Stein began the illustration in FreeHand 3 and finished it in FreeHand 4, taking advantage of some of the features of the upgrade. For example, he used the ability to define an off-center radial fill to produce the appearance of a rounded indent in the center of a button.

The first step was to create a beveled button. Stein drew a black rectangle, cloned it, and changed the clone's fill to light gray. Then he ungrouped the clone in order to select and delete one of the corner points, changing the shape into a triangle. Another rectangle, smaller than the original, was drawn in the center of the button and filled with a white-to-black radial blend.

Finally, Stein used the Locate Center option in the Inspector palette to offset the center of the radial fill, making the button look as though it had a concave surface ⓫. He cloned the button several times and changed the fill colors to produce a set of grayscale and color buttons ⓬.

ADDING COMPLEX ELEMENTS

When Stein created more complex imagery, he expanded on the drawing techniques he had used to produce the gears and the buttons — cutting sim-

❼
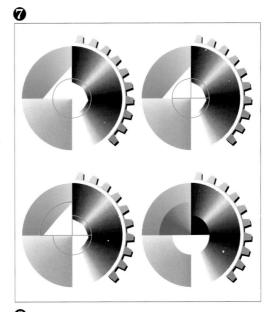

❽
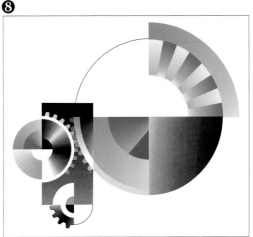

❾ ❿
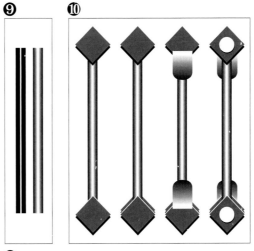

⓫
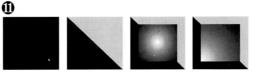

7 To cover up the ragged edges in the center, Stein drew a small circle and cut it into a half circle and two quarter-round shapes. After enlarging one quarter circle, Stein pasted a blend inside it. He filled the other quarter circle with black and the half circle with white.

8 The same technique (breaking circles into segments and pasting blends inside them) was used to draw additional gears.

9 To create a rod, Stein drew a fat black line, cloned it, then changed the stroke and color of the clone to create a thin white line. Blending between the two rounded out the rod shape.

10 A rotated square was used to build a bolt. Stein cloned the rotated square, filled the clone with black, and offset it behind the original to create a shadow. The bolt and shadow were cloned to make another bolt at the bottom. Stein cloned the original rotated square again, filled the clone with white, and placed it behind the bolt and shadow to add a white highlight to the bottom bolt. The bottom bolt and shadow were cloned and the clone was placed in back. To create connectors, Stein drew a gradient-filled shape and reflected a copy of it. The two connectors were placed in back. He finished the bolts by drawing a white circle in the center of each rotated square, then cloning the circles to produce black shadows.

11 To create the beveled button, Stein drew a black rectangle, cloned it, filled the clone with gray, and deleted a corner point to turn it into a triangle. He drew a smaller rectangle on top and added a radial fill. Shifting the center of the radial fill to the lower left corner gave the button a rounded, indented look.

12 Stein produced a set of three-dimensional buttons, cloned from the original. He filled some of the buttons with black tones and others with colors to create a transition between the grayscale gears and the color areas in the illustration.

13 To draw a stylized ladybug, Stein began with an oval shape. After the oval was cut in half and the resulting shapes were closed, Stein cut the tops off the two half ovals.

14 A circle formed the basis of the ladybug's head. Stein cut the circle twice to complete the head.

15 A rainbow blend, created by blending between five circles, was pasted into a black-filled ladybug wing, and a set of purple-to-white gradients was pasted into the other half of the bug's body. Finally, a clone of the wing was reflected to produce the second wing.

⑫

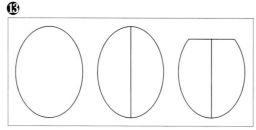

⑬

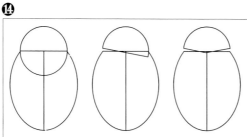

⑭

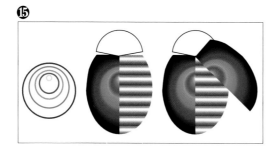

⑮

ple shapes apart, closing the cut shapes, and filling them with blends or gradients.

He used a complex set of blends to create a surrealistic ladybug, but he relied on the simplest of shapes to draw the creature: an oval for the body and the wings ⑬ and a circle to define the head ⑭. A five-step blend added a rainbow effect to the ladybug's wings, and a purple-to-white gradient (cloned and reflected several times) brought a neon look to the body ⑮. The ladybug's legs were arcs, cut from circles and joined to produce crescent shapes.

To create the centaur archer, Stein used the pen tool in conjunction with the circle tool to combine freeform shapes with perfect curves. To draw the legs, for example, he used arcs cut from circles to define the hips, knees, and ankles, then joined the shapes by drawing between them with the pen tool. Once he had completed the basic outline of the leg, he cut it into sections in order to apply different colored fills.

BUILDING THE BORDER

FreeHand's Union command made it possible to create an outline framing the entire finished illustration. Stein had drawn different sections of the illustration on different layers, and he planned to use cloned elements from several of those layers to produce the outline. So he began by selecting New in the Layers palette to define a new layer named *Outline.* Then he carefully selected all the elements in the illustration which fell along the perimeter (except for the centaur's hand and the arrow, which Stein wanted to float above the outline). All the perimeter elements were cloned, and while the clones were still selected, Stein clicked on the name *Outline* in the Layers palette. This placed the cloned elements on that layer.

Several of these cloned contours held pasted-in blends, and Stein didn't want to include these blends in the outline. So after he released the pasted-in blends (Command-Shift-X) and deleted them, Stein reselected everything on the *Outline* layer and chose the Union command from the Arrange, Path Operations submenu to combine them into a single shape. He filled the shape with gold and then dragged the name *Outline* to the bottom of the list in the Layers palette to place it in the back of the illustration. ☛ *The Union function will not work if the selection is too complex, so be careful not to select too many elements when applying this command.*

Stein then increased the stroke width of the gold shape so that its edge extended beyond the edges of the illustration. To create a hairline black border around the gold outline, Stein cloned the gold shape, filled the clone with black, sent it to the back, and increased its stroke width slightly. ■

FREEHAND
Spirited Shapes

■ *by Sara Booth*

CREATED IN FREEHAND by a playful mind," reads Darlene Olivia McElroy's self-promotional art sample. McElroy gives her FreeHand illustrations a lively, spontaneous look by quickly roughing in gradient-filled shapes to give her artwork depth, then using a pressure-sensitive tablet to "paint" highlights, reflections, and suggestions of movement.

When McElroy created the jungle-theme artwork for the American Cancer Society's annual black-tie fund-raiser, she incorporated her illustration into the invitation, a wine bottle label, and a T-shirt. The invitation was to be printed together with an invitation cover, which used metallic ink. To avoid adding another ink to the print job, she sacrificed black, building her colors entirely from percentages of the other process inks so that she could reserve the black plate for the gold ink used on the cover. The black used for the linework, for example, contains 100 percent of each of cyan, magenta, and yellow.

McElroy began the illustration by creating a detailed black-and-white sketch, which would serve as linework in the final illustration. After scanning the sketch, she used Adobe Streamline to convert it to PostScript contours ❶. Because her drawing style is loose and organic rather than geometric, she was able to set a fairly loose tolerance in Streamline's Conversion Setup dialog box (Options, Conversion Setup or Command-J), instructing the program to create shapes with longer segments and fewer anchor points, even if that meant not following her scan precisely. This

Darlene McElroy of Santa Fe, N.M., works in two distinctive visual styles. To avoid confusing potential clients, she identifies this style — characterized by highlights created with FreeHand's freehand drawing tool and a pressure-sensitive tablet — by her middle name, Olivia.

1 McElroy's black-and-white sketch, scanned and converted in Streamline, was opened in FreeHand and used as a guide as she drew color-filled shapes.

2 McElroy followed her linework fairly closely for the upper part of a spiky bush (shown in red), but roughed in the bottom because it would be covered by other shapes. And she drew the butterfly (shown in black) and many other shapes very quickly, knowing that the black linework would cover the uneven edges.

3 Once the main shapes were drawn, McElroy added contours with contrasting gradients, which, together with the black linework, add the appearance of curvature to the surface of the leaf.

4 The flower's bottom contour is filled with a gradient from pink to purple. The upper contours are filled with gradients between white and the same pink, making them appear to flow into each other.

resulted in both a smaller file size and smoother curves.

When McElroy opened the converted sketch in FreeHand, she cleaned it up further by deleting unnecessary anchor points and smoothing some curves. ☞ *To reduce the number of anchor points FreeHand uses to define a contour, choose Arrange, Path Operations, Simplify (or Xtras, Cleanup, Simplify).*

McElroy created a new layer for color by choosing New from the popout menu of the Layers palette, then dragged the layer name down in the palette to place it behind the linework layer. Keeping the linework visible as she worked, she used the pen tool to create the large shapes that define the foliage, flowers, and animals in her jungle. She used her black linework as a guide, but didn't worry about following it precisely ❷; if her color shapes had rough edges, the linework would cover them.

McElroy's color method, like her drawing style, is informal and interactive. She mixed new colors by eye in the Color Mixer palette (trusting her calibrated monitor and her own experience with

printed color to help her predict what the finished colors would look like), then dropped swatches onto contours to fill them. As she went along, she added new colors to the Color List palette for future use by dragging swatches onto the Color Drop box (the arrow in the palette's upper right corner). ☞ *To add every color used in your illustration to FreeHand's Color List, choose Xtras, Color, Name All Colors. The colors will be assigned names that reflect either their CMYK or RGB values, depending on which box is set in the Preferences dialog box. To change the naming convention, choose File, Preferences, click the Colors category, and click either Use CMYK Values or Use RGB Values.*

Once McElroy had filled a contour with a flat color, she often changed it to a gradient, using FreeHand's drag-and-drop capability to define the angle and type of gradient fill on the fly, reapplying the gradient until she was satisfied with the way it looked. ☞ *To change a flat-color fill to a graduated fill in FreeHand, first fill the object with one of the desired colors. Then pick up a swatch of the second color and drag and drop*

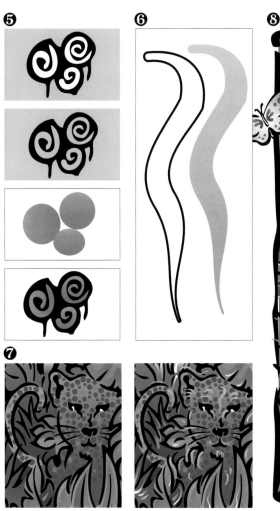

❺ **❻** **❽**

❼

it onto the object, holding down the Control key to create a linear gradient. Or hold down the Option key to create a radial gradient with the second color on the inside. Where you drop the second swatch determines the gradient's angle (for linear gradients) or the location of the center (for radial gradients).

McElroy's approach to gradients is stylized rather than realistic, but she still finds them useful for adding a hint of three-dimensionality. For example, after filling leaves with a dark gradient, she added shapes in lighter gradients to mimic the natural curves of foliage ❸. She created flowers using gradients that shared a color, giving them a more natural look ❹, or combined a single gradient with "petals" created by black linework ❺. A rectangle filled with a gradient of two shades of green, placed on its own layer behind all the other elements, assured that no white areas would show through any gaps between shapes.

Next, McElroy switched to the freehand tool in Variable Stroke mode to draw the "squiggles" that add a sense of light and movement to her illustration ❻. Some of these shapes follow the linework,

softening the contrast between the black and the other colors; others function as highlights or reflections ❼. ☞ *When you draw with the freehand tool in Variable Stroke or Calligraphic Pen mode, the resulting shapes often contain unnecessary points, especially when the shapes cross over themselves. Free-Hand can remove the overlaps while you draw (if you first double-click the freehand tool in the toolbox to display the Freehand Tool dialog box, then choose either Variable Stroke or Calligraphic Pen and check Auto Remove Overlap), but this slows the program down. To remove overlaps after a contour has been drawn, choose Arrange, Path Operations, Remove Overlap (or Xtras, Cleanup, Remove Overlap). To simplify two paths that cross over each other, select both paths and choose Arrange (or Xtras), Path Operations, Union.*

The finished illustration was die-cut along several of the black shapes; the corners of an invitation (printed in gold ink on vellum) were tucked into these cuts ❽. The vellum allows a mysterious glimpse of the illustration to show through. ■

5 Streamline rendered the roses as white contours in front of black contours (left), but McElroy wanted the spiral shapes to be open areas so contours behind them would show through. So she selected all four shapes and chose Arrange, Join Objects (Command-J). Because she was joining closed paths, FreeHand joined the objects together as a compound path, so gradient-filled ovals placed behind it would show through the spirals.

6 McElroy worked with the freehand tool in Variable Stroke mode, with no stroke and a graduated fill, so Free-Hand drew each of her "squiggles" as a gradient-filled contour. After drawing a contour, she often used FreeHand's drag-and-drop option to change its color.

7 Because of their gradient fills, the "squiggles" seem to develop gradually out of the colored shapes, softening their highlight effect.

8 Die-cuts — designed to hold a smaller sheet of vellum (shown in white) printed with event information in metallic ink — follow the lines of the drawing.

Better Blending

■ *by Grant Jerding*

THE NEW VERSION OF FreeHand introduces an incredible level of control of pasted-inside objects (now called clipping paths) and more accessible, powerful blends. These changes enabled me to create an auto-alarm illustration for *Consumer Reports*, with a total of 108 blends, in about two-thirds of the time it would have taken to do the same graphic in version 5.5.

For me, FreeHand 7's greatest new asset is that when objects are pasted inside clipping paths, they remain fully editable. By holding down the Option key while selecting them, I could tinker with numerous blends (and other paths) inside a single clipping path — without continually pasting the objects inside the path to see the end result and then cutting the contents to further edit the blend. As I pasted more and more objects into the same clipping path, I was also able to reorganize by sending objects to the back or front inside the clipping path.

When I needed to select all the objects pasted inside a single clipping path at once, I hit the tilde (~) key repeatedly to continue up the hierarchy until all the shapes pasted inside were selected. Hitting the tilde key once more selected the clipping path itself. This technique is especially helpful when trying to select a clipping path that is part of a group. In this case, Option-clicking on the shape will first select any object inside the clipping path, not the clipping path itself. To select the path itself, the tilde key must be used.

Furthermore, blends themselves are now even easier to edit because Option-clicking anywhere

FreeHand 7's improved control of blends and objects pasted inside other objects made it much faster to create this infographic, but much slower to wait for the screen to redraw.

along the blend will automatically select either the beginning shape or the end shape — whichever is closer. After I had adjusted all the points of a blend, I hit the tilde key to select the entire blend so I could check the number of steps. ☞ *To double-check the number of blend steps in all the blends, use the Edit, Find & Replace, Graphics command (Command-Option-E). You can speed up the document's redraw by initially setting all the blends at a relatively low number of steps until the illustration is finished, then using Find & Replace to increase the number of steps for high-resolution output.*

That's the good news, but here's the bad — this 315K illustration took nearly 20 seconds to redraw at 100% in version 7. (This same file takes less than 6 seconds to redraw in FreeHand 5.5 on the same Mac.) FreeHand 7's "improved" redraw lets the user continue to work (enter commands, select things, and so on) while the program redraws the image in chunks. (This is similar to the way Adobe Photoshop handles redraw.) However, that's clearly not worth the huge sacrifice in redraw speed. Most of the time I change views to see the entire portion of the illustration on the screen, so I end up waiting for the often painfully slow redraw anyway.

And speaking of painful, due to an obvious programming glitch you can no longer Control-click down through a series of grouped objects by pressing Option-Control, although the manual plainly states that you should be able to. (The Control-click function still works if the objects are not grouped.)

Another problem: The blends are not editable when the document is exported in FreeHand 5.5 format to send to the client. All the blends in a FreeHand 7 file become a group of uneditable shapes in 5.5, preventing the client from making even the slightest color adjustment. ∎

1 To create realistic modeling on the automobile, I first created a skeleton car of the basic shapes.

2 I then began building the highlights and shadows with blends. I drew an initial blend shape with the freehand tool, simplified it by choosing Xtras, Cleanup, Simplify (setting the Amount at 1), and cloned that shape to create the other end of the blend. After quickly scaling down the top shape, I selected both contours and hit Command-Shift-B to create the blend. I then cut this rough blend and pasted it (Command-Shift-V) into the basic bumper shape, making that shape a clipping path.

3 I continued to use pasted-inside blends to build up the shading and reflections on the bumper. After a blend was pasted inside a clipping path, I could still edit it. Even the raised strip (which I constructed by pasting a blend inside a path, then pasting that path inside the bumper shape) could still be edited without cutting the contents.

4 FreeHand's graphic find-and-replace function let me find all the blends in the illustration with less than 10 steps and increase the steps. I used the command to make sure I didn't get any blends with visible steps.

5 I found out while working on this illustration that pasting objects into a composite object (for example, pasting the shadow blend inside this alarm part) can become a dicey situation. If you Option-click a single shape of a composite path without selecting the entire composite path, then try to paste an object into it, a message appears, "Could not complete the Paste Inside because an error occurred." Then the object you tried to paste into becomes unselectable or disappears entirely, and FreeHand sometimes crashes.

❶

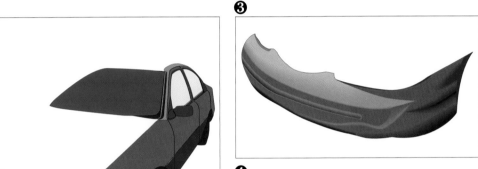

❷

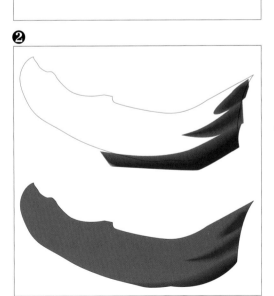

❸

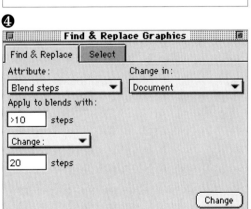

❹

❺

PostScript Airbrushing

■ by Lynne
Breckstein

I CAN'T REMEMBER the last time I used a straight gradient fill in FreeHand. I prefer radials. The rounded graduations have a more natural look to my eye, closer to the effect I used to get with an airbrush. And by positioning the center of the radial judiciously, I can achieve some dramatic fade effects. The airbrushed look is especially pronounced in thin elements — sweeping lines drawn with a pressure-sensitive tablet. Frequently, I use the Multi-Color Fill option (in the Xtras, Colors submenu) to define my radials, but I couldn't do that when I was asked to create a menu cover for a new restaurant because the budget limited me to two spot colors.

I experimented with traditional two-color approaches when I began working up thumbnails, roughing out the lettering with markers. I tried using one color for the lettering with an accent color for design elements. Then I tried coloring one or two of the letters in an accent tone. But I wasn't happy with the results — they didn't give me the sophisticated look the client wanted. It didn't occur to me to use my radial/airbrush technique simply because I had never tried it in a two-color project before. But I finally realized that there's no reason why it wouldn't work. And it did. In fact, I was perfectly happy with the results I got when I filled the restaurant logo with only one color (using it at 100 percent to define one of the colors in the radial and at 25 percent strength for the other). But I did get a chance to put the second spot color to good use: I created a radial-filled background that gave the foreground design a misty, other-worldly shimmer.

1 To create a menu cover, I began by drawing a swash in FreeHand, tracing a scanned sketch with the freehand tool and a pressure-sensitive stylus.

2 My initial plan was to cut the swash with the knife tool so I could fill each loop separately. But the knife merged the overlapping segments into unified shapes, not the individual loops I wanted (top). So I undid the cut and used the Split Object command (Command-Shift-J) to divide the swash into sections (center), which I filled with radial gradients (bottom).

3 After setting the restaurant's name in Goudy, I deleted serifs from the *A* and *v* and replaced them with swashes. I also added a swash to the *e* and lengthened the leg of the *d* before applying a radial fill to all the letters.

4 I wanted the menu cover to have an airbrushed look, and the first step in creating the effect had been filling the separate pieces of the lettering and the swash with a radial fill, defined by using a warm, rusty spot color as the Outside color of the radial and a 25 percent tint of the same tone as the Inside color. At that point, I decided to scale the swash 110 percent horizontally.

❶

❷

❸
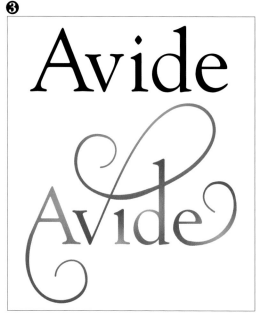

❹

The first step in the project was designing the restaurant logo, and for that, I worked in black-and-white. First, I double-clicked on the freehand tool icon to open the tool's dialog box, where I chose the Variable Stroke setting with a maximum width of eight pixels and a minimum of two. Then I drew a swash, tracing a scanned sketch I had created earlier. For me, at least, it takes a lot of sketching and erasing and replanning to come up with a calligraphic swash that looks spontaneous. So I always work the shape out in pencil before I ever approach the computer. And I count on the Simplify command (Xtras, Cleanup, Simplify) to eliminate the unnecessary points I invariably impose into a line when I draw with a pressure-sensitive stylus. I start out by setting the Allowable Change slider close to Max in the Simplify dialog box, and if that distorts the shape I've drawn too much, I undo the simplification and try again, moving the slider down a bit.

For the restaurant name, I chose Goudy because I felt that the thick-and-thin strokes of the lettering complemented the swash without looking too florid (and believe me, the italic faces I tried first led to some embarrassing results).

Once the black-and-white version was finished and approved, I could begin working on the two-color design. I placed the swash and the lettering on separate layers, and I turned the lettering layer off so that I could color the swash without the distraction of seeing black-and-white elements on the screen. My first step was to cut the swash roughly down the middle with the knife tool so that I could fill each loop with a radial, but that didn't work out the way I expected it to. Instead of slicing the design into free-standing loops, the knife turned it into a complicated compound path. So I hit the Undo command and tried again.

This time, I used the old-fashioned method (old-fashioned for FreeHand, that is) to divide the swash into sections: the Split Object command. Before I began splitting the swash, I moved into

magnified view so I could get a good look at the contours, and I selected the path so I could see the individual points. I looked for places where two points — one on each side of the shape — were located close together, then selected and split them. As I completed each split, I clicked the Closed button in the Object Inspector palette. And I made sure the Even/Odd Fill button was de-selected so that I wouldn't get any unfilled holes where the line segments looped back and crossed over themselves.

When all the loops had been cut free and I had applied the radial fill to the first one, I chose New from the Styles palette Options menu while the filled loop was still selected. That way, I could select the other loops and fill them by simply clicking on the style name in the palette. When I had filled them all, I selected each one and repositioned the center of the fill to make the color fade in and out as it swept around the swash. I moved on to the lettering once the swash was colored, using the same radial to fill the letters and adjusting the center of the radial in each one. ∎

5 To enhance the airbrush effect, I used another spot color, fading to white, to create a radial fill for the background. But I wanted to avoid the bull's-eye look that results from applying a radial fill to a rectangle. So I drew a much larger shape than I needed for the cover, filled that shape, and used the Paste Inside command (Command-Shift-V) to place the large radial-filled shape inside a smaller rectangle, drawn to the size I needed (including bleed) for the menu cover.

6 On the finished cover, the lettering and swash took on an iridescent sheen against the background.

❻

❺

Adding Elegant Style to Linework

■ *by Janet Ashford*

THE STYLIZED FASHION DRAWINGS featured in *Vogue* magazine during the early 1900s inspired a graceful and subtly colored poster created in FreeHand by David Guinn of Design 1 in Asheville, N.C. For the past several years, Guinn has designed promotional material for the national sales meeting of Doncaster, a company that produces women's clothing. *A Grand Tradition* was the theme for Doncaster's 1994 meeting, and Guinn felt that the art style complemented the theme.

After looking through books of *Vogue* cover designs and examining works by Aubrey Beardsley and other art deco illustrators, Guinn created a pencil sketch of a woman. In the background, he roughed out the buildings and grounds of Asheville's Grove Park Inn, where the Doncaster sales meeting was to be held.

Guinn reduced the sketch on a photocopier so that he could slip the copy under the transparent plastic cover of his 6 x 8½-inch Wacom ArtZ tablet. Then he opened FreeHand, selected the freehand tool, and used the stylus to draw over the figure on the tablet. ☞ *To minimize the number of points you draw with the freehand tool, make sure the Tight Fit option is deselected in the Freehand Tool dialog box (accessed by double-clicking on the freehand tool icon in the toolbox). And you can remove excess points in FreeHand 4 by selecting a line and choosing Arrange, Path Operations, Simplify.*

Once the figure was complete, Guinn drew the background elements. Here he worked directly on the screen, following his sketch as a reference but

To create this poster illustration, David Guinn began by drawing black-and-white lines, then used FreeHand's Styles palette to recolor the linework and vary the width of the strokes, bringing a hand-crafted look to the image.

no longer tracing it. He drew more detail than the original sketch included, especially in the leaves in the foreground and the stones in the building ❶.
☞ *If you make a mistake while drawing with the freehand tool, you can "erase" the path or part of the path — as long as you have not released the mouse button — by pressing the Command key and "backing up" over the line.*

COLORING THE LINE ART

The next step was to add color to the line drawing. Although some of the lines were closed shapes (the hand in the foreground, for example), most of the linework consisted of open paths. So Guinn colored the woman by placing blocks of color behind the lines, using the freehand tool and the tablet to draw shapes that could be filled and then sending the shapes to the back (Command-B). To color the building and the landscape in the background, Guinn drew over his original linework to create closed shapes that could be assigned both a line and a fill. After redrawing these shapes, he deleted the original lines.

Most of the shapes were filled with solid color, but Guinn used radial fills to shade the woman's parasol and hat brim and to bring delicate color to the face ❷. He also applied graduated fills to the sky and several of the background elements to add depth to the imagery.

Earlier in the process — when Guinn traced the linework in the sketch — he had used Free-Hand's default settings, so all the lines were drawn in black at the same weight ❸. But Guinn wanted a more painterly look for the illustration. So he used the Styles palette (Command-3 or Window, Styles in FreeHand 4 and View, Windows, Styles in FreeHand 3) to recolor all the lines and to vary their weight.

First, he selected one line, gave it the color and stroke width he wanted, and chose New in the Styles palette pop-out menu. The values of the selected element were automatically entered as the specifications of the new style, and Guinn could then give other lines the same properties by simply selecting them and clicking on the style name in the palette. (Later, when Guinn refined his color selections, the style colors were updated automatically.)

ADAPTING THE PALETTE FOR PRINTING

Early in the process, when Guinn applied color to the illustration, he chose tones that looked good together on his monitor, selecting his palette from the Pantone Process library, accessed through the Options menu in the Color List palette. But he knew that the printed colors would vary from the on-screen effect, so once the illustration was complete, he edited his color selection in order to get

❶

❷
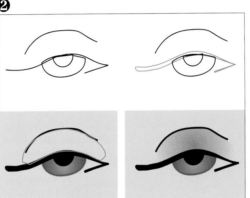

❸

1 Using a pressure-sensitive tablet, Guinn traced his pencil sketch with the stylus to reproduce the illustration in FreeHand. This black-and-white version of the art was printed in gold ink on white 9 x 12-inch envelopes used for a conference mailing.

2 To add detail to the original drawing (top left), Guinn drew filled shapes on top of the lines that defined each eye (top right).

He applied a radial fill to the iris and assigned a dark blue outline. Then he shaded the eyelid by drawing a shape over the eye (bottom left) and applying a radial fill that graduated from lavender in the center to the flesh tone at the sides (bottom right). Additional radial fills, fading to the skin tone at the outer edges, were used to color the cheeks.

3 The black linework didn't produce the delicate effect Guinn wanted for the poster. So he changed the color of individual lines, choosing hues that related to the colors in the filled shapes.

4 After converting the type to outlines and ungrouping, Guinn edited the *A* and *R* by Option-clicking to select (and then reposition) one point and Option-Shift-clicking to select multiple points. The *O* was scaled, and tiny squares were drawn below it with the rectangle tool.

5 Guinn altered a copy of the original design to produce name tags, moving all the lettering below the illustration and adding two lines to provide space for handwritten names.

6 When he created a grayscale version of the illustration, Guinn specified gray tones for some of the linework to soften the details in the face and to make a few of the trees seem to fade into the distance.

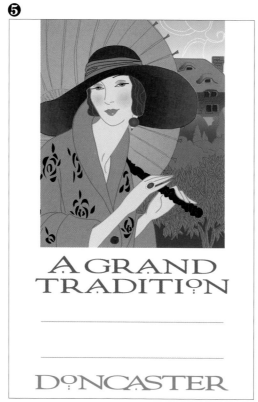

the printed results he wanted. Using a swatch book, Guinn selected printed colors that matched the hues he saw on his screen. Then he changed the CMYK specifications of the on-screen colors, replacing the original specifications with the percentages listed in the swatch book.

Guinn finds that he develops more interesting color relationships when he chooses his on-screen colors freely and then alters the tones for reproduction. Working with "print" colors limits the options he sees on the screen.

Once he finished editing the color palette, Guinn trimmed off the illustration's rough edges by selecting all, cutting the artwork to the clipboard, and using the Edit, Paste Inside command (or Command-Shift-V in FreeHand 4) to place the artwork inside a rectangle which had been assigned no line and no fill.

CREATING THE TYPE

To complement the style of the illustration, Guinn created custom type, based on the lettering of the Arts and Crafts movement of the early 1900s. He began by setting the type in Goudy Regular and then elongating the letterforms, scaling them about 200 percent horizontally. As he resized the lettering, Guinn worked by eye, placing the left edge of the type along the left side of the artwork and stretching the type out until it spanned the width of the illustration.

After converting the type to outlines (Type, Convert To Paths), Guinn could edit individual characters to match lettering he had seen in reference books ❹. Then he placed the company name below the illustration and set *A Grand Tradition* lettering above the artwork to complete the poster illustration. This design was reduced and modified slightly to produce name tags for the meeting ❺.

PRODUCING A GRAYSCALE VERSION

The client also requested a grayscale version of the illustration that could be placed in the company newsletter and used to produce one-color conference materials. To create the grayscale file, Guinn opened the poster and chose File, Save As (or Command-Shift-S in FreeHand 4) to save a copy of the artwork under a new name. After selecting the illustration, he chose Edit, Cut Contents (or Command-Shift-X in FreeHand 4) to release the artwork from the rectangle he had used to square off the edges. Then he carefully substituted a tint of black for each of the colors, trying to match the tonal values of the original colors while adjusting the lightness or darkness of the tints to provide contrast between adjacent shapes. Finally, he pasted the illustration into the rectangle again ❻. ■

Painted Textures in PostScript

■ *by Sara Booth*

COMPLEX GEOMETRY and crisp lines are PostScript specialties, and illustrator Si Huynh used them to his advantage in a WPA-inspired image for a freelance art director. But for an added boost of surface interest, Huynh went beyond PostScript, using FreeHand's ability to place and manipulate TIFFs to add texture.

Many of Huynh's trademarks (exaggerated perspective, organic figures built of simple shapes) were already present in his ink sketch ❶. Huynh scanned this sketch at low resolution and placed it in FreeHand, putting it on its own locked layer "so I didn't have to worry about it moving about on me," then used it as a guide as he drew his illustration with black-stroked, unfilled shapes. ☛ *Layers which appear below the dividing line in FreeHand's Layers palette (Window, Layers or Command-6) are treated as sketches: They are displayed in dimmed form, and they don't print. If a dimmed display isn't clear enough, simply drag the layer's name up the palette until*

When Si Huynh (Nanaimo, British Columbia) was asked to design an identity for a freelance art direction firm called Creative Direction, he used placed TIFF textures to add interest to his retro traffic cop. "It got good response," he says. "People didn't expect that kind of image for a design firm."

1 Huynh's ink sketch contained the basic shapes that would make up the illustration, but he added many details as he worked in Free-Hand, including much of the shaping in the face.

2 Huynh used lighter colors in the background to make the figure and the car the center of attention. Some shapes, such as the rows of dots, were grouped first; then Huynh could add color to the entire group by dragging a swatch into the Fill well in the Color List palette.

3 For the lines around the figure's head, Huynh drew an arc with the pen tool, then selected one of the dash patterns from the popout menu of the Path Inspector palette. The line width is four times the dash length, creating the impression of lines coming out from the center.

4 Huynh created two textures for the illustration, both using black ink on rough white paper: a coarsely airbrushed graduation for the background and curved strokes with a fan brush for the car.

❶

❷

❸

❹
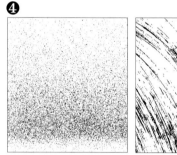

it's above the dividing line. Before printing, move the layer back below the line or delete it.

Because his illustration contained so many contours, Huynh found it easier to build it as two separate files, one containing the figure and car, the other containing the background elements. When they were complete, he copied them into a single image. ☞ *To select a contour that is behind other contours, press the Control key as you click on the frontmost object. FreeHand will select each contour in the "stack" in turn.*

When the black-and-white outline was completed, Huynh chose his colors from a swatchbook, aiming for a retro feel by choosing a palette that consisted mostly of neutrals. He defined his palette in FreeHand by entering CMYK percentages in the Color Mixer palette (Window, Color

Mixer or Command-Shift-C), then dragging a swatch and dropping it on the arrow at the upper right of the Color List palette (Window, Color List or Command-9). To add richness to the image without changing its muted feel, Huynh mixed as many as five shades of each color. "It looks like there's not much color in this image," he says, "but really there's a lot." He colored the art by dragging swatches onto selected contours ❷. ☞ *To toggle the Color Mixer palette on and off, double-click any color swatch in the Color List.*

FreeHand's dashed lines provided a shortcut for repeating elements such as the circle of lines around the figure's head ❸. Huynh also used dashed lines to create the toothed border of the image itself, which is simply a white dashed line placed in front of the other elements. Choosing

❺

❻

❼

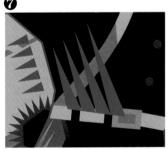  

5 The graduated texture, filled with tan, was placed in front of the background elements but behind the figure. The outer ellipse around the figure's arm covered the texture, so a second copy was pasted inside the inner ellipse.

6 After changing black pixels of the curved texture to dark tan, Huynh pasted it inside the black car shape.

7 Filling a set of triangles with blue, Huynh cloned them, cut the clones to the clipboard, and pasted them inside the shoulder strap contour. When he filled the original triangles with darker blue, they appeared to change color where they crossed the strap.

different dash patterns and line widths in the Path Inspector palette (Window, Inspector or Command-1) resulted in different dash effects. ☞ *To create your own dash pattern in FreeHand, first choose a pattern in the popout menu of the Path Inspector palette. Then Option-click on the menu to open the Dash Editor dialog box, where you can enter numbers for the length of dashes and gaps.*

"For every job I do," Huynh says, "I create a new texture or two." For the traffic cop illustration, he painted two textures, one using an airbrush and the other using a fan brush ❹. He scanned these textures in TIFF format at a fairly low resolution (100 pixels per inch) so that pixelation would add to their natural texture. When he placed them in FreeHand, he checked the Trans-

parent box in the Inspector palette to change their backgrounds from white to transparent. Dragging a color onto the images changed all the black pixels to color ❺. And by using the Paste Inside command (Edit, Paste Inside or Command-Shift-V), he could place the images inside a shape that was filled with a contrasting color ❻.

Huynh also used Paste Inside extensively to simulate transparency by creating shapes that appear to change color where they cross other shapes ❼. ☞ *Using FreeHand's Paste Inside command to paste large objects inside small shapes can slow printing, because the printer must interpret the entire pasted object even if only a small portion of it is visible. For faster printing, keep pasted objects close to the size of the path that contains them.* ■

Blends for Speed

■ *by Tom Gould*

C ALLED UPON TO DO a series of editorial spot illustrations for a politically oriented magazine, I went through the list of short items for inspiration. One quotation seemed to offer possibilities: "Why drag every government power to Washington so that a vast centralized government may devour the states and the liberty of individuals as well? I say this amendment [the 16th, concerning instituting an income tax] should be more carefully considered than it has yet been considered." — Republican Rep. Samuel McCall of Massachusetts, in 1909.

Despite the overly dire tone about what we now know to be one of our most beloved and benevolent institutions, I felt some imagery might come out of this as a theme. My first thought was a map of the United States being sucked up as a kind of octopus shape into the Capitol dome. It would take lots of work to bring off the scrunched map, and, though dramatic, the idea lacked something to hook the images together intellectually as well as visually.

❶

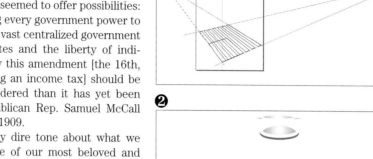

❷

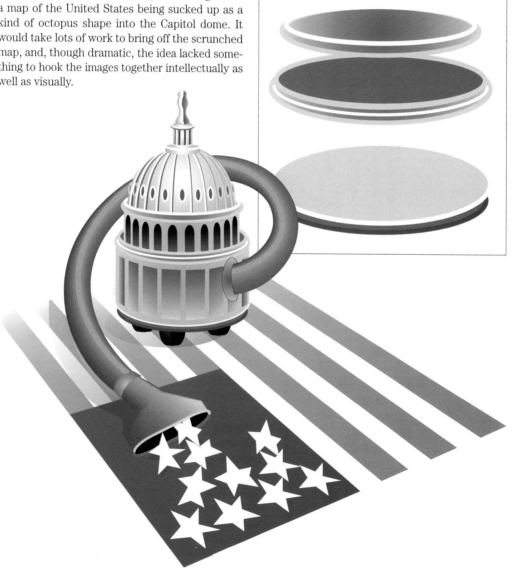

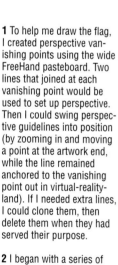

1 To help me draw the flag, I created perspective vanishing points using the wide FreeHand pasteboard. Two lines that joined at each vanishing point would be used to set up perspective. Then I could swing perspective guidelines into position (by zooming in and moving a point at the artwork end, while the line remained anchored to the vanishing point out in virtual-reality-land). If I needed extra lines, I could clone them, then delete them when they had served their purpose.

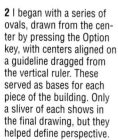

2 I began with a series of ovals, drawn from the center by pressing the Option key, with centers aligned on a guideline dragged from the vertical ruler. These served as bases for each piece of the building. Only a sliver of each shows in the final drawing, but they helped define perspective.

The Capitol dome, come to think of it, looks a little like a '50s-era vacuum cleaner. I could add a hose to get that little dual connectivity that makes a concept (remember those?) out of an image.

But what about the map? Use a 3-D/Bryce/Distorto power-user series of apps and map a stock U.S. map onto a scrunched-rug shape? Someday maybe I'll be hot to get into that action, but for now, simplicity and the budget rule.

Another symbol for states is the 50 stars on the flag. I could show them being sucked up one by one into the vacuum. And I could make them more graphic with the little shift from a flat field as they lift up and disappear into the hose. My first sketch went off by fax with some other proposed spots, and the vacuum idea was one of those accepted by the editors and art director.

I took the sketch and began to develop it with my Capitol dome reference in hand. The blue field of the flag would help convey the states idea, and why not add the stripes as well? To help me give the flag a convincing 3-D look, I roughed in a rectangle in perspective, then zoomed out to establish vanishing points on a horizon line extending to both sides onto the pasteboard.

Blending was the key to creating the stripes. I began by drawing a line at the top edge of the flag, then cloning (to be sure that points on each line would correspond) and dragging the clone to the bottom edge. Blending in 12 steps set up the 14 lines needed to make 13 even stripes. I ungrouped

the result, then drew short connecting lines to create closed paths for the top and bottom stripes. I filled these two stripes with red in a linear blend to white at the far edge. After throwing away the remaining intermediate lines, I blended the two outer red stripes in five steps to produce 13 alternating stripes. The blue quarter field was layered on top and filled with a gradient from full-strength blue to a middle value to follow the fading away of the stripes.

I stacked up a set of ellipses to define the vacuum, following the perspective by eye. The basic shapes of the building were defined, then filled with warm or cool grays to add dimension. Some of the contours would be hidden behind partial ellipses simulating cornices and moldings. The bottom was set up with blue stripes, linear-filled at different angles, with a passing resemblance to our trusty shop-vac.

The hose was made of blended lines, one on each side to make a highlighted center. A minimum number of blend steps was used to maintain a little anatomy. The nozzle and the stars were probably the only bits of the original sketch to make it this far. They were tweaked, and the nozzle got a blended highlight.

Shadows cast on the flag by the vacuum were defined and colored to match the various backgrounds: light grays where they fell on white, and shades of red or blue cloned from the same shapes and pasted inside the stripes or field. ▪

3 I used radial fills, rather than blends, for the Capitol. I didn't need more detailed perspective — I planned to layer stripes and arches and ribs and oval windows over everything, and I knew these would provide more than enough dimension cues to kid the eye into seeing rounded forms.

4 For the ribs, I drew white lines, then recolored them to match the shady side of the dome. They were then grouped, cloned, and horizontally scaled a bit, colored darker gray, and moved behind and to the right of the original light-colored lines. Scaling offset them enough to create variable-width darker sides.

5 I drew one arch next to the center, cloned it, moved the clone out to the edge, and distorted it appropriately, then blended to set up a sequence (top). Next, I Option-selected items from the blend group and moved them up or down to follow the curve of the vacuum cleaner body (center), then reflected them across a vertical axis (bottom). Other details of the dome were created the same way.

6 The hose was created in two parts, using opposite blends, to get shadows on the same side of the hose as it curved around. The dome would hide the join.

7 Side-by-side blended lines made up the hose. I used few blend steps: five for the inside curve, six for the outside. This provided texture to avoid a rubber-hose look.

8 Cast shadows used lower-key versions of background colors, with matching gradients. A shadow was made for each color. The red and blue versions were pasted inside the stripe and field shapes. Light gray shapes (for shadows that appear on the white background) were sent behind the stripes.

❸
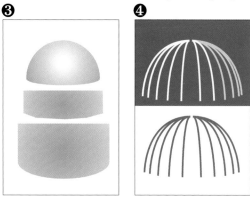

❹

❺

❻

❼
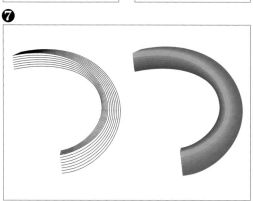

❽

"FreeHand 5.5 is in many ways a very capable program, but its capabilities are not things I need," says Peter Alsberg. So he continues to use version 3.1, which has everything he uses in his illustrations — layers, styles, custom colors, and the pen and curve tools.

1 Alsberg created his drawing in three layers: first the linework on top, then filled shapes behind it, and finally a third layer sandwiched between them for color lines that define shadows and other details.

2 Straight lines and simple Bezier curves get a more hand-drawn look from rounded caps and joins. Alsberg has saved his most-used lines as styles (by selecting a line with the desired specifications and choosing New from the popout menu of the Styles palette).

3 Alsberg constructed the word "Ethernet" almost entirely with straight lines, using the same heavy pen-drawn lines that make up the linework.

FREEHAND

Simulating Marker Lines

■ *by Sara Booth*

THICK, ROUNDED LINES make Peter Alsberg's FreeHand illustrations look like marker drawings. The Takoma Park, Md., illustrator uses heavy line weights and rounded joins and end caps to create flowing strokes with the pen tool. He saves time by defining a handful of often-used line specifications as styles.

For an editorial illustration for *PC Magazine*, Alsberg began by placing a scanned sketch on the background layer, then created a new layer (by choosing New from the popout menu of the Layers palette) where he drew his linework with the pen tool using a line weight of about 3.5 points. He used areas of flat color to define the objects in the image, adding a heavy stroke to round out these color-filled shapes, and finished with color linework using a slightly lighter line weight ❶.

Alsberg tries to use a minimum of points for his lines, but they still look more hand-drawn than electronic, thanks to their rounded end caps and joins ❷. In keeping with this hand-drawn appearance, even the word "Ethernet" was created with strokes rather than a typeface ❸.

Once all the elements were in place, Alsberg began subtly changing line weights. "There's a balance I'm after," he says. "If the lines are too thin, everything looks weak and spindly, but if they're too thick, it looks blotted." The final step was to use the curve tool, clicking from point to point, to draw a shape that outlines the entire illustration. Then he cut the artwork to the clipboard, selected this outline, and chose Edit, Paste Inside (Command-Shift-V). ☞ *The curve tool draws straight segments between points. Press the Option key as you click to create curves instead.* ■

FREEHAND

Scribbling to the Top

■ *by Janet Ashford*

POSTSCRIPT SHAPES masquerade as brush strokes in an illustration James Miceli of Fairport, N.Y., created for Gannett Newspapers. Gannett had asked only for an image that combined newspapers and sports. So Miceli developed a series of thumbnail sketches, depicting a football player running for a touchdown holding folded newspapers instead of a football. After the thumbnails were approved, Miceli looked through Gannett's extensive photo library to find shots of the Buffalo Bills in action. Using these photos as reference, he drew a more detailed pencil sketch and scanned it for use as a template. Then he used FreeHand 4 in conjunction with a pressure-sensitive tablet to produce flowing lines that are more characteristic of painting than of computer art.

DRAWING WITH A PAINTER'S TECHNIQUE

Miceli planned to render his illustration by building up layers of freeform shapes, much as a painter builds up strokes of paint. To keep his work organized, he used the Layers palette. He began by choosing New from the palette's Options menu to create a new layer called *TIFF Sketch,* where he placed the scan (File, Place or Command-Shift-D). He wanted to be able to draw on top of the sketch and then delete it easily, so he placed the sketch in the back by highlighting its name in the Layers palette and dragging it below the *Foreground* layer. ☞ *If you want to be able to keep a scanned template in a FreeHand file but be sure that the scan will not print, place it on FreeHand's default background layer or create a new layer and drag its name below the*

Layers of "scribbled" shapes add up to a dynamic illustration. James Miceli created the design in FreeHand, using a pressure-sensitive stylus and varying the freehand tool's Width settings often so that he could draw broad, expansive shapes in the background and precise details in the foreground.

1 A set of blue-filled shapes, drawn on top of a scanned sketch, form the foundation of the illustration (left). Although many of the larger shapes look as though they are defined by a single path, Miceli frequently built up the shapes by layering several sribbled strokes (right).

2 Miceli created a new layer and placed it behind the one that held the blue "foundation" shapes. After drawing a set of forms that model the figure and fill in the face, he "deleted" the hand by drawing a hand shape, Shift-clicking to select the background elements and the hand, and choosing Arrange, Path Operations, Punch.

3 After decreasing the maximum width setting for the freehand tool, Miceli added details to the hands, face, and torso.

4 A set of green and yellow strokes appear to fly off the shoulder of the football player, adding a sense of motion to the design.

5 To create a background, Miceli used the freehand tool to draw two large free-form shapes. He then drew an outline around the figure and filled the outline with white to keep the background color from showing through open areas in the illustration.

❶

❷

❸

dotted line in the Layers palette. All layers set below that dotted line are non-printing.

Miceli added a layer named *Base Shapes* and began to block in the figure, using the freehand tool in its pressure-sensitive mode to draw thick-and-thin shapes that follow the dominant forms in the sketch. To set up the tool, he double-clicked on its icon in the toolbox to bring up the Free-hand Tool dialog box, selected the Variable Stroke option, and set the Width to vary from zero to five points. (In FreeHand 3, the Pressure Sensitive option in the Freehand Tool dialog box activates the variable-stroke feature.) Then he "scribbled" over the scan, building up strokes of blue until he got the effect he wanted. In pressure-sensitive mode, the freehand tool automatically converted each scribble into a closed path ❶. These blue shapes formed a foundation for the drawing and a starting point for Miceli's color palette. (See "Developing a Palette," page 13.)

Once the general outline of the figure had been roughed in, Miceli returned to the Freehand Tool dialog box and increased the maximum width setting so that he could draw broader shapes to add volume to the figure ❷. Returning to the thinner stroke specifications he had originally set for the tool — and working on a new layer, set in front of the others — Miceli continued to build up color, bringing definition to the hands and face ❸ and adding motion to the design ❹.

When he drew the foreground elements, Miceli "shuffled" the layering, bringing his scanned template forward (by highlighting the layer name and dragging it up through the Layers palette) so that the shapes defining the body would not obscure details in the scan. And he periodically made the scan invisible (by clicking beside its name in the Layers palette to turn off the check mark) so that he could see the illustration clearly and evaluate the effect. Once the figure was complete, Miceli

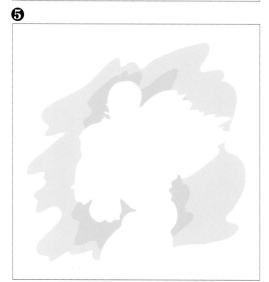

C 80 M 65 Y 0 K 0	C 100 M 55 Y 10 K 0	C 95 M 30 Y 0 K 0	C 70 M 20 Y 0 K 0
C 15 M 25 Y 15 K 0	C 0 M 5 Y 5 K 0	C 25 M 50 Y 70 K 0	C 40 M 55 Y 65 K 0
C 0 M 15 Y 30 K 0	C 0 M 10 Y 25 K 0	C 0 M 7 Y 20 K 0	C 50 M 90 Y 0 K 0
C 0 M 20 Y 90 K 0	C 0 M 55 Y 35 K 0	C 100 M 40 Y 0 K 0	C 30 M 85 Y 70 K 0

Developing a Palette

Many illustrators develop a standard color palette, a selection of reliable favorites they use again and again. But that method doesn't work for James Miceli. He chooses surprising colors for each of his illustrations — and because much of the surprise relies on using tones that contrast vividly with the subject matter, Miceli selects a new palette for every drawing he creates.

When he drew a football player for Gannett Newspapers, Miceli built his palette (as he always does) around a single color, in this case, a deep blue-violet that was used to rough in the figure. Then Miceli expanded the palette by selecting tones that harmonized or contrasted with that initial shade.

First, Miceli selected harmonizing colors: three softer shades of blue to model the forms that had been defined in the original blue-violet and two pastel lavenders to add bright highlights to the illustration. (Miceli feels that tints tend to look washed out. So instead of building tints of his base tone to define the highlight colors, he selected new colors from a swatch book.)

Next, Miceli chose the dominant flesh tone, a cool shade of brown with a lot of cyan that would relate to the blue-violet base color. Then he selected a set of shadow and highlight colors to complement this flesh tone.

Finally, Miceli defined a few accent colors — an intense shade of yellow, a bright lime green, and three rosy tones — that contrasted dramatically with the rest of the palette. ∎

highlighted *TIFF Sketch* in the Layers palette and chose Remove from the palette's Options menu to delete the scan. Then he created a new layer, placed it behind the others by dragging its name down through the Layers palette, and drew a set of freeform background shapes.

Before drawing the background, Miceli opened the Freehand Tool dialog box and checked the Freehand option (so that the tool would no longer respond to pressure) and made sure the Tight Fit function was unchecked (in order to draw a smooth shape with as few points as possible). When he filled the background shapes, the color was visible through the gaps in the rest of the drawing, so Miceli used the freehand tool to draw an outline around the edges of the figure. But this time, he activated the tool's Tight Fit function to be sure that the outline would hug the figure. This outline was filled with white and used to mask out the background color ❺. ∎

Color Made Simple

■ *by Sara Booth*

"Dusty colors may be a trend," says Richardson, Texas, illustrator Diana Craft. "but I like colors that have life and movement." To be certain she chooses colors that retain their brightness in CMYK printing, and to make her work more efficient, Craft creates custom color libraries in FreeHand to store her favorite palettes.

VIBRANT COLORS and clean shapes are the hallmarks of Diana Craft's illustrations. Careful preparation, from sketch through scan to Streamline conversion, helps the Richardson, Texas, illustrator retain a hand-drawn look as she converts her art to PostScript contours. And FreeHand's color management tools make it easy for her to create, save, and access colors to sim-

plify the creation of final artwork. Craft created a Native American-inspired image for a planned T-shirt licensing project. When the T-shirts didn't pan out, the illustration became a successful self-promotion.

SWEATING THE DETAILS

When Craft creates an illustration, she spends more time on her sketch than on any other part of

the process. She went through several rounds of thumbnails and pencil sketches before she arrived at her ink-on-tissue sketch, which closely resembles the final illustration ❶. At this stage, she doesn't even think about color, preferring to work out the geometry of the piece in black-and-white. Later, she may experiment with several color palettes before settling on one.

When Craft had a final sketch she was happy with, the next step was to scan it. Many artists would have considered themselves finished when the scan was made, but while she tries to maintain the spontaneity of her pen-drawn lines, Craft is a perfectionist about her line quality — and she finds it easier to correct imperfections on the scan in Photoshop than to wait until the artwork is converted and make changes in FreeHand. "The pen will sometimes leave a little extra glob when I make a circle," she says. "When it's vectorized, it's an extra point, and it takes more time to clean up."

In Photoshop, Craft uses the pencil tool to edit individual pixels, narrowing excessively thick lines and evening out thin ones ❷. ☞ *If you have reset Photoshop's foreground and background colors, you can return them to the default black and white with a single keystroke by typing the letter* D. *Rather than switching to the eraser tool, you can apply white pixels with your current tool by exchanging the background and foreground colors: type the letter* X.

Craft also took this opportunity to be certain her drawing was entirely made up of closed shapes; if any shape wasn't closed, she used the pencil tool to stop up the gap. Her goal was to simplify her FreeHand tasks so that she could add color with a simple click-and-fill technique. ☞ *To test whether a shape is closed in Photoshop, click in the area with paintbucket tool and see if any color overflows.*

When she had the scan cleaned up to her satisfaction, Craft saved it in TIFF format and opened it in Streamline. She wanted Streamline to maintain a hand-drawn look while smoothing out a few rough spots. So in the Conversion Setup dialog box (Options, Conversion Setup or Command-J), she changed the default tolerance of 3 to a somewhat looser 4, instructing Streamline to make curves smoother, even if that meant not being as accurate to her scan. She also moved the Curved and Straight Lines slider toward the Curved end to 4, so that Streamline would use mostly curved, rather than straight, segments to convert her art. Finally, Craft saved the document in FreeHand 3.0 format (which can be read by later versions of FreeHand). ☞ *To save frequently used Streamline conversion settings, first choose Options, Conversion Setup (Command-J) and Color/ Grayscale Setup (Command-B), enter your*

❶

❷

1 Craft creates her final sketch in ink on tissue. She doesn't use a straight-edge, preferring the slight unevenness of a hand-drawn line.

2 If Craft used Streamline on an unedited scan (top), tiny splotches of ink in the scan would become extra points in the conversion (shown in blue). For a smoother conversion, Craft edited the scan in Photoshop to remove these irregularities (bottom).

3 Streamline creates linework by drawing white contours in front of slightly larger black contours. Craft filled the large linework shapes with tan and other outline colors, then filled the interior shapes.

4 To achieve the appearance of gold without the expense of metallic ink, Craft uses one of two colors: medium tan (23M 43Y 18B) when her image contains many colors (top), and a lighter shade of tan (10M 35Y 10B) that works best against black (bottom).

5 Craft has created several custom libraries of colors that are reliably lively when printed in CMYK. She uses these libraries as she would a spot color palette, loading them through the Options popout menu of the Color List palette.

❸

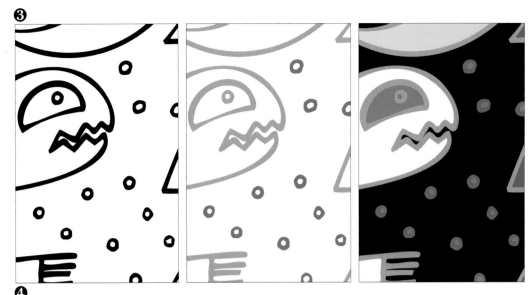

❹

desired settings in each dialog box, and click OK. Next, choose Options, Settings (Command-T), name your settings file, and click Create. To use a custom settings file, choose Options, Settings (Command-T), choose your custom file from the list, and click OK.

COLOR MANAGEMENT

Once she opened the image in FreeHand, Craft's goal was to add color as quickly and easily as possible **❸** — and to keep the colors energetic. Custom libraries give her easy access to colors she uses often, including a rich black (54C 63M 63Y 100K) that matches Photoshop's default black, as well the two shades of tan that she substitutes for gold **❹**. To avoid losing color vibrancy when her art is printed in CMYK, she has also saved a palette of colors "that still have some spunk when they're printed" **❺**. As she creates her imagery, Craft can easily access these custom color libraries from any FreeHand document. ☛ To define a document's Color List as a FreeHand custom color library, choose Export from the Options popout menu of the Color List palette to display the Export Colors dialog box. Choose the colors you want to include in your custom library (using the Shift key to select multiple colors). When you click OK, FreeHand will prompt you to enter both a file name and a library name (the library name will be shown in the Options menu), specify the number of rows and columns, and enter any notes (which will be displayed when you open your new library and click the About button). Click Save As and save the file into the Color folder inside your FreeHand folder. ☛ To load all or part of a custom palette into a document's Color List palette, open the custom library, shift-select the desired colors, and click OK. ∎

❺

C 0	C 0	C 0	C 0	C 0	C 0	C 0
M 0	M 15	M 31	M 15	M 43	M 60	M 76
Y 51	Y 94	Y 94	Y 76	Y 87	Y 0	Y 6
K 0	K 0	K 0	K 0	K 0	K 0	K 0
C 0	C 0	C 31	C 43	C 43	C 100	C 100
M 43	M 56	M 28	M 38	M 6	M 9	M 31
Y 6	Y 6	Y 0	Y 0	Y 0	Y 0	Y 0
K 0	K 0	K 0	K 0	K 0	K 0	K 6
C 51	C 100	C 76	C 65	C 43	C 0	C 0
M 0	M 0	M 0	M 0	M 0	M 56	M 94
Y 19	Y 69	Y 91	Y 100	Y 79	Y 87	Y 87
K 0	K 15	K 0	K 0	K 0	K 0	K 0

PostScript Photorealism

■ *by Janet Ashford*

To launch a new product line, a company often needs realistic pictures before the merchandise has been manufactured. Etonic had built models of a new line of running shoes, but photos of these painted prototypes wouldn't have looked convincing in the brochures and posters the company needed for advance sales. So Etonic asked Michael Scaramozzino of Dream-Light Studios in Stoneham, Mass., to create photorealistic illustrations. Working in FreeHand, Scaramozzino combined simple line patterns with graduated fills and blends to produce believable cloth textures for the shoes.

CREATING CONSISTENT SCANS

Etonic wanted exploded views showing the shoe structure. So DreamLight was provided with a prototype of each shoe, along with models of its separate components. Scaramozzino planned to photograph the elements and use scans of the photos as templates. He began by setting up a simple system to make sure that all the components were photographed at the same angle so that their positions would be consistent in the exploded view.

After placing a piece of cardboard on a table, Scaramozzino set a prototype shoe on top of the cardboard and connected a stationary video camera to his Macintosh so that he could see the prototype on screen and adjust its position. When he was satisfied with the angle, he drew an outline around the shoe on the cardboard ❶, scanned the image at a video resolution of 640 x 480 pixels, and saved the scan as a TIFF. Then he followed the outline to position the other shoe elements when he photographed them ❷.

Each scan was placed into a FreeHand document, and Scaramozzino used the pen tool to trace the basic shapes, using artistic license at times to make some of the curves more aesthetically pleasing ❸. As he worked, Scaramozzino used the Layers palette to organize the complex

When Michael Scaramozzino began working on this exploded view of a running shoe, one of a series of illustrations he created for a new line of Etonic shoes, the manufacturer had yet to finalize the color selection. But Scaramozzino didn't let that interfere with progress. He drew every detail down to the texture in the shoelaces, then edited the specifications later in Free-Hand's Styles and Color List palettes to color correct the art.

1 Scaramozzino had been given a prototype of each shoe and its components. He wanted to photograph all the elements at a consistent angle, but some of the prototypes had been created for the left foot and others for the right. So Scaramozzino began by placing a right-foot prototype on a piece of cardboard and drawing an outline around it. Then he drew another outline, perpendicular to the first one, this time tracing a left-foot prototype. Later, when he photographed the other components, he placed right-foot elements inside the original outline and left-foot elements in the other.

2 Once he had scanned all the components, Scaramozzino used Photoshop to flip the left-shoe elements (Image, Flip, Horizontal) so that all the parts appear to belong to a right shoe.

3 Scaramozzino drew over the scans in FreeHand, producing closed shapes that could later be filled with solid colors, gradients, or blends. In the early stages, most shapes were assigned a black line and white fill.

4 A two-step blend was used to simulate the look of shiny nylon. To make sure the blending paths had the same number of points — so that there would be no irregularities in the blend — Scaramozzino selected the original shape (shown in black), cloned it twice, and reduced the clones. Then he reshaped the clones to create the blending shapes he needed. He executed a blend between the outside contour and the larger inside shape to round out the form and give it a 3-D look. A blend between the two inner shapes produced a shiny highlight.

❶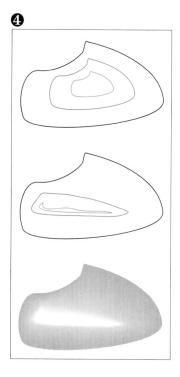

❷

❸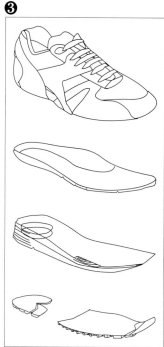

❹

drawings. He estimates that the scanning and tracing process shaved hours of work off the time usually needed to render the 3-D models.

MANAGING COLOR CHANGES

When Scaramozzino began working on the shoe illustrations, Etonic's color choices had not been finalized, and that meant the colors would have to be changed as the project progressed. So Scaramozzino used the Color List and Styles palettes to handle the changes efficiently. When he drew the first shoe, he modeled it carefully, naming colors and styles as he worked — but the CMYK values he specified were arbitrary. Once Etonic chose the final colors, Scaramozzino could work within the palettes to update the illustration.

Scaramozzino has found that he can simplify color management in a complex illustration by basing color names on function rather than hue — *Suede* rather than *Blue* and *Nylon* instead of *White*. And if he fills two different elements with the same color, he still defines two separate colors in the Color List palette in case he needs to edit one or both of them later. For example, in an early stage of an illustration, he might use the same shade of blue in the suede and the smooth leather trim. But rather than use the *Suede* color swatch to fill the leather, he will duplicate the color (by highlighting its name in the Color List palette and choosing Duplicate from the Options menu) and then change the name of the duplicate to *Leather*. By using separate names, he could simply change the CMYK specifications for those colors through the Color Mixer and Color List palettes to update the image. Flexibility and speed was crucial for

this artwork, which contained a lot of blends and small parts. ☞ *When editing a color in Free-Hand (by dragging the color swatch from the Color List palette into the color well area of the Color Mixer palette, adjusting the values, and then dragging the swatch back to the original color swatch in the Color List), you can open and close the Color Mixer palette by double-clicking on a color swatch in the Color List palette. When you open the Color Mixer palette by double-clicking on a color swatch, that color is selected in the Color Mixer.*

Scaramozzino also speeded up color editing by defining base colors (like *Suede*) and using the Tints palette to produce variations (for example, *Suede HLT* for highlights and *Suede MD* for a medium tone, midway between the base color and the highlight). Changing the CMYK specifications of the base color updated the color values in the tints as well. Scaramozzino also used the Styles palette to facilitate changes. As he had done when he built the Color List, Scaramozzino created style names that referred to function. And he exploited the Set Parent feature to define related styles that could be edited globally by modifying the parent. (See "Base Colors and Parent Styles" on page 10.) ☞ *When you edit a color in the Color List palette, all blends and gradients created with that color are automatically recalculated, and all styles created with the color are updated.*

RENDERING TEXTURES

The key to making the shoes look realistic was the careful use of texture effects. One of the simplest treatments was simulating the look of shiny nylon.

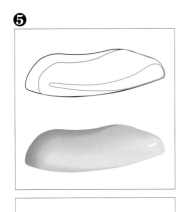

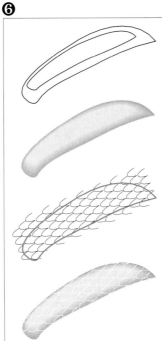

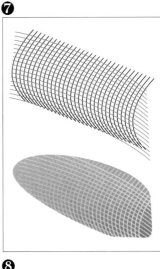

❺ Another two-step blend was used as the basis of a bubble texture. First, Scaramozzino created three shapes and defined blends between them. This set of blends was grouped to produce a bubble. After cloning the bubble, Scaramozzino reshaped some of the blending paths to construct two different bubble pads.

❻ To render the shoelace, Scaramozzino drew each section of the lace with an inner shape that could be used as a blending path. The blend rounded out the form. On top of the blend, he drew a tiny U-shape and cloned it to create a knit-look texture (shown in black). He cloned the outside contour of the shoelace (shown in blue), then cut the knit texture to the clipboard, selected the cloned outline, and chose Edit, Paste Inside (Command-Shift-V). The blended shape shows through the "holes" in the knit.

❼ To create webbed fabric, Scaramozzino drew two curved lines and defined a blend between them (shown in black), then repeated the process to produce another set of curves (shown in blue). This produced a mesh pattern which was pasted into a gradient-filled background shape.

❽ To create the look of top-stitching, Scaramozzino started with a shoe shape, cloned it, scaled the clone down, and moved individual points to produce an inner "stitching" line. He gave this line a darker stroke color than the background, then cloned it and changed the clone to a dashed line in a lighter color.

Scaramozzino generally used a two- or three-step blend, one or two blends to sculpt the shape and another to define the bright highlight **❹**. ☞ *When using a blend to model a 3-D object, it's important to draw the blending paths with the same number of points. The tonal transitions in a blend move from point to point. So if the two blending shapes have a different number of points, the blend will appear skewed or misshapen.* ☞ *To be sure blending paths have the same number of points, it's a good idea to use clones of a single path. As long as the two paths have the same number of points, those points can be repositioned, and the shape of the paths can be edited dramatically without interfering with the smoothness of the blend.*

Two-step blends were also used to create a bubble texture for the shoe's insole. Blends can be reshaped interactively in FreeHand, and Scaramozzino used that feature to mold clones of the original bubble, reforming the clones to produce different blend effects without having to redraw the original paths **❺**. ☞ *When you create a blend in FreeHand, the original paths and the intermediate blending steps between them are automatically grouped. To edit a blend, press the Option key and click on one of the two original blending paths to select it and then reshape it or change its color. The blend will be reblended automatically, so long as it has not been ungrouped.* ☞ *Pressing the Option key lets you select a single element within a FreeHand group. Once you've selected an element in a group, press the tilde key (~) to expand the selection to include all the elements in the group. This is especially helpful when you have groups within groups (a grouped set of blends, for example) and you want to select one of the subgroups.*

To create a realistic cloth texture for the shoelaces, Scaramozzino used blends to make each section of the shoelace look three-dimensional, then placed a "knit" pattern over each blend **❻**. He used a similar technique to simulate webbing, placing a mesh pattern on top of a gradient-filled background **❼**. And the look of top-stitching was created by layering a dashed line over a darker solid line **❽**.

Gradually, as all the elements in the shoe were colored and filled with textures or blends, the artwork acquired a photographic look.

ADAPTING THE BASE ILLUSTRATION

Rendering the first shoe involved the most work. But as the project progressed, elements from the first illustration could be reused. For example, the plastic bubble pads and insole were copied and pasted into later illustrations.

Scaramozzino could also paste the custom colors and the styles he had created into subsequent drawings and then edit the Color List and Styles palettes to update the specifications for a new shoe model. ☞ *When you paste an element from one FreeHand document into another, all the color and style specifications associated with the pasted-in element will be added to the Color List and Style palettes. Even if you delete the element, the color and style names remain in the palettes, so you can apply their specifications to new items as you create them.* ∎

Base Colors and Parent Styles

Michael Scaramozzino's technical drawings are often mistaken for photographs (see "PostScript Photorealism," page 157), but photographs were never this adaptable. Scaramozzino creates his photorealistic effects in FreeHand, and he relies on editable colors and Styles options to update his imagery easily.

When Scaramozzino creates a set of related colors to simulate realistic highlights and shadows, he always begins by defining a base color. First, he creates the color in the Color Mixer and adds it to the Color List palette by choosing New in the palette's Options menu. Then he double-clicks on the default color name so that he can type in a new name, pressing the return key to finalize the name change. When he enters the name for a base color, he includes a bullet (Option-8) so that base colors can be readily identified in the list ❶.

After creating the base color, he drags its swatch from the Color List palette to the Tint palette, selects the tint (or tints) he needs to create the highlights, and drags the tint swatch to the Color List palette. If he edits the base color later, the values in the tints change correspondingly. ☞ *Tints created from a base color that has a custom name can be added to the Color List by dragging the color from the Tint palette to the Color List palette. A tint created from an unnamed base color can be added to the Color List palette only by selecting New in the palette's Options menu.* ☞ *Only tints defined with the drag-and-drop method (by dragging the tint swatch onto the Color List palette) will be updated automatically when the base color is modified. If you add a tint to the Color List by choosing New from the pop-out menu, it will not be changed when the base color is redefined.*

To create shadow tones, Scaramozzino adds black to the base color or clicks on the HSL button in the Color Mixer and drags the slider down to produce a darker shade. When he chooses New in the Options menu in the Color List palette to add the new color to the list, he renames it, giving it a name that corresponds to the base color. ☞ *Unlike tints, colors created by darkening a base color are not updated when the base is modified. You must change these shadow tones manually by dragging the base color swatch to the Color Mixer and darkening the tone. Then drag and drop the new color to replace the original tone in the Color List palette.*

In addition to base colors, Scaramozzino uses parent styles to facilitate color changes in his artwork. After applying stroke weight, fill style, and color to an element, he chooses New in the Styles palette Options menu so that he can apply the same attributes to other elements (by simply selecting them and clicking on the style name in the palette). To create related styles (*Suede* and *Suede Side*, for example) he first modifies the basic style (*Suede*) by applying it to a selected element, then changing the specifications as needed and choosing New in the Style palette Options menu. While the new style's name is still highlighted in the Styles palette, he chooses Set Parent from the Options menu and clicks on *Suede* in the Set Parent dialog box. That way, if he later modifies the parent style — and in case he needs to edit the specifications, he uses a pair of bullets when he names a parent style to make it easy to identify in the Styles palette ❷ — the changes are reflected throughout the substyles.

By defining base colors and parent styles, Scaramozzino could redefine a few specifications to make sweeping changes in an illustration, a process that let him produce color and style variations for an entire line of women's running shoes with a minimum of trouble ❸. ■

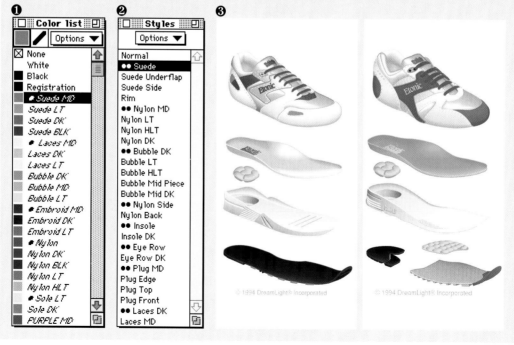

❶

❷

❸

© 1994 DreamLight® Incorporated

© 1994 DreamLight® Incorporated

Fast, Friendly Lettering

■ *by Sara Booth*

WORKING FOR a newspaper will make you into a speed demon," says Dan Hubig. In his work for the *San Francisco Chronicle,* Hubig has learned to use FreeHand efficiency features to best advantage. For example, he has saved a custom FreeHand Defaults document that contains six layers, about 20 styles, and nearly 100 colors that he uses frequently. When he was asked to illustrate the cover for a schedule of arts events, Hubig used his FreeHand shortcuts to keep the complex illustration in order so he could concentrate on the playfulness of the design.

Hubig doesn't own a scanner and has never wanted one. He has a conventional fax machine and a fax modem, each with its own phone line, and when he needs to "scan" a sketch into the computer, he faxes it to himself. When he had worked out a final sketch for the arts preview, he used this technique to transform it into a 72 dpi TIFF image, which he imported into FreeHand

When Dan Hubig created the cover for the *San Francisco Chronicle*'s schedule of fall arts events, he wanted each letter to function as its own little illustration — but also to be readable as a letterform. Hubig, who divides his time between Santa Barbara and San Francisco, put FreeHand through its paces using a variety of techniques, with gradients, blends, and clipping paths playing the starring roles.

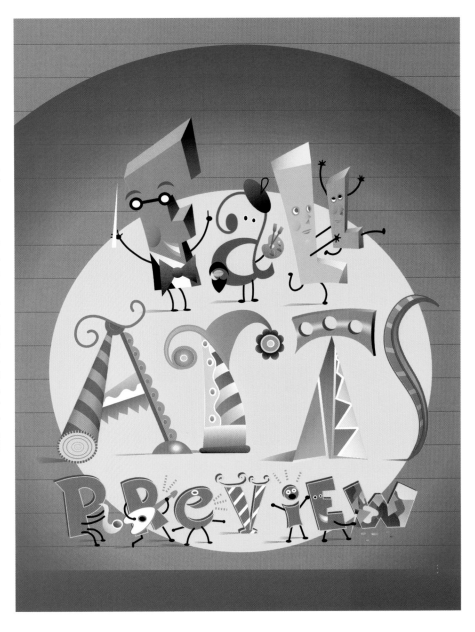

1 To add dimension to the left side of the *A*, Hubig made two blends, cloned them four times, and pasted one set inside each of a series of stripes.

2 Hubig cloned the blends he used above, darkened them, and pasted them inside a cone. Then he pasted the stripes inside the same cone.

3 Hubig drew most of the *A* as flat shapes to contrast with the three-dimensional cone. "I was trying to make it look contradictory, so you'd look at it and think, 'That couldn't really happen,'" he says.

4 The upright of the *R* is constructed of a variety of shapes pasted inside a path: a series of gradient-filled stripes, a curved shape with dots, and a gradient-filled bottom shape.

5 To create the stripes in the *S*, Hubig blended between two rectangles, then rotated and repositioned one, causing the blend to spread out into a fan. He pasted the stripes inside the gradient-filled *S* shape. He drew another shape to add dimension, filled it with a gradient, added a stroke, and sent it behind the letter.

6 FreeHand can't fill a stroke with a gradient, so for the upright of the *T*, Hubig simulated the effect by copying two triangles, filling the copies with gradients, offsetting them, and placing them behind the originals.

7 Hubig added a pink zigzag shape, created a white-filled copy, offset it slightly, and sent it behind, then pasted the shapes inside a triangle.

8 The crossbar of the *T* began with a blend between a stripe and a rough arc.

9 The circles look like holes punched in the letter, but they were created by drawing dark circles for shadows, then making three slightly offset copies, filling them with the background color, and pasting them inside the shadow circles.

❶

❷

❸

❹

❺

❻ ❼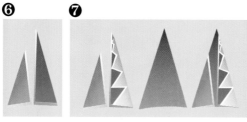

❽ ❾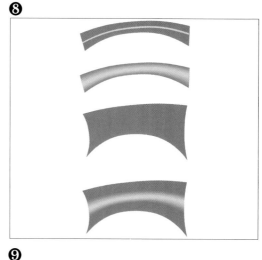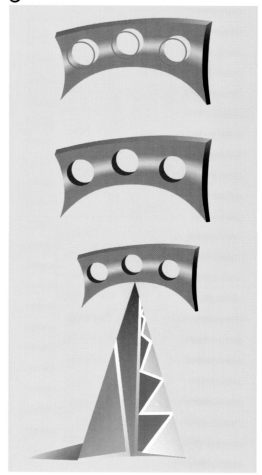

and redrew with a black stroke and no fill, using the bezigon tool because he finds it easier to work with than the pen tool. ☞ *To select the bezigon tool, press 8 or Shift-F8. By default, the bezigon tool makes corner points. To make curve points, Option-click; to make connector points, Control-click.*

When he has finished redrawing a sketch, Hubig selects all the contours and applies one of his styles: a white fill and a black stroke. This allows him to check the stacking order without the distraction of color. Then he begins adding flat colors. As he continues to work, he replaces many of the flat fills with linear gradients, choosing Logarithmic from the Taper popout menu of the Inspector palette because he feels it gives a more realistic sense of volume. ☞ *To give an object a flat-color fill, drag and drop a swatch from the*

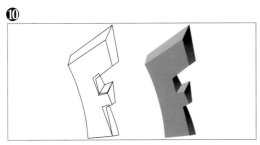

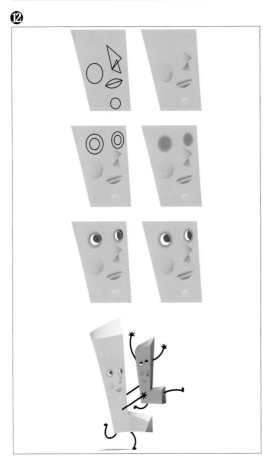

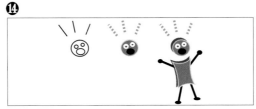

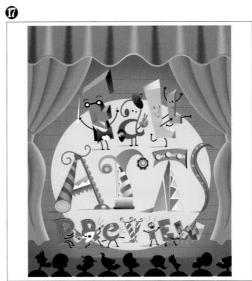

10 To create the *F*, Hubig roughly drew a 3-D form. To increase the sense of dimension, he used the same gradient for all the surfaces that define the right side of the letter; the other shapes have flat fills.

11 He added features by pasting shapes representing the cheek and tuxedo inside the surface of the letter, then added the glasses, bow tie, mouth, arms, and legs.

12 Gradients and blends give a soft look to the face of an *L*. Hubig first used gradient-filled shapes for the nose, mouth, cheek, and chin. For the eye sockets, he blended between two concentric ellipses. Then he created the eyes by pasting two dark circles (for pupils) inside two white circles.

13 When he redrew his sketch, Hubig looked for ways to save time. For shapes that didn't need to vary in width, like the thin curve of the *a*, he used strokes (shown in blue) rather than filled objects.

14 The "sound lines" on the *i* are actually dashed strokes. The stroke (3 points) is wider than each dash is long, so the dashes appear to be separate lines.

15 The colorful shapes of the *W* were roughly drawn, then pasted inside the letter's outline. The gaps are filled with the outline's dark-blue fill.

16 Hubig blended between two white stripes, then made three copies of the blend and pasted one inside each of the outline shapes of the *V*. The flourishes at the tops of the letters were drawn with strokes, not filled shapes.

17 For the final cover, Hubig placed the letters on their own stage. He used blends extensively in creating the stage — from the planks on the floor to the shadows and highlights in the curtains.

Color List, Color Mixer, or Inspector palettes. To assign a linear gradient, Control-drag a swatch; the swatch will become the end color of the gradient, and where you drop it will determine the angle of the gradient. To assign a radial gradient, Option-drag; the swatch becomes the center of the gradient, and where you drop it determines the placement of the center. If you drag a swatch onto an image that *already contains a gradient, the color will replace one of the colors in the gradient. Shift-drag to replace a gradient with a flat-color fill.*

Where Hubig wanted to give the impression of rounded surfaces, he pasted blends into shapes rather than filling them with gradients. He wanted other objects to look painted, so he built playful patterns of geometric shapes, then pasted these inside contours. ■

Rounding it Out

■ *by Dave Lavaty*

WITH TRADITIONAL AIRBRUSH illustration, the quality of the finished art relies entirely on the friskets. I can correct or cover up almost any other mistake, but if I don't cut my friskets carefully, I'll end up with a mess. And the same thing holds true when I work in FreeHand, using blends, gradients, and radial fills to create airbrush-look images: The most important aspect of the project is building smooth "frisket" forms.

As long as I create fluid shapes, I can cut corners in other areas. When I define small blends, for example, I often keep FreeHand's Printer Resolution set to 300 dpi in the Inspector palette. Using low-resolution blends cuts down on the size of the finished file, and the stair-stepping (as long as it's confined to small areas) simply adds to the texture of the artwork the way a few spatters add texture to my airbrush work. Of course, when I'm blending across broad shapes or defining strong

focal points, I first set the Printer Resolution to 2540 dpi to make sure that the color transitions in the blend are smooth.

Before I begin working on a illustration, I sketch out the design in pencil, scan the sketch at 600 dpi, and place the scan on the background layer in FreeHand. I block out the forms with the pen tool, drawing simple, straight-line shapes, and then convert some of the corner points to curves so that I can adjust these rough-cut pieces into "friskets" that fit the contours in the sketch. This is similar to the way I handle airbrushing, when I cut the masking film into rough forms that cover key areas in my sketch before going in and carefully recutting the film to shape.

One of the advantages of working in FreeHand is that I can reuse my friskets. For example, when I drew a toucan illustration as a "mascot" for a local bar, I drew the beak as one shape and then drew another shape to define the line that divided the top and bottom halves of the beak. By using clones of these shapes with the Punch and Intersect function, I could divide the beak — and all the dots I placed on top of it as decorations — into separate sections. The original shapes disappear when Punch or Intersect is applied, so I always keep copies safe on another layer so I can use them again if I need to. And because FreeHand can come up with some surprising results if I use Punch or Intersect with more than two shapes at once, I went through several clones of the original shapes in the process of creating all the pieces of the beak, one at a time.

Once I had "cut out" the beak pieces, I grouped the top section and the bottom section of the beak so that I could rotate them. I could never have done anything like that with an airbrush frisket: cutting it into detailed shapes and then repositioning the set of shapes as a unit. And I cloned some of the friskets to produce blending shapes for the beak, the feet and the feathers. (With simpler forms like the toucan's eye and the flowers, I applied radials and graduated fills).

I can also experiment with color on the computer more freely than I can with an airbrush, and I find FreeHand's Color List and Styles palettes invaluable for these experiments. In the early phases of creating an illustration, I apply "raw" colors, shades of yellow, magenta, cyan, and black. But as I apply these raw colors, I define them as styles and give the colors names like *Beak, Beak dots,* and *Feathers.* And when I plan to apply blends or gradients, I define a second raw color (*Beak dots 2* and *Feathers 2,* for example). Later when I try different color combinations, I can "repaint" the entire image by simply changing the CMYK definitions of my raw colors. So I can experiment up to the last minute without having to redo any of my work.

One of the habits I hang onto from my "traditional" work is the way I handle detail in an illustration. I like strong, graphic imagery — bold forms and punchy colors. And if I add a lot of fussy details to an illustration, I'll detract from the graphic effect. So I've made it a rule to restrict myself to only three detailed areas in any image, and I keep these detailed areas away from each other. In a large illustration, the detailed sections may be expansive. But with a small design like the toucan, even the details were fairly simple: the beak, the cluster of flowers on the right side of the image, and the curling branches with more flowers on the left side.

Those curling branches were easy to produce. I drew a looping line with the freehand tool, set to Variable Stroke. This gave me closed paths that could be joined to the branch shape I had created earlier (by using the Union command in the Path Operations submenu). ∎

❶
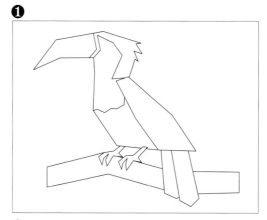

❷
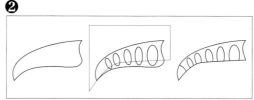

❸

❹
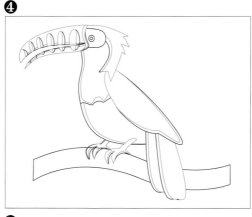

❺
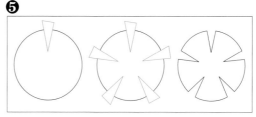

1 To draw the toucan, I began by roughing out the shape in FreeHand, drawing straight lines and then re-shaping the contours by selecting individual points and changing them to curves (by clicking the curve point icon and the Automatic button in the Object Inspector.

2 Once I had reshaped the beak, I added small oval dots, rotating each one to follow the angle of the beak. I cloned the beak elements, moved the clones to a new layer, and created an "intersect" shape (shown in blue). I selected the intersect shape, along with each element, and applied the Intersect command (in the Xtras, Path Operations submenu) to create the top of the beak. I used the same shape as a punch (Xtras, Path Operations, Punch) to produce the bottom of the beak.

3 I created styles for all the elements in the image, using black, gray, cyan, yellow, and magenta. Then, when I finalized my color choices later, I could recolor all the elements quickly by editing entries in the Styles and Color List palettes.

4 I planned to use the Blend command (Xtras, Create, Blend) to give the image an airbrush look. And I began by cloning several elements and reshaping the clones slightly so that I could use them as blending shapes.

5 As a last touch, I added a set of flowers. To create the first flower, I drew a circle, placed a wedge on top of it, and rotated clones of the wedge around the circle. I used the wedge shapes and the Punch command to slice into the circle. (To finish the flower, I drew a star shape in its center with the polygon tool.)

Efficient Infographics

■ *by Grant Jerding*

CREATING INFORMATION GRAPHICS can be relatively simple — throw a hasty illustration next to a table, list, or chart and move on. But doing them well requires much more than that. An infographic artist must not only create a sophisticated illustration, but also integrate it with clear, concise information.

When I illustrated an article for *Insight* magazine on medical technology in foreign countries, I noted that although specific technologies were mentioned in the article, none was discussed at length. So an illustration of a particular device was out — especially since most complex medical devices are not readily recognizable by the average reader of a weekly newsmagazine. Therefore, I brainstormed for simple ideas that said "medical

❶

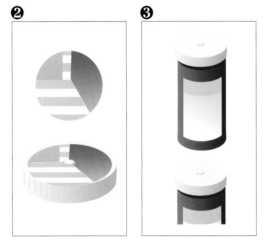

1 Although DeltaGraph Pro can export charts in Illustrator 3.2 format, I find it just as easy to copy and paste the chart into FreeHand. Either way, the chart comes in as fully editable points and lines.

2 I used the 3-D Rotation tool from FreeHand's Xtra toolbar (accessed by choosing Windows, Other, Xtra Tools or Command-Shift-K) to push the pie graph into perspective with the top of the bottle.

3 To cut off the bottom of the medicine bottle at the frame of the illustration, I first double-clicked the knife in the toolbox to display the Knife Tool dialog box, where I checked the Close Cut Paths option. Then I used the knife to cut a straight line across each of the objects that hung over the frame.

❷   ❸

technology" — coming up with beakers, lab coats, pills, powders, and scales.

I try to build graphics using objects whose shapes can easily be adapted to display information: repetitive rectangles or cylinders for bar charts and, naturally, ellipses for pie charts. Since I had recently drawn a medicine bottle for an illustration that was never used, I decided to use its top for the pie charts. Although medicines are usually the result of medical technology, not the technology itself, I decided to use the bottle for its immediate recognition value and because time was a major consideration: Unlike other kinds of illustrations, infographics illustrate actual facts and figures provided by the editorial side, so much of the available time may be spent waiting to receive information.

I use DeltaGraph Pro to plot data, even for simple charts like these, because it's efficient and it ensures that the graphic will be accurate. DeltaGraph generated only the skeleton of the two graphs — color choices, shading, depth, and so on would be added manually in FreeHand. Entering the data, choosing the type of chart, and plotting took less than five minutes and saved painstaking measuring methods that would have been needed to create the charts accurately in FreeHand.

When I press Command-N in FreeHand, the new document automatically contains all my application preferences, my freelance logo and nameplate, commonly used styles (such as a hairline stroke with no fill and a black fill with no stroke) in the Styles palette, extra layers in the Layers palette, and a set of 60 colors I use frequently (from water and land to fleshtones and clothing colors) in the Color List. I created this template document by manipulating the file called *FreeHand Defaults*, located in the application folder. Any changes made to this document will appear in each new document.

Some of the colors I used in the illustration were already present in my default Color List, but I created the others as I went along. I base color names on the objects they're used for, not their hues (for example, *medicine dark* rather than *red dark*), because that makes it easier to go back and edit the colors of objects independently as the illustration evolves.

To make the illustration match the graphs I had generated in DeltaGraph, the Layers palette was a very important organizational tool. Since this graphic was not complicated, I was not concerned with layering everything. But I locked the layers that contained the ground and sky shapes and the chart skeleton from DeltaGraph (by clicking the lock icon by their names in the Layers palette) so I could line up elements with the skeleton chart without accidentally modifying the chart itself.

After the chart took shape, I decided on a light

shining from above left to enhance the feeling of three-dimensional space. To be believable, all the large objects had to be shaded taking this lighting decision into account — for example, cylinders are all shaded with a graduated fill from light (left) to dark (right). But the most effective way to define three-dimensional space was with shadows. After creating the shadows that the beakers cast on the ground, I added the shadows they cast on the rack. Since the rack was slightly raised off the table, I offset the shadows on the rack from the shadows on the table.

To add motion and a sense of importance to the information, I often include small people interacting with pieces of the graphic. The minuscule scale of the people makes the central objects look gargantuan. I drew a small man in a lab coat placing the 1995 beaker by the row of earlier beakers. This also allowed me to include more of the medical technology symbols I had brainstormed earlier. Because I had dead space between the charts, I also created a woman carrying a pill to balance the man and further integrate the two charts. After I drew the shapes for the woman, I copied the attributes (Edit, Copy Attributes or Command-Option-Shift-C) of the man's coat and pasted them (Edit, Paste Attributes or Command-Option-Shift-V) onto her coat. The Copy Attributes command gives the second object the same fill and stroke as the copied object and is more efficient than creating a style if there are only one or two objects that need the same fill and stroke. ∎

④ 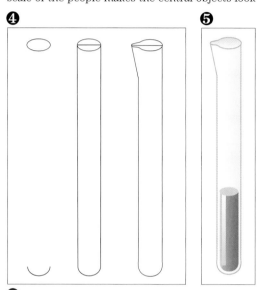 **⑤** **⑥**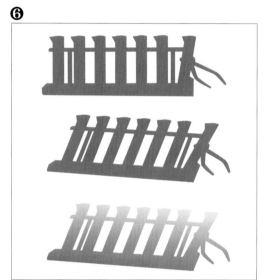

⑦

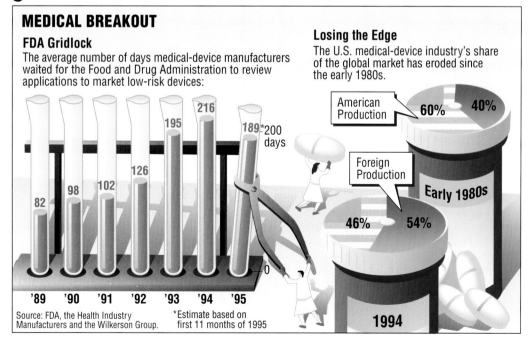

4 To create a beaker, I drew an ellipse for the top, then cloned it and Shift-dragged it down for the bottom. It was too shallow, so I used the Scale tool to scale it vertically. Then I used the knife tool (with Close Cut Paths unchecked) to cut away the top half of the ellipse. Finally, I chose View, Snap to Point (Command-'), so when I used the pen to connect the cut points to the top of the beaker, the shapes snapped together.

5 The best way to represent the glass sides and bottom of the beaker was to not draw them at all. By insetting the liquid from the sides of the beaker, I made the glass look thick. I cloned the beaker, selected the clone, and chose Xtras, Path Operations, Inset Path, setting the Inset at 1.5 points, to draw the liquid that serves as the values of the chart. After using gradients to add color and highlights to the beaker and liquid, I cloned and duplicated to make six other beakers.

6 To create a shadow for the row of beakers and clamp, I cloned them, selected the clones, and chose Xtras, Path Attributes, Union to make them into a single shape. I double-clicked the scale tool, unchecked Uniform, and dragged to scale the shadow about 40 percent horizontally. I used the skew tool to skew the shape about 20 degrees horizontally and -3 degrees vertically until I was satisfied with the angle. Finally, I gave the object a graduated fill from a dark table shadow color to the actual color of the table so the shadow appeared to fade out.

7 Setting the shadow gradient to an angle (82 degrees in this case) that created graduated steps parallel with the horizon made the shadow appear to rest flat against the ground.

Roughing Up PostScript Art

■ *by Sara Booth*

Straight-line segments add a spontaneous look to Robert Oswald's food cart logo. Oswald "grouped" elements with FreeHand's Paste Inside command, using the outline of each vegetable or fruit to mask out the unfinished edges of quickly drawn shadow and highlight shapes.

NERGY WAS THE EFFECT that South Carolina's Richland Memorial Hospital wanted in the logo for a cart that sells healthy foods to hospital employees and visitors. So Lexington, S.C., designer Robert Oswald used a quick-sketch technique to create lively fruits and vegetables in FreeHand using only straight lines.

The client gave Oswald a list of fruits and vegetables, chosen not for their visual compatibility but for their cancer-preventing benefits. Oswald's challenge was: "How can I put apples and broccoli together and still make them look appetizing?" The roughness and spontaneity of his pencil sketch of foods bursting from a bowl appealed to Oswald and his client. To maintain the same "quick, down-and-dirty" look in his final design, he used the pen tool to click from point to point, roughly following a scan of the sketch. He created the vegetables entirely out of straight lines, using curves only for the type and the background circles.

PLANNING FOR CONSISTENT COLOR

Once Oswald had chosen the basic hues he would need for the illustration, he used his color inkjet printer to print swatches of various Trumatch colors. He and the hospital's graphics manager, Tim Floyd, used these printed swatches to choose a final palette of "colors that you'd want to eat." He believes he can trust his inkjet printer to give him fairly reliable color because he has checked its accuracy by comparing its results with his final printed output.

To make this palette more convenient to use once the colors were chosen, Oswald added each color to FreeHand's color list by choosing the Trumatch selector from the Options menu of the Color List palette, scrolling to the color, clicking OK to add it to the Color List palette, and giving it a new, more descriptive name. For most of the vegetables' colors, he chose a slightly darker color for shadows; for the greens, he also chose a lighter shade for highlights.

MODELING WITH PASTE INSIDE

Oswald used FreeHand's Paste Inside command to add modeling while keeping his file simple . After creating a vegetable, he used a darker color to draw a rough shape in front to serve as a shadow. Rather than closely following the edges of the vegetable, he simply roughed in the edges. Then he cut the shadow to the clipboard, selected the vegetable, and pressed Command-Shift-V to paste the shadow contours inside the selected path. If he needed to make changes to the shadow contours, he chose Edit, Cut Contents (Command-Shift-X), and FreeHand released the pasted-in contours, placing them in front of the vegetable.

Oswald also used Paste Inside to create a transparent effect in the bowl. After creating a blue background and a dark yellow burst, he pasted them both inside a masking oval with no fill and no stroke, then placed a light yellow copy of the burst behind them to make the burst appear to change color as it leaves the bowl.

Oswald used the Layers palette to keep his work organized and to avoid accidentally changing or deleting one element as he worked on another. His scanned sketch went on the Background layer until he had traced and deleted it. He placed the type and the background circles on one layer, the wheat on a second, and the fruits and vegetables on a third, then locked the layers he wasn't working on by clicking the padlock icons beside their names in the Layers palette.

Oswald used the logo to create what he calls a "brochure shell," a letter-sized sheet that can be folded vertically to enclose a menu or other literature. To create the paler copies of the fruits and vegetables that free-fall randomly across the shell, Oswald dragged a swatch of each color from the Color List palette into the Color Mixer palette, then adjusted the CMYK percentages by eye to get the tints he wanted . ☛ *To lighten or darken a color without changing the proportions of its CMYK values, click the HLS button in the Color Mixer palette and drag the slider.*

Oswald rotated and rearranged paler fruits and vegetables to get a random scatter ❸. "I would step back from the screen," he says, "and if I saw too much green in one area, I would delete green elements until the design was visually balanced."

The logo was also used for a cut-vinyl sign that stands near the food cart, stickers, T-shirts, and one-color coupons, as well as a backlit sign on the cart which is actually a color print mounted to an acrylic panel. Using so many media, Oswald had to be vigilant to achieve color consistency, and in some cases this was impossible. "On the vinyl sign, we couldn't get the yellows to match up, because there are a limited number of vinyls out there," he says. "I just picked the closest match I could." ■

1 Oswald used the Paste Inside command to add modeling to the vegetables. The top of the broccoli was filled with medium green. Next, he drew a highlight shape and a shadow shape. Contours that would show were carefully rendered, but those that would be cropped were drawn with a few rough lines. He selected both contours, cut them to the clipboard, selected the main shape, and pressed Command-Shift-V to paste them inside.

2 To create lighter versions of the vegetables, Oswald used the Color Mixer palette to adjust colors by eye. The bright red on the original apple is 100 percent magenta and 100 percent yellow. For the lighter version, Oswald preferred a different proportion: 35 percent magenta and 20 percent yellow. For the pea pod, the original green is 85 percent cyan and 85 percent yellow. When Oswald lightened those percentages to 25 percent, he also added six percent black.

3 Oswald arranged the lighter fruits and vegetables in a random scatter across the brochure shell, adjusting placement, rotation, and size by eye. The inside of the brochure was left blank so that menus, price lists, or other information could be printed later in black only.

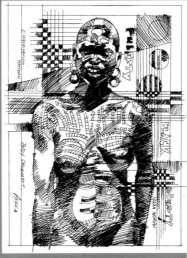

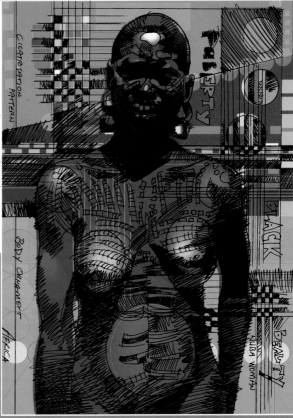

The jet plane part of Steve Greenberg's dove-to-jet morph was relatively simple: Modelmaker Matthew Mees put together a miniature plane, and Greenberg photographed it with a digital camera and added windows in Photoshop to make it look like a bigger jet.

The challenge was getting a photograph of a dove in flight. Animal trainer Charlene White of Animal Episodes, who provided the cage of trained doves, suggested tying fishing line to a bird's leg and letting it fly in front of a blue screen. "I had no idea how fast a dove's wings moved," Greenberg says. "There was no way I was going to catch this and freeze the bird in flight."

Plan B was to take a photo of a bird resting on someone's hand. "We found that if you quickly lowered the hand, the bird's wings shot out," Greenberg says. "After repeating the movement a few times to get our rhythm, the bird got the hang of it and we had our shot. Every once in a while a bird got bored with this and took off. No problem — we had plenty of doves. At the end of the shoot I looked up to see six doves perched on the sprinkler pipes above my head. I quickly put on a hat!"

The bird used for the final shot was a composite of three photographs: one bird's head and feathers from two others, put together in Photoshop. For more of Greenberg's morphing adventures, see "Reality Check" on page 196.

Designer Charly Palmer uses his copier almost as much as his computer, and to get the effect he wants, he'll experiment with just about anything that comes to hand. For the illustration below, he used an unusual tool to give his electronic image a rough, non-mechanical look: sandpaper.

First, Palmer scanned a pen-and-ink drawing, converted the scan to Bitmap mode in Photoshop, and saved it as an EPS image with transparent whites so that he could place colorful shapes behind it in Illustrator. When he took a look at the finished effect, he decided the linework in his scanned illustration was too heavy. He tried softening the linework by adjusting the contrast in Photoshop, but he didn't like the results. So he made a photocopy of the original drawing and broke down the lines by rubbing the copy with fine sandpaper. When he scanned the photocopy (left), he gave it the same name as the original scan so that it replaced the image in the Illustrator file automatically without needing to be repositioned (right).

"Posterizing in PostScript," page 109, describes how Palmer uses Adobe Illustrator to give scanned sketches and photographs a hand-painted look.

AMP, an on-line magazine produced by MCA Records, hit the World Wide Web in November 1994. And judging by reader response, it stands out from the typical on-line offerings: "Beautiful graphics." "Kudos to your art department." "After looking around a bit, all I can say is, Wow! You have done a wonderful job of producing a web page that is not only informative, but visually stunning." Almost as an afterthought, one reader added, "And the content is equally good."

David High, the designer who gives AMP its flair, finds the comments particularly gratifying because the magazine is his first venture into an exclusively electronic arena — and because he succeeded on his own terms, as an inventive layout artist and not a technical wizard. In fact, High prefers to leave many of the technical aspects of the project to others. "I turn the files over to the MCA people," he says, "and they make the buttons work."

In its short history, AMP has already undergone several stages of evolution. For the first issue, MCA asked for QuarkXPress layouts, planning to convert the files to a portable document format before uploading them. But before the issue was published, MCA technicians decided that the only way to maintain the integrity of High's imagery was to start with bitmap files. So High started again, working in Adobe Illustrator and Photoshop. First, he placed EPS versions of the background photos into Illustrator and arranged the type on top of the photos. When he was satisfied with the composition, he deleted the placed imagery from the Illustrator documents, opened the files in Photoshop, and pasted the type on top of the photos. Three of the resulting layouts are shown below.

High changed his production methods again when he composed the second issue of the magazine. Photoshop 3 had recently been released — and because High could use the new layering feature to arrange elements and to create dramatic type effects, he produced the layouts entirely in Photoshop. For more information about High's approach to layering, see "Photoshop As a Layout Tool," page 41. And you can browse through AMP online at http://www.mca.com/ on the World Wide Web.

When Hermann Hospital asked Chris Lockwood to design a cover for the "High-Tech at Hermann" issue of its quarterly magazine, the Houston illustrator wanted to show the transition between old-fashioned and high-tech. He gave a sepia-tone look to a photo of hospital founder George Hermann by opening Photoshop's Curves dialog box (Image, Adjust, Curves or Command-M) and adjusting the midtone section of the curve in each color channel, subtracting cyan and adding magenta and yellow.

Next, he opened a copy of the face to work on the high-tech side. Opening the Curves dialog box, he used the pencil tool to scribble a rough curve to bring up exaggerated color changes, experimenting with different color combinations until he found one he liked. Then he selected one part of the face with the lasso, added a feather to the selection, and applied the Mosaic filter to create the pixelated effect. Other elements were imported from Illustrator. For a look at Lockwood's 3-D work, see "Where 2-D Meets 3-D" on page 211.

Painting With Texture

■ *by Sara Booth*

PUTTING COLLAGE techniques to a novel use, Mark Shaver uses scanned, hand-painted images to add texture to his artwork. The Santa Monica, Calif., illustrator paints or spatters high-contrast abstract images in gouache on paper or board, then uses Photoshop to make multiple variations in shape, color, and contrast. The Paste Into function allows him to fill any selection with the scanned texture of his choice.

When the city of Beverly Hills asked for an illustration of its new recycling bins in action, Shaver began by making a detailed marker sketch, in which he worked out the composition and line weights of the final illustration without the distractions of shading and color. After scanning the sketch and opening it in Illustrator as a template, he hand-traced it with the pen tool. Then he began experimenting by filling contours with color.

"When I'm adding flat color in Illustrator, I'm thinking of the patterns I'll be using later on in Photoshop," Shaver says. After developing his palette, using a relatively neutral background to play up the saturated colors used in the foreground elements, he sent the Illustrator file to the client for approval ❶.

Shaver keeps a file of abstract painted textures, created by brushing, dripping, or spattering gouache on paper or board. He reuses these textures often, but each one goes through so many changes before it finds its way into a final illustration that the same texture can be used several times in the same image. For the recycling art, Shaver chose four textures from his file ❷, then altered them in Photoshop ❸, picking up flat colors from his Illustrator file to use in the textures. Finally, he used the magic wand to select each flat-color area in his Photoshop file, then chose Edit, Paste Into to fill it with the pattern. Shapes that were not in the original Illustrator file were added in Photoshop ❹.

Hand-painted textures add a variety of surfaces to the work of Santa Monica illustrator Mark Shaver. For a recycling brochure, he used Photoshop to make many variations on scanned textures, then used the Paste Into function to place these textures in selected areas.

When he sees how a pattern looks in the context of the final illustration, Shaver may decide that its color or contrast needs adjustment. He can make changes while the area is still selected. Favorite techniques include using the Image, Adjust, Levels (Command-L) or Image, Adjust, Curves (Command-M) dialog box, or simply floating the selection, filling it with a new foreground color, then adjusting the floating selection's opacity using the slider in the Layers palette. ■

1 Shaver began his work in Illustrator because he finds the task of adding flat color faster there. Once the client approved the Illustrator file, Shaver opened it in Photoshop (rasterizing it in the process) and began selecting flat-color areas with the magic wand tool so that he could fill them with textures.

2 For the recycling image, Shaver scanned four handpainted textures: a small-scale stipple for the truck, the sidewalk, the man's pants, and the shadows in the faces; feathery brushstrokes for the hair and the woman's mouth; diagonal brushstrokes for the tan background; and a rougher pattern for the cans and the upper background.

3 To generate the texture behind the truck, Shaver first scanned the spatter pattern and chose Image, Distort, Scale to flatten it into the desired shape. Opening the recycling illustration, he used the eyedropper to pick up the color of the background shape; this would be the darkest color in his texture. Returning to the texture file, he selected all, then filled with the foreground color; choosing Color mode in the Fill dialog box caused the fill to change the color pixels but leave the white ones untouched. To add the lighter color, he filled again, this time choosing Darken mode so the darkest areas wouldn't be affected.

4 For the shapes that define shadows and highlights on the bins, Shaver used the same pattern, but with color variations. Once the shape was filled with a pattern, he created a shadow by making a jagged selection, then using the eyedropper to pick up the darkest color in the pattern and filling the selection with this color at low opacity. A similar technique, using white as the foreground color, was used to make the highlights.

❶

❷
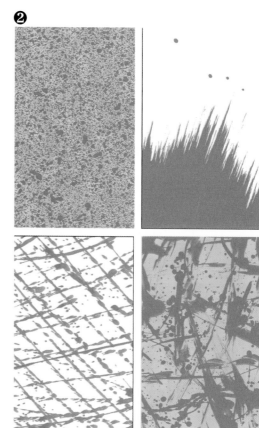

❸
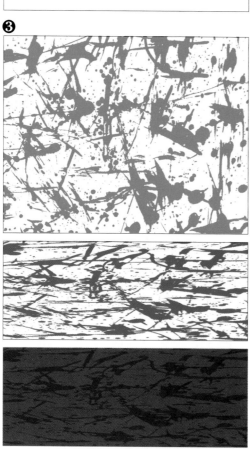

❹

Painting with Light

■ *by Sara Booth*

AIRBRUSHED SHAPES fill the art of Elliott Park with halos of light and movement. The South Lake, Texas, illustrator draws linework in Illustrator, then adds a slight feather to Photoshop selections so that his brushwork resembles paint applied using an airbrush with a loose frisket. When a hotel wanted an illustration for a brochure promoting its jazz nights, the art director asked Park to provide an image that was richly colored and dark enough to work as a backdrop for white type. So Park set out to create a piece that had the low-light atmosphere of the music it illustrated.

Park worked out many aspects of the illustration, including the thick-and-thin lines that characterize his work, at the pencil sketch stage. With a sketch so complex, he knew Illustrator's template function wouldn't preserve enough of the details to be useful. So instead, Park created a new layer in his Illustrator

Elliott Park had only about 12 hours to complete an advertising brochure for a hotel's jazz nights. "The speed contributed to the looseness and creativity," he says. Park created the linework in Illustrator, then used Photoshop's layers and paths to speed the application of an evocative color palette with the airbrush tool.

1 Park created the linework in Illustrator, filling the contours with a black that also contained about 30 percent each of cyan, magenta, and yellow for a richer look.

2 The path called *Mask* is a series of related subpaths. When Park closed one subpath, Photoshop automatically started a new subpath with the next click.

3 Two subpaths define the curves above the mouth of the saxophone. Park used the airbrush tool to paint along the left side of each subpath, then chose Select, Inverse and painted along the right side of each subpath, to get a total of four curves. He used the blur tool to soften the right side of each curve.

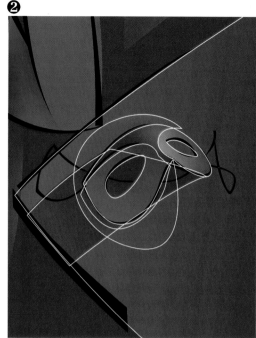

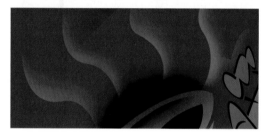

document for the sketch. He saved the scanned sketch in EPS format, placed it in Illustrator, and double-clicked the name in the Layers palette to display the Layer Options dialog box, where he checked the Lock option to prevent changes to the layer and the Dim Placed Images option to tone down the sketch, so that he could trace it in the top layer.

Park wanted to keep the template visible as he worked, so he didn't want to cover it up with filled shapes — and he didn't have the option of working in Artwork mode, because placed EPS images are visible in Preview mode only. So before he began tracing the sketch, he set a default fill of None and black stroke in the Paint Style palette, so that they would be applied automatically to each contour he created. As he worked on the linework, he used a stroke weight of 0.1 point, because that weight would display as a fine line even when he zoomed in very close. When he had finished his Illustrator work, he selected all the contours and changed their fill to a rich black and their stroke to None **1**.

Park wanted to bring these black contours into Photoshop, but he knew that he would also want access to the PostScript paths. So he selected all of the contours in his Illustrator document and copied them to the clipboard. He opened a new Photoshop document and created a new layer in it by clicking the New Layer icon at the bottom left of the Layers palette. The black linework would go in one layer while Park painted color into another.

Park activated the linework layer and pasted the contents of the clipboard twice: first as pixels, then as paths. ☞ *When the clipboard contains contours copied from Illustrator, pasting in Photoshop displays the Paste dialog box, where you can choose to paste your selection as pixels (with or without anti-aliasing) or as paths.*

While the linework paths were still selected and displayed in the Paths palette as Work Path, Park double-clicked their icon in the palette to name and save them as a single path. ☞ *To save a work path: Double-click the path's name in the palette. Or drag the path's icon in the palette onto the New Path icon at the bottom of the palette. Or choose Save Path from the palette's popout menu. Any of these options will display the Save Path dialog box, where you can name your path.*

4 Park made two duplicates of the path that defined the saxophone player's shoulder, then used the arrow tool to reshape each path before turning each one into a selection and airbrushing blue inside it. The same technique was used for the musician's head, this time with black to reflect his hair.

5 When he had activated the path that defines the light and made it a selection, Park chose Select, Inverse so that the selection would mask what was inside the shapes, rather than what was outside. A darker shade of the background color, airbrushed along the edges of the paths, created shadows.

WORKING WITH PHOTOSHOP PATHS

Other paths would be needed, too, to use as masks as Park painted color into the illustration. For complex paths, he used Illustrator to create contours with no stroke or fill, then pasted them into his Photoshop file as paths. But most of his paths were simple enough that he could create them in Photoshop, using the pen tool and the path-editing tools from the Paths palette. ☛ *When the pen tool in the palette is selected, holding down the Command key will display the arrow tool. When the arrow tool is selected, holding down the Command and Option keys will display the delete-anchor-point tool when you move the cursor over a point, and the add-anchor-point tool when you move the cursor over a segment where there is no point.*

Rather than saving each contour as a separate path, Park often drew several related contours (for example, all the shapes that make up the Mardi Gras mask at the bottom of the art ❷) as a single path. When he was ready to paint, he activated the path, selected only the subpaths he wanted to use, and converted them to selections. ☛ *When a path contains several subpaths, you can use the arrow tool with the Shift key to select only some of the subpaths. When you choose Make Selection, only the selected paths will be used to create selections.*

ADDING SOFT COLOR

Park began his color work by filling the *Background* layer with maroon, but for his other color areas, simply selecting and filling resulted in color that was too flat. Instead, after creating a new *Color* layer between the *Background* layer and the *Linework* layer, he used paths as masks, painting color into the illustration using the airbrush in various sizes and a pressure-sensitive tablet.

After he mixed each new foreground color in the Color Picker (consulting a swatch book as he chose colors), Park closed the Color Picker and added the color to the Swatches palette by moving the cursor into the blank area at the bottom of the palette (where the cursor turned into a paint bucket) and clicking. These swatches remained in the palette until he deleted them by Command-clicking to cut each unwanted swatch.

To avoid having a hard edge where an airbrush stroke met a selection, Park added a small feather

6 Park likes to use cool tones to give nearby warm tones more impact. When he had created a highlight color (by adding yellow to the flesh tone and removing both cyan and black) and airbrushed it along the right side of the trumpet player's hand, Park brushed a bit of purple onto the left side of the hand for contrast.

7 Park activated the *Instruments* path and selected only the subpath that follows the bell of the saxophone, then turned it into a selection. He set the foreground color to gold, then double-clicked the airbrush tool to display the Airbrush Options palette, where he set the Fade to about 20 steps and chose a large brush. When he chose Stroke Path, the stroke (masked inside the selection) followed the upper curve and faded out before it rounded the corner.

❻

❼

to each selection. "I was after the look of a conventional airbrush with a loose acetate mask," he says, "where a little of the spray would bleed underneath the mask." ☞ *The Make Selection function can be used to add a feather to a path as you turn it into a selection. Choose Make Selection from the Paths palette's popout menu or Option-click the Make Selection icon at the bottom center of the palette to open the Make Selection dialog box, where you can type in the feather radius.*

In the Airbrush Options palette, Park set the pressure slider to a fairly low number so color would build up as he layered brushstrokes. Then, beginning with larger areas and darker colors, he converted paths to selections, chose colors, and began airbrushing. ☞ *To change a tool's pressure or opacity without having to move your mouse or stylus away from your painting, type a number key — 1 for 10 percent, 2 for 20 percent, and so on, with 0 for 100 percent. Likewise, to change brush tips from the keyboard, used the left bracket ([ ) to move to the left and up in the Brushes palette, the right bracket ( ]) to move to the right and down.*

To further smooth the effect, Park dragged the blur tool along the edge of the airbrush stroke that didn't touch the mask ❸.

Faint shapes around the figures add a sense of movement ❹. To create two shapes around a musician's shoulder, Park duplicated the path that defined the suit (by dragging its icon to the New Path icon at the bottom of the Paths palette) and used the arrow tool to enlarge and reshape the path before converting it to a selection and airbrushing in color. Airbrushing next to another set of paths created shadows in the background ❺.

To add a suggestion of volume to the musicians, Park airbrushed highlights and shadows around the edges of the figures. Unconventional color choices add to the atmosphere of a smoky club — for example, shadows that are blue or purple, rather than black or gray ❻.

To save time, Park sometimes automates the process of brushing color along a path by selecting the path, choosing Stroke Path from the palette's popout menu, and choosing the airbrush as the stroking tool ❼. Photoshop applies all the airbrush's defaults, including opacity and fade, when it strokes the path. ▪

Creating Electronic Cut Paper

■ *by Sara Booth*

LIGHT IS THE KEY to cut paper, says Green Village, N.J., illustrator John Hovell. To capture that look in an electronic image, Hovell used Illustrator's radial gradients to establish a light direction, then placed his Illustrator shapes one by one in Photoshop to add soft shadows. When Hovell began working on a self-promotion using his cut-paper style, he made a pencil sketch, but rather than scanning it, he preferred the freedom of using his sketch for reference only, using Illustrator to try out different shapes until he got the effect he wanted ❶. "One of my problems is making myself pull back from making things too realistic. I'd draw something, and then have to backtrack and simplify it," he says.

Hovell consciously adds roughness to his illustrations. For example, his original mammoth leg was too smooth until he deleted a section and redrew it to give it a furry look ❷. To make the spear less geometric, he turned to the Roughen filter ❸. To define the wrinkles in the mammoth's trunk, he drew a triangle, Option-dragged to copy it, and blended between the two to generate a row of triangles, then adjusted points to resize the middle ones.

Hovell drew many of his shapes with Illustrator's pen tool, but he also built shapes, such as the mammoth's body, the caveman's body and head, and the clouds, out of circles, sometimes using the Pathfinder, Unite filter to join them with other shapes ❹.

The Pathfinder, Divide filter was useful in adding "folds." For example, Hovell used the pen tool to draw the four parts of the frame, then drew lines for folds and used the Divide filter to

"I've done a lot of technical illustration, but I wanted my self-promotion to be a little more stylish," says John Hovell. The Green Village, N.J., illustrator combines Illustrator and Photoshop for a convincing electronic simulation of cut paper. Gradients are crucial to the illusion, and Hovell has developed a way to transform a radial gradient into an elliptical one.

1 Hovell used Illustrator to experiment with different treatments of the mammoth. He tried making the trunk curved, using a circle for the top of the head, and applying the gradient in the legs at different angles.

2 The original mammoth leg was too smooth. So Hovell selected two points and deleted the line segment between them, then used the pen to reconnect those two points, this time drawing a jagged shape for fur.

3 To make the spear look more uneven, Hovell chose Filter, Distort, Roughen, using very low Size and Detail settings and selecting the Smooth option.

4 For clouds, Hovell drew a series of circles (shown in red) and chose Filter, Pathfinder, Unite. He drew a rectangle (shown in blue), chose Filter, Pathfinder, Divide, and deleted some contours, then applied the Unite filter again to join the remaining contours into a single shape.

❶

❷

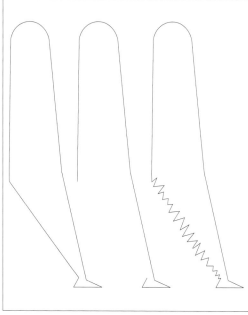

❸

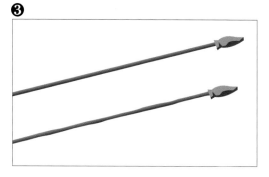

❹

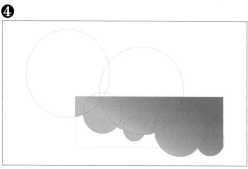

separate each side of the frame into two shapes. When he filled both shapes with the same gradient at the same angle, the repetition gave the appearance of shadows cast by a fold. A similar technique added shape to the spearhead **❺**. ☞ *To quickly apply gradients and other attributes to several Illustrator contours, select them, then use the eyedropper tool to double-click on an object with the desired attributes.*

Gradients were Hovell's primary Illustrator tool for indicating a light source. He filled the back-ground shapes with simple linear gradients — for example, to create the mist at the base of the mountains. But nearly all the shapes that make up the mammoth and caveman are filled with radial gradients, hinting at both a three-dimensional shape and a slight shininess in the "paper."

After applying the gradient to a shape, Hovell dragged the gradient tool to place the highlight at the top left. To make the mammoth's eye and ear recede, he dragged the gradient in the opposite direction, placing the highlight at lower right.

In some cases, what Hovell wanted was a slight variation on radial gradients. "In Illustrator, there's no such thing as an elliptical grad," he says. "But you can make one" — by scaling a shape after a radial has been applied to it **❻**. Hovell used this technique for the caveman's forehead and lips and the mammoth's tusks. "It takes a little experimenting to get it to look right," he says.

A few linear gradients used on the elements (for example, the spear, the base of the mammoth's tusk, and the caveman's clothes) required a different lighting strategy. Hovell made a copy of the original mammoth gradient (by clicking the Duplicate button in the Gradient dialog box), changed its shape from radial to linear, then added a lighter color between the starting point and the ending point for a highlight.

Once Hovell had all the pieces in place, he made a laser print of the entire illustration to use as reference as he positioned pieces and added shadows in Photoshop. Then he copied groups of contours that could all get shadow treatment at once (for example, the frame, the mountains, the clouds and background gradient, and the caveman

❺

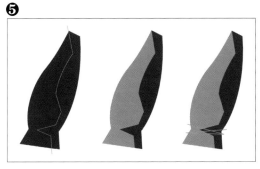

❻

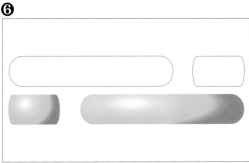

❼

and mammoth) and pasted each group into a new Illustrator file.

Hovell opened a new Photoshop document and began using Edit, Place to import these Illustrator files as pixels, placing each on its own layer. He began by importing the sky, then applying the Gaussian Blur filter with a radius of about 9 to smooth the edges of the clouds.

On a new layer, Hovell imported the mountains. Then, to add a shadow behind them, he placed a new layer behind the mountain layer and imported them again. The mountains were placed as selected pixels. Hovell offset the selection slightly, filled it with black, and applied the Gaussian Blur filter with a radius of about 4. Then he set the layer's opacity to 30 percent. He used the same technique, varying the blur radius and the layer opacity, to import the caveman and mammoth and add a shadow. ☞ *To reapply the same Photoshop filter with the same settings, type Command-F. To reopen the last-used filter's dialog box so that you can enter new settings, choose Command-Option-F.*

Hovell knew that some elements, such as the mammoth's legs and the caveman's facial features, would cast shadows not only on the background, but also on other elements. So he returned to his Illustrator file and copied these shapes into new Illustrator documents. On a new layer, he placed the mammoth's legs and added a shadow. Then, with the shadow layer active and the mammoth layer visible, he used the eraser to remove the parts of the shadow that overlapped the legs, leaving only the parts behind the legs. ☞ *Typing the letter* E *selects Photoshop's eraser tool. Type* E

again to toggle through the eraser options: Air-brush, Paintbrush, Pencil, and Block.

Hovell applied shadows behind the caveman's nose, eyebrows, and cheeks the same way. For smaller shadows, like the one the spear casts across the caveman's chest and the one where the spear enters the mammoth's leg, he used the pen tool ❼. The final step was to import the frame. Hovell placed it on its own layer in Photoshop, added a shadow, and then applied the Add Noise filter to give it a slightly rougher appearance. ∎

5 Hovell drew the spear-head, drew a line where he wanted the color to change, and chose Filter, Pathfinder, Divide to split it along the line. A gold-filled stroke, drawn with the pen tool, represents the thong used to tie the head to the spear.

6 To create the elliptical gradient on the caveman's forehead, Hovell drew a round-cornered rectangle, then selected the points at one end and dragged until the shape was the right size. He used the scale tool to reduce the shape horizontally, then applied a radial gradient and scaled the shape back to its original size. The gradient was scaled along with the shape.

7 The mammoth and caveman both cast a single shadow on the background (top). "The tricky part was some of the extra shadows," Hovell says. For the shadow cast by the spear on the caveman's chest, Hovell traced the spear with the pen tool to make a shadow, then used the eraser to remove the parts of the shadow that extended beyond the body. He used the same technique for the shadow of the caveman's wrap on his legs.

Seeing Is Believing

■ *by Lisa Belhage*

WHEN I CREATE photorealistic medical product illustrations, I try to work with the product in hand so I can really see how light plays on it and with it, instead of trying to intellectualize how it should look. So with a Urias urine collection device in hand, I used Illustrator and Dimensions to generate convincing outlines of all the parts. Then I took these outlines into Photoshop as paths. In concert with Photoshop's painting tools and layers, they allowed me to render the device realistically, even the tricky transparent parts.

To generate the paths I would need, I began by measuring each part of the product and replicating it on a two-dimensional plane in Illustrator. Then I imported each shape into Dimensions, where it was extruded and rotated according to the actual dimensions of the product. To produce a final 3-D model of the product in Dimensions, I assembled the parts, keeping the perspective at None and flipping around to different views as I worked to line them up precisely.

When the model was finished, I looked at the layout from the art director to choose the view and perspective (in this case, I set the view to Front and the perspective to Wide Angle), then grouped all the parts and rotated them into position. I tried to plan ahead and make sure I had all the parts I was going to need built up so I could rotate them all together at the same time.

Finally, I rendered the image and exported to Illustrator. It doesn't matter to me how the image is filled in Dimensions, because I never use the

❶

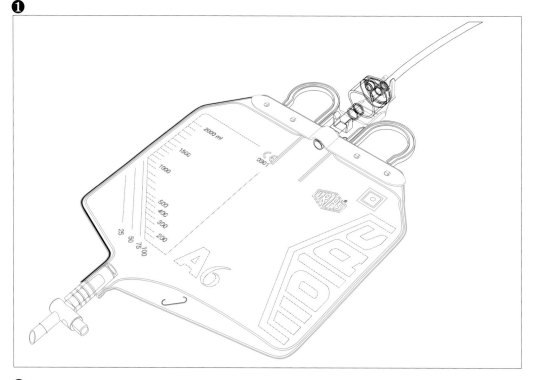

1 I used Illustrator and Dimensions to create paths to use as "friskets" for my Photoshop painting. When the paths were finalized, I placed related contours on the same Illustrator layer (each layer is shown in a different color), then drew a rectangle the size of the final image and copied it onto each layer. That assured that when I copied the layers into Photoshop as paths, they would register precisely — plus, when I copied the first layer onto the clipboard and opened a new Photoshop file, Photoshop automatically made the file the same size as the Illustrator layer.

❷

2 When I began painting the transparent portions of the device in Photoshop, the very back layer consisted of the rims of the cylinder. Then came the tubes and valve that ran down through the cylinder. I applied a small mask to this layer to allow the back rims of the previous layer to show though, and I painted in a little of the blue color from the plastic shining through the tube as well.

resulting shading. For the same reason, I stick to draft render to save time.

Using Illustrator again, I cleaned up the image and created the paths that I would use as "friskets" in Photoshop. Dimensions generates a lot of unnecessary (for me) lines that I have to delete. I use the Pathfinder filters Minus Front, Minus Back, Intersect, and Unite to create discrete areas that define the shape of the product. The resulting "sketch" I faxed to the client for approval. In this case, the client requested the cylinder be rotated a bit, which I did manually in Illustrator rather than going back into Dimensions.

To prepare for my Photoshop work, I organized layers in Illustrator so that each layer represented a part of the product to be rendered. Layer by layer, I copied the Illustrator file over to the Photoshop file as paths.

To begin my work in Photoshop, I usually fill the entire area to be worked with a base color, then check Preserve Transparency for the active layer in the Layers palette. That way no unintentional painting occurs outside the area I'm working on.

All non-transparent parts I painted fully and in no particular order. I used the paths I created in Illustrator to create selections, generally using no feathering because it is faster. (The rough edges are smoothed later with a blur over the entire image.) Any light lines left over along the selection lines are eliminated by choosing an appropriate darker color, making sure the Preserve Transparency box is not checked in the Layers palette, then choosing Edit, Fill and setting the fill mode to Behind.

To create the transparent parts, the important first step was observing exactly the order in which the parts overlay each other. They were painted with close observation, only applying paint to the areas that obscured the structures below. To place highlights and shadows on tube shapes, I sometimes draw straight-line paths, then stroke them with the airbrush tool. ■

❸

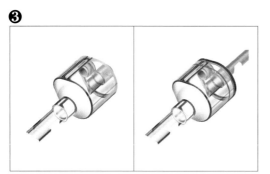

❹

❺

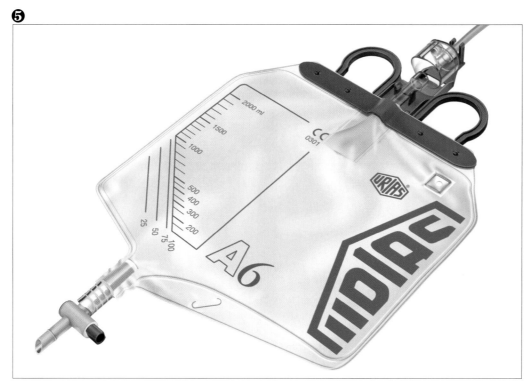

3 The third layer I painted was the cylinder itself. Here all I did was paint the highlights and reflections that concealed the structures behind them. Strong reflections and highlights will generally increase opacity. They are very effective at establishing the depth of a transparent image. The final layer was a simple painting of the top rims and hose.

4 To replicate the way the blue plastic parts behaved as seen through the cylinder, I created another layer and copied onto it the parts of the blue plastic behind the cylinder (using the cylinder paths to make the selection). Then I used varying Gaussian blur settings (from 1 behind the bottom of the cylinder up to 4 for the areas behind the tubes). Using the smudge tool, I dragged across a few areas where the clear plastic created distortions. Finally I desaturated the blurred layer by 20%.

5 After the layers were completed, all that remained was to run a blur over the entire image to get rid of the rough edges and enhance the photorealistic quality.

Flexible Duotone Color

■ *by Janet Ashford*

BETTER-THAN-LIFE PHOTOREALISM was the goal when Rubbermaid sought illustrations for pressure-sensitive labels for its Rough Tote containers. The illustrations also had to be in a form that made it easy to change the colors on the labels to match the containers. The designers at Logos Studio of Cleveland, Ohio, found that duotone artwork provided just the solution they needed. Art director Fred Wypasek worked out the details with illustrator Gary Cirino.

Duotone illustrations seemed the best solution for two reasons: First, because of the registration problems inherent in flexography (the standard method for printing on pressure-sensitive adhesive stock), duotones of a spot color and black would be easier to print accurately than four-color process. Second, product colors could be changed on press by simply changing the custom ink color without changing the color plate.

CONSTRUCTING THE TUBS AND LIDS

The four containers in the Rough Tote line vary in size, but the lids are the same shape. Cirino took a wide-angle photograph of a tub and and a lid and scanned them in grayscale. To get the most detail for tracing, the scans were made at 200 percent of the actual photo size, at 300 dpi. They were opened in Photoshop and saved in EPS mode so they could be imported into Illustrator as art, rather than as low-resolution PICT templates.

Cirino traced the scans in Illustrator, using the pen tool to create the top of the tub and the left part of the bottom, reflecting a copy of the left side to make the right. He used Illustrator's Gradient dialog box to fill these shapes with complex gradients composed of grays ❶. A similar process was used for the lid.

The Illustrator files for the bases and lid were opened in Photoshop at twice the size needed for the label; again, the resolution was 300 dpi. The next step was to create a clipping path to silhouette the tub when it was placed in the label. Cirino used the magic wand to select the background and inverted the selection to select the tub. He converted this selection to a path, adjusted points for a better fit, and saved it to use as a clipping path.

ADDING REALISTIC LIGHT

Cirino converted the files to RGB and opened them in Painter so he could use the Apply Lighting function to make them look more realistic ❷. (This could also have been done in Photoshop 3 with the Render, Lighting Effects filter.) ☛ *In Photoshop as in Painter, a file must be in RGB mode in order to apply lighting effects.*

The Painter files were saved as TIFFs and opened in Photoshop, where Cirino added punch to the lighting after first converting the artwork back to grayscale mode ❸. Cirino also replaced the shaded gray background with a 60 percent black fill so that when the duotone was made and the container silhouetted, any background pixels

Duotone artwork made it possible to print labels for an entire line of Rubbermaid's RoughTote containers using a single set of plates. Logos Studio's Gary Cirino, working with art director Fred Wypasek, changed each illustration to match the container color by simply changing the spot color used to print the label.

1 In Illustrator, Cirino traced a scanned photo to create the base, then filled the contours (shown in red) with complex gradients. By choosing Object, Gradient and moving sliders while viewing the art in Preview mode, Cirino could adapt the gradient for realism: Gradient-filled objects update interactively as sliders are moved. A photo of a single tub was used to generate the art for all four products: Two of the containers have the same proportions, so the same art could be used for both, and differences of proportion for the other containers could be handled in Illustrator by moving the bottom points.

❶

❷

❸

❹

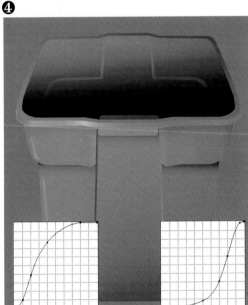

❺

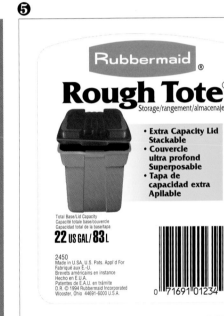

Rubbermaid ®

Rough Tote ®
Storage/rangement/almacenaje

- **Extra Capacity Lid Stackable**
- **Couvercle ultra profond Superposable**
- **Tapa de capacidad extra Apilable**

Total Base/Lid Capacity
Capacité totale base/couvercle
Capacidad total de la base/tapa

22 US GAL/ **83** L

2450
Made in U.SA, U.S. Pats. Appl'd For
Fabriqué aux É.-U.
Brevets américains en instance
Hecho en E.U.A.
Patentes de E.A.U. en trámite
D.R. © 1994 Rubbermaid Incorporated
Wooster, Ohio 44691-6000 U.S.A.

0 71691 01234 4

2 To emphasize highlights, shadows, and reflections, Cirino opened the file in Painter and chose Effects, Surface Control, Apply Lighting. He specified white ambient light and positioned a white light source to shine across the container from the upper left. After adjusting brightness, distance, and other parameters, he saved the settings (by clicking Save in the Apply Lighting dialog box) so he could apply the same effects to the other bases and the lid.

3 To create highlights in Photoshop, Cirino drew shapes with the pen tool to accentuate the reflections he had created in Painter. He turned each path into a selection by dragging its name to the Make Selection icon in the Paths palette, and feathered to soften the edges, then filled each selection with a lighter gray than the surrounding area. For shadows under sharp edges, Cirino painted in an unfeathered selection with the paintbrush in Multiply mode. He saved his paths so he could adjust them for use on the other containers.

4 Cirino converted each file to duotone mode in Photoshop, specifying black and a spot color. He adjusted the duotone curves so the spot color (left) reached 100 percent coverage at about 70 percent in the gray scale. The settings for the black curves (right) left little or no black except in shadows.

5 The finished duotone art was saved in EPS format with a clipping path so it could be incorporated in a final label layout in Illustrator, along with type and logo elements. Each label was printed in five spot colors: red, yellow, black, plus one color for the lid and another for the container.

that might be included in the selection wouldn't make a contrasting outline when the tub was placed in the label.

CONVERTING TO DUOTONE MODE
Once the gray illustrations were finished, Cirino opened the illustration of one base and chose Mode, Duotone. He then chose Duotone from the Type popout menu in the Duotone Options dialog box. He specified a spot color as his second ink, then adjusted the duotone curves so that the spot color would be applied at 100 percent opacity starting in the midtone range of the image, while the black ink would be applied primarily in the shadow tones. Because the result was virtually

solid color in the midtones, this combination worked best to create a good match between the appearance of the product itself and the color of the illustration on the label. He then saved the duotone curves so that he could apply the same values to the lid and the other tub illustrations, changing only the spot colors ❹.

The duotones were saved in EPS format and imported, along with their clipping paths, into Illustrator ❺, where Cirino added type, the UPC symbol, the die-cut outline, and the Rubbermaid logo. The Illustrator file was then turned over to the printer, who distorted the label to compensate for stretching as the soft flexography plates wrap around the paper stock on a roller. ■

Electronic Batik

■ *by Lee Risser*

COULDN'T HAVE BEEN older than eight or nine when I spotted my first batik print. (All right, it was an imitation. But what did I know about reality at that age?) My mother had taken me to the fabric store to buy material for an Easter dress, and naturally, I picked out the batik pattern with a row of ochre and brick red elephants marching around the border. Mom said no, but I never forgot that shopping expedition or the pattern.

I didn't know at the time that my beloved elephant print was a batik look-alike. I didn't discover the word *batik* — or the technique — until high school years when I stumbled onto an eye-opening article in *Smithsonian* magazine and took my revenge on Mom by turning the bathtub into a dye vat. The dye could be rinsed out of the tub easily, but it tended to splash on things that weren't readily rinsed. And that mess was nothing compared to the messes I generated by painting with melted wax. (In traditional batik, wax is applied to fabric and then dyed. The wax resists the dye to produce the pattern.)

It's been years since I had the time to indulge in sloppy hobbies, but I never lost my fascination with batik prints. So when I accepted a pro bono assignment to design T-shirts for a jamboree held at a summer camp for at-risk children, I decided that it was a good opportunity to do some exploring and develop an electronic version of batik. I always hesitate to experiment on paying jobs because I can't ask clients to foot the bill for my trial-and-error time. But with pro bono work, I don't have to worry about per-hour productivity.

1 To create an electronic "batik" print, I drew a simple design in FreeHand with a pressure-sensitive tablet and the freehand tool. (First, I double-clicked on the tool's icon in the toolbox to open the FreeHand Tool dialog box and chose Variable Stroke and Tight Fit.)

2 After adding color, I exported the file in Illustrator 5.5 format so it could be opened in Photoshop.

3 Using the original colors as a guide, I repainted the image with Photoshop's airbrush tool to produce richer tones. I used the magic wand tool to select by color and painted inside the selection border. (After I made the selection, but before I began to paint, I chose New Layer from the Layers palette and airbrushed each color on its own layer.)

4 For the cracked-wax look of batik, I began with a photo of a bare tree. I lifted out a small section and boosted the contrast (Image, Adjust, Brightness/Contrast or Command-B) until I was left with nothing but spidery lines. Then I changed the black fill to brown and chose Edit, Define Pattern to turn the lines into a pattern fill.

❶

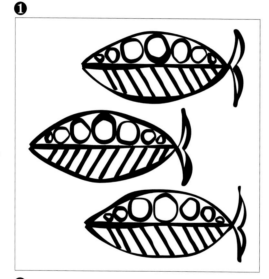

❷

❸

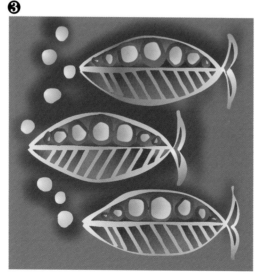

❹

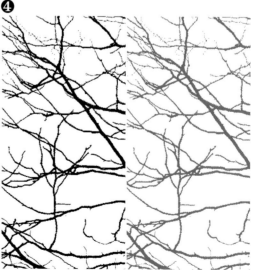

All in all, it was easier than I expected it to be (I could have billed a client for the work without feeling guilty). The tricky part, naturally, was creating the cracked-wax effect that characterizes batik. Just before I started the project, I had been putting some family photos in an album, and a picture of my son playing outdoors in the winter caught my eye. In the background was a tree, and the texture of those bare limbs came awfully close to the crackled effect I wanted. Even so, I anticipated unforeseen problems converting bare limbs into batik-like crackling. But luckily, this was one of those rare times that the solution came quickly. All I had to do was scan the photo on my grayscale scanner and use Photoshop's contrast controls to turn the tree limbs into a spidery pattern that looked convincingly like cracked wax.

I selected a small section of the limbs, looking for an area with a lot of fine lines, and turned it into a repeating pattern in Photoshop. I didn't even have to make the pattern seamless. When I began building the Photoshop file for the electronic batik pattern, I placed each color on a separate layer and sandwiched a copy of the cracked wax pattern between each layer. That way, I could move the pattern around on top of each color to find a position where the seams didn't show (or didn't show enough to cause any problem).

The exception was the background layer with the blue water. I needed to use the entire width of the pattern to fill the background, and the seams were clearly visible. So I took another crop from my tree limb photo and used it as a pattern fill in a separate layer. Although the seams were obvious in each layer, they disappeared when the two patterns were combined — the repeating sections were created at different sizes, so together, they form a random pattern. ■

❺

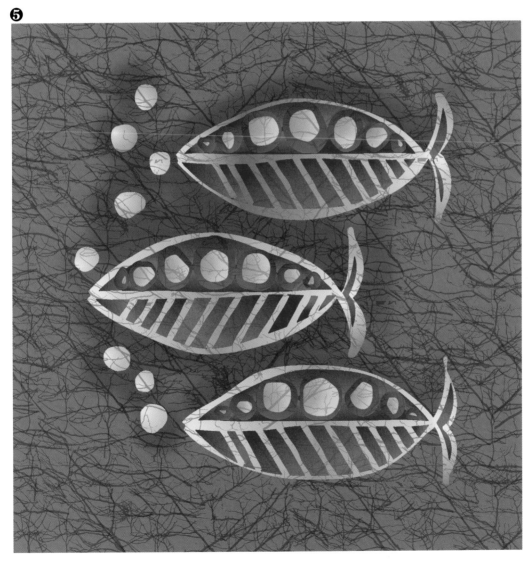

5 I placed a new, blank layer on top of every color layer in the Photoshop file, then filled each of the blank layers with the cracked wax pattern by choosing Edit, Fill and selecting Pattern as the Use option. Although I used the same brown pattern in each layer, I was able to change the color to correspond to the tone in the underlying layer by selecting Multiply in the Layers palette and adjusting the opacity. I also repositioned the wax pattern on each layer (by pressing the *V* key to access the move tool) so the cracks wouldn't match up from one layer to the next. I wanted random crackling, and not a continuous pattern.

Electronic Block Printing

■ *by Talitha Harper*

WHEN THE PHONE RANG, Kay Alwyn was pushing deadlines on paying jobs, and the last thing she wanted to hear was a request for pro bono work. But this project was close to the Philadelphia illustrator's heart. A community children's center was sponsoring an African-American festival, and a vendor had promised to print T-shirts for free — if the center could provide the artwork. Alwyn decided she could devote an hour or two to the project, and that meant keeping the job simple. Fortunately, the center's request was modest: a colorful design with no type so the children wouldn't feel that the T-shirts were outdated once the event was over.

Since she needed to work quickly, Alwyn went directly to the computer and roughed out a stylized gnu in FreeHand, using the ellipse and rectangle tools to define basic shapes and then repositioning individual points to give the form a more graceful

Philadelphia children's illustrator Kay Alwyn allowed herself two hours to produce this pro bono T-shirt design, using FreeHand to build the basic forms and Photoshop's layer modes to give the image a rough texture. Laser prints were used to produce screen printing plates.

shape ❶. To create a horn, she drew two overlapping circles and turned them into a crescent with the Punch command. This crescent was cloned (Command-=) to produce the other horn ❷.

BUILDING THE OUTLINE

Alwyn planned to color the design in Photoshop. She wanted to give the image the rough look of hand-printed textiles, and she felt that Photoshop's filters and brush controls could give her the primitive look she wanted. So she built the Free-Hand design in black-and-white, defining white shapes with thick black outlines.

To create the outline, she first selected all the elements forming the gnu and merged them into a single contour by choosing Xtras, Path Operations, Union. This shape was cloned, and the clone was given a broad stroke and placed behind the white-filled contour. But this caused some problems. The outline's sharp corners added definition to the gnu's hoofs and tail — but the same sharp points looked clumsy around the ends of the horns. So Alwyn used the Undo command (Command-Z) to back up a few steps, eliminating the cloned outline and breaking the united contour into its original parts. Then she created separate outlines for the horns in order to use different Cap and Join settings: butt caps and pointed joins for the body (so that the line around the hoofs and tail would be squared off) and rounded caps and joins for the horns (for more graceful crescents) ❸.

After adding a few details (a collar around the gnu's neck, bands on the horns, and a horizon line in the background), Alwyn exported the image (Command-E) in Illustrator 5.5 format so that she could open it in Photoshop ❹.

MUTING THE OUTLINE

Once she opened the file in Photoshop, Alwyn applied the Diffuse filter to break down the black outline. But the filter didn't give her the ragged look she wanted, so she used the Mode options in the Layers palette to rough up the black linework.

Alwyn reopened the file in Photoshop to get a fresh copy of the image with no diffused edges, then selected all and used the Select, Float command (Command-J) to create a floating copy. This copy was turned into a separate layer by clicking on the words *Floating Selection* in the Layers palette and dragging to the new layer icon at the bottom of the palette. (This opened the Make Layer dialog box, where Alwyn entered the name *Gnu* for the new layer.) Then she clicked on the name *Background* in the palette to activate that layer and deleted the original image. Once the artwork was lifted off the background layer, Alwyn could choose Dissolve mode to break up the black tones ❺. ☞ *Photoshop's layering modes cannot*

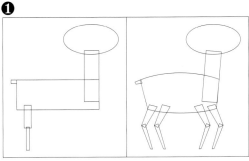

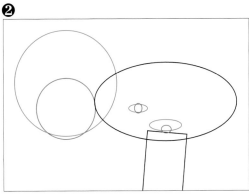

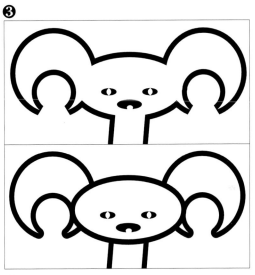

1 Alwyn used basic shapes to rough out a gnu in Free-Hand. After rotating the neck, she ungrouped the rectangles forming the tail, body, and legs so that she could reposition individual points to reshape the form. Corner points in the body were converted to curve points by selecting each point and clicking on the Curve icon in the Inspector palette. After reshaping one leg, Alwyn cloned it, then reflected copies of both legs.

2 To create the eyes, nose, and horns, Alwyn drew a set of circles and ovals (shown in blue) and placed smaller shapes on top (shown in red). When she applied the Punch function (Xtras, Path Operations, Punch), the shapes on top punched holes through the underlying forms. Clones of the horn and eye were reflected across the center of the ellipse forming the head.

3 The original Cap and Join specifications (in the Path Inspector palette) produced a blunt, squared-off outline around the horns. So Alwyn changed the shape of the contour by clicking on the round Cap and Join icons in the Path Inspector. (She also created a separate outline for the gnu's head to give it more definition.)

4 After drawing the collar, Alwyn Shift-clicked to select all the collar elements and used the Send Backward command (Command-]) to place it behind the head.

5 In Photoshop, Alwyn selected the *Gnu* layer by
clicking on its name in the
Layers palette, then chose
Dissolve from the Mode
menu and set the opacity
to 90 percent.

6 After the black channel
was duplicated and inverted
(Image, Map, Invert or Command-I), Alwyn selected the
black area around the gnu
with the magic wand tool
and chose Select, Inverse.
Deleting filled the selection
with white (the background
color). This channel was
named *Gnu Outline.*

7 Alwyn created a new,
black-filled channel, then
Shift-clicked on the name
Gnu Outline in the Channels
palette to activate the selection in the new channel. She
chose Select, Modify, Border and set a 20-pixel radius
in the Border dialog box to
create a new "outline" selection (shown in blue). She
pressed the Command key
and used the lasso tool to
delete the bottom half of the
horizon line from the outline
selection and deleted to fill
the outline with white.

8 Using a large soft-edged
brush, Alwyn applied color
at 75 percent opacity.

9 The paint opacity was
changed to 100 percent to
add brighter color around
the inside of the horns.

❺

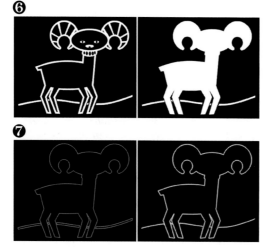

❻

❼

❽

❾

*be applied on the background layer. You must
place the art on a layer above the background
before selecting an option from the Mode menu.*

When she saw the Dissolve effect, Alwyn decided to use Photoshop channels make the black
lines even rougher. She temporarily selected Normal mode and 100 percent opacity for the *Gnu*
layer so that the linework returned to solid black.
After activating the black channel, she chose Duplicate Channel from the Channels palette menu
and inverted to turn the black linework into white
selection areas. Alwyn wanted to use the channel
in combination with Photoshop's Border function
to select only the outer fringes of the lines. But the
border would surround all the white tones in the
channel — and in this case, that would include
areas Alwyn didn't want to alter. So she modified
the selection channel by filling the gnu entirely
with white ❻ before defining the border ❼. She
then reapplied the Dissolve effect, Shift-clicked
on the name of the border channel in the Channels
palette to load the selection, and deleted. (The
Border function creates a feathered selection. So
deleting removed a feathered fringe of pixels from
the linework, creating a tattered effect.)

Alwyn used a soft-edged brush to apply color
on the background layer, working from muted
tones ❽ to deeper colors ❾. Once she completed
the painting, she selected all and applied the Add
Noise filter on the background layer to churn up
the color, creating a mottled effect that complemented the ragged border.

Opening the Image, Canvas Size dialog box,
Alwyn added a half inch to the height and width.
Then, working on the *Gnu* layer, she drew a black
frame around the edges of the canvas. Because
the layer was set to Dissolve mode at 90 percent
opacity, this frame took on a rough, pixelated look.
She selected the outside margin of this black border, gave the selection a 20-pixel feather (by
choosing Select, Feather and entering 20 in the
Feather Selection dialog box), and deleted.

OUTPUTTING THE DESIGN

Because this was a rush job — and because the
screen printer planned to use an 85-line screen —
Alwyn output color separations directly from her
laser printer. To set the image to print at 85 lpi,
she chose File, Page Setup and clicked the Screen
button to open the Halftone Screens dialog box.
She entered 85 as the Frequency setting and
chose Line as the Shape option. Clicking OK returned her to the Page Setup dialog box where she
selected Registration Marks. Finally, she chose
File, Print (Command-P) and activated the Print
Separations function at the bottom of the dialog
box. The laser prints were used as camera-ready
art to produce the screenprinting plates. ■

Hand-Painted Effects with Channels

■ *by Sara Booth*

AIRBRUSH FREEDOM AND PostScript precision — that's what Mike Schmalz got when he used FreeHand to generate channels to use in Photoshop. The Dubuque, Iowa, illustrator used multiple blends in FreeHand to create the graduated waves, then airbrushed in color in Photoshop. Applying filters to some channels made it easy to brush in hand-painted texture.

When he was asked to design a poster for an annual jazz series, Schmalz first made a rough sketch for composition. When this was approved, he worked out tight pencil sketches for the clock tower and the dancers. He scanned the sketches, then redrew them in FreeHand, placing each element on its own layer. For the dancers and the clock tower, he also created outlines that he would use to paint a glow around them ❶.

To make later work easier, Schmalz drew a white, unstroked rectangle the size of the final art, then cloned it onto each layer. When the layers were imported into Photoshop, lining up these rectangles would assure accurate registration.

Once he had finished the main figures, Schmalz began working on the image's biggest challenge: the waves. He used circles to generate one wave shape ❷ and adjusted it by eye ❸, then created a four-step blend ❹ in a smooth arc across the page. Then he fine-tuned the placement of each wave to be sure its relationships with the dancers and the clock tower were pleasing.

Before he began generating his final blends, Schmalz opened FreeHand's Document Inspector and entered 2540 dpi as the resolution so that FreeHand would use the proper number of steps for each blend. ☛ *FreeHand chooses the number of steps in a blend based on two variables: the color differences between the blended objects and the printer resolution set in the Document Inspector palette. To change the number of steps once the blend is created, display the Document Inspector while the blend is still selected and enter a new number of steps.*

The waves were grouped into five large light-to-dark clusters. To make painting those clusters easier, Schmalz generated light-to-dark blends in

To create a poster for an outdoor jazz festival, Mike Schmalz (Dubuque, Iowa) used FreeHand to generate the building blocks for a Photoshop painting. To give dimension to the waves in the background, Schmalz generated a series of gray-to-black blends in FreeHand, then imported them into Photoshop as channels, allowing him to load the graduated selections and paint inside them.

1 Schmalz knew he would want a glow around the outer edges of the figures and tower. So once he had redrawn his sketches in FreeHand, he roughly traced the outer edges with the pen, filled this path (shown in red) with black, and saved it in its own file.

2 To make a wave, he drew a circle, Option-dragged a copy, and scaled it to 30%. He blended, ungrouped, and dragged the circles until they touched.

3 Schmalz changed the circles to ellipses by scaling them 50% vertically. He used the knife to cut away half of each ellipse and joined the points. The result was still too rough, so he selected the joined points and converted them to curve points (by clicking the Curve Point icon in the Object Inspector palette), then adjusted individual curves for a more fluid path.

4 Schmalz first worked out the waves' basic fan shape by drawing a line, rotating a copy, and blending between them. When he was happy with the arrangement, he used the same settings to fan copies of the wave.

5 To shade the waves, Schmalz needed a Photoshop channel with a gradient that followed the wave. He used blends in FreeHand to create it. First, he cloned the middle four waves so each area was defined by a pair of waves. He gave a white stroke to the top wave of each pair and a black stroke to the bottom, cloned the pairs onto a new layer to use later, and blended between each pair.

6 Schmalz also needed a blend for each individual wave. In the layer he had just created, he applied a 10-step blend between each pair of waves to create the outlines of the new blends. Again he cloned the middle waves so each area was defined by a pair of waves, gave the bottom waves a black stroke and the top ones a 20% gray stroke, and blended.

❶

❷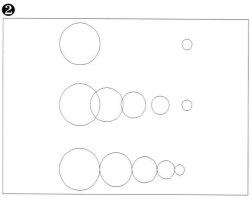

❸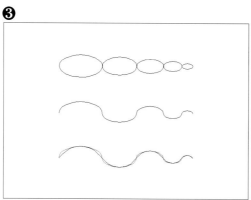

❹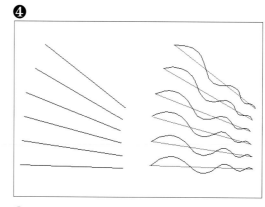

❺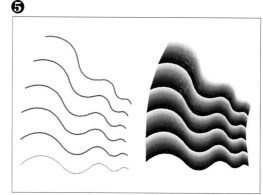

❻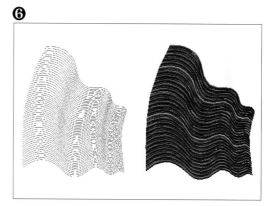

FreeHand by blending between the waves ❺. He prepared smaller blends to allow him to paint each individual wave ❻, and he made another blend to help him to create a fade effect at the left and the top ❼. Finally, he saved each layer as a separate file and exported them in Illustrator format so that he could place them in Photoshop.

When he works on complex illustrations in Photoshop, Schmalz begins by saving a composite file, in which he places each of the elements in its own channel, giving the channel the same name as the original file it was made from. "It can be tricky to get blends into Photoshop," he says, "and some of the complex blended files take 10 to 20 minutes to open in Photoshop." So having them saved in a single file means he can always access the original grayscale file without having to spend the time importing it from FreeHand again.

Before he began painting the illustration, Schmalz selected a palette in Photoshop ❽. He began by filling squares with his chosen colors; when he was happy with the entire palette, he loaded the colors into Photoshop's Swatches palette by clicking each color with the eyedropper, then Shift-clicking a square in the palette.

Schmalz painted the dancers, the clock tower, and the waves in three different files to keep file sizes workable. To paint the dancers, Schmalz opened his composite file, copied the channel that contained the sketch of the dancers, and pasted it into a channel in a new file, where he would use it as a guide as he painted. The sketch had a closed outline around each color area, so he could activate the channel and select an area with the magic wand. He chose Select, Expand to enlarge the selection by one pixel, then returned to the docu-

7 Blending between two corners gave Schmalz a shape he could use to make the image fade out at upper left.

8 Because he knew the art would be used on T-shirts as well as posters, Schmalz used only two process inks for many of his colors to make things easier for the screen printers. He also mixed a warm black (which he used for shading in warm areas like the skin and the clock tower) and a cool black which he used for shading in the waves and other cool areas.

C	100	C	100	C	100	C	100
M	70	M	95	M	45	M	0
Y	0	Y	0	Y	0	Y	100
K	100	K	0	K	0	K	36
C	85	C	40	C	0	C	0
M	0	M	0	M	100	M	50
Y	100	Y	90	Y	100	Y	100
K	0	K	0	K	0	K	0
C	0	C	0	C	30	C	0
M	15	M	100	M	100	M	100
Y	100	Y	0	Y	0	Y	100
K	0	K	6	K	18	K	100

9 To add texture to the waves, the edge of the wave area, and the shading on the clock tower, Schmalz used the Graphic Pen filter. Copying a channel (left), he applied the filter to create a textured version (right). He loaded the channel as a selection and painted in it.

ment area and painted inside the selection with the airbrush tool.

To add the glow around the dancers, Schmalz created a new layer below the figures. In that layer, he loaded the outline channel he had made earlier and filled it with yellow, then airbrushed in red. When he was happy with the way the outline looked, he merged the two layers. Finally, he used an airbrush with a very small brush to paint in the tiny black outlines that define the figures, following the outline in the channel.

For the waves, he loaded the channel with the narrow waves and painted inside it with shades of blue and violet, varying the colors but working generally from light to dark. Because each of the original waves graduated from gray to black, the channel masked out more paint at the top of each wave than at the bottom for a dimensional effect.

When he had painted all the waves, Schmalz loaded the channel with the broad waves and painted in it with cool black to add the large-scale shading. Finally, he gave some areas rough diagonal brushstrokes by painting in a channel created with the Graphic Pen filter **9**. ☞ *The Graphic Pen filter is included in Photoshop 4.0 in the Artistic submenu of the Filter menu. It is also available as a plug-in in the Adobe Gallery Effects package.*

The final step was to mute the colors and add texture by applying the Add Noise filter to each file, using an amount of 40 and checking the Gaussian button. The filter added noise to both the figures and the background, so in each file Schmalz loaded the outline channels to select only the figures, which he copied and pasted into the final file. ■

Changing Seasons

■ *by Mike Hill*

THE GREATEST BENEFIT an illustrator can gain from using a computer is flexibility. The ability to make seamless changes, even late in the process, is a huge plus. The computer also makes it possible to work in new ways that expand the scope of what an illustrator can offer a client.

I discovered one such technique while working on a project for Loyola College in Maryland. I've worked on several projects for them in the past, and although they have been fair about budgets, cost is always a factor. In this case, the project was an invitation to an alumni Christmas party — a small print run with a very tight budget.

At first I was inclined to take the project on anyway, despite the budget limitations, because Loyola had always been such a good client. Then I had an idea. What if I could produce a multi-purpose piece of art? The clients agreed that if I could provide an illustration that they could use in several different ways, they could justify paying a higher price for the art.

So I created a file that had a basic piece of black-and-white line art at its base. When layers were turned on and off, the scene changed from summer to winter, and Christmas decorations could be displayed or hidden. The result is a single piece of art that can be used several differ-

❶

1 I placed my grayscale scan in Painter, cloned it (File, Clone), and filled the clone with black. To use the original clone source as a template, I turned on the tracing paper option (Canvas, Tracing Paper or Command-T, or click the tracing paper icon at the upper right corner of the screen). With the scratchboard variant of the pen tool and white defined as the paint color, I used the sketch as a guide to rough out the image, then turned tracing paper off and continued to work, using a range of brush styles and sizes.

2 I placed the Painter woodcut in its own locked layer in FreeHand, then added color-filled shapes in layers behind it. To allow the color to show through the white areas in the woodcut, I checked Transparent in the Object Inspector palette.

3 By displaying other layers, the clients could turn on the Christmas decorations and the stars. Note that the Christmas tree, which is on its own layer, completely covers the smaller tree in the base file.

❷

❸

ent ways with only a minimal amount of extra effort on my part.

I began by sketching a prominent campus building, using felt marker because it allows me to draw in a style that captures the look of a woodcut. After the clients approved the sketch, I scanned it and opened it in Painter to use as a template while I created the final drawing using the scratchboard tool on a black background. One of the things I like most about working this way is the ability to change my mind. If I scratched out an area and wanted to make a change, I simply changed my paint color to black and worked back over the area. After I filled the spot back in, I changed back to white and reworked the image. When the art was finished, I save it as a TIFF file.

The next stage was to create multiple layers with the simple, flat color that I like. This could be done in any program that supports layers — I used FreeHand. First, I imported the TIFF file and assigned it to its own locked layer, then made the white areas transparent by checking Transparent in the Object Inspector palette. This was essential because any color placed behind the art needed to be able to show through. At this point, I just began creating layers of color and placing them behind the art to achieve the effect I was after. I also placed smaller images, such as the stars and the Christmas tree, on their own layers so that they could be turned off when they were not needed.

Displaying and hiding layers has also come in handy for other projects. For example, if a client is using an illustration, but I retain the rights to it, I can place the client's logo on its own layer. That way, I can hide the logo when I want to use the piece for other applications. ■

④

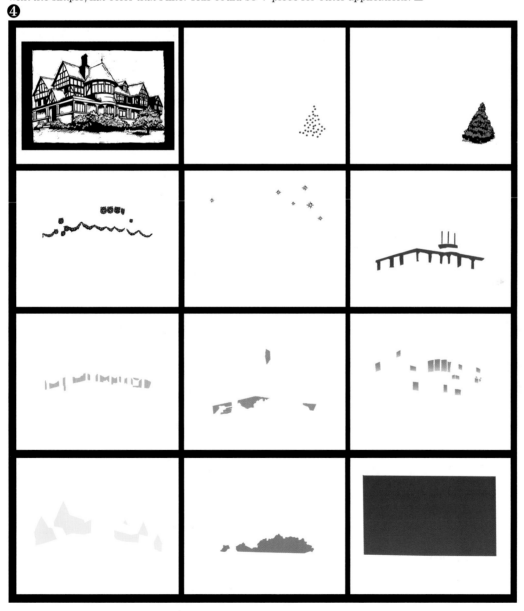

4 The black-and-white scratchboard drawing (top left) could be used alone or with the addition of Christmas decorations in the next three layers. Other layers could be turned on to add stars and color.

Reality Check

■ *by Steve Greenberg*

①

An ad for Fidelity Investments began with a morph created in Elastic Reality. I used Live Picture instead of Photoshop to composite the morph steps because I could move files around quickly and not get bogged down by file size. I layered the frames together, feathering and adjusting opacity as I went along.

1 I placed the caterpillar and butterfly sketches in Elastic Reality's two roll windows. In the Edit window, I drew a path around each shape with the pen tool and put in a few correspondence points to control what part of the first image moved into the second. But once I rendered a test QuickTime movie, I discovered that the effect was blobby.

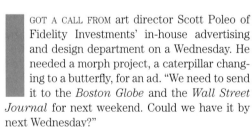

GOT A CALL FROM art director Scott Poleo of Fidelity Investments' in-house advertising and design department on a Wednesday. He needed a morph project, a caterpillar changing to a butterfly, for an ad. "We need to send it to the *Boston Globe* and the *Wall Street Journal* for next weekend. Could we have it by next Wednesday?"

I had only played around with morphs. I organized my thoughts during the walk back to my studio, then hit the phones in search of butterflies and caterpillars. I've shot dead butterflies before, but the color is not as vibrant as in live ones and they usually are in disrepair. So I called my stylist, Leslie "I can get anything fast" Fenton, and told her to get a few live swallowtails and a monarch (now I'm a butterfly expert). "So where you gonna get them?" I asked. I could hear Leslie smiling.

"Relax and have another cup of coffee," she said. "At the butterfly farm, where else?" Leslie never gives me a straight answer and always tells me to relax and drink more coffee. But she found a business in Westford, Mass., called The Butterfly Place that raises butterflies to sell to schools.

I looked for stock photos of caterpillars, but didn't find anything big enough. Leslie suggested I call Boston modelmaker Matthew Mees, and he said he'd deliver a 6-inch foam model by Tuesday.

The next step was to decide which software to use, Gryphon's Morph or Avid's Elastic Reality. I called a few of my tech-weenie friends and I got the expected answer: They all loved whichever program they were using and couldn't tell me why. I decided to test both programs.

After running through a few demos, I chose Elastic Reality. Just a gut decision, but it had one

❷

2 The final morph had three parts: caterpillar, thorax, and butterfly. I drew a short control line midway up the sides of the thorax, then went to the finished butterfly and drew a corresponding line around the outline of the wings. I also drew a closed shape along the inside of the thorax as a barrier. This kept the black interior of the thorax from morphing into the wings.

feature I liked: I could switch between wireframe and normal editing modes to check the motion of edges without getting confused by the image. Now I had to become an expert morpher by Monday.

Not having any images to play with yet, I drew a crude caterpillar and butterfly in Photoshop, saved them as PICTs, and brought them into Elastic Reality. I drew paths and connected points. (I'm really cruising now — watch out, Industrial Light and Magic!) But when I rendered the test to a QuickTime movie, I sadly watched a caterpillar blob into a butterfly.

I decided that the caterpillar needed to change into a mid-shape, such as the thorax of the butterfly, then wings could grow from the thorax. But I still was working with drawings.

Leslie showed up Monday with six gorgeous live butterflies and a smile. "I'll bet you want to know how to make them sit still, don't you? Put them in the fridge. The farmer said the cold will slow down their metabolism and they'll be still. It won't hurt them." We put a chilled butterfly on the set and turned on the lights. Like magic, the wings opened. We shot a few rolls on all the butterflies (stock images for later).

I photographed Mees' caterpillar model and silhouetted it using the bluescreen software Photo-Fusion (a Photoshop plug-in). I did the preparation and retouching in Photoshop, then saved the images as PICT files and placed them in Elastic Reality. When I was satisfied with the corresponding points, I rendered the image.

I brought the steps into Live Picture to collage together. At last I rendered the Live Picture file, sent it to Fidelity's production department, and sat down to finish my coffee. ■

Improving on Black and White

■ *by Kathy López*

TWO TO ONE is a dependable scan ratio for grayscale and color images, but that formula (multiplying the line screen by two to establish the scan resolution) isn't sufficient for Lydia Hess. Hess of Portland, Ore., is a scratchboard artist, and she needs high resolution to hold the clarity of her handwork when she scans it in black-and-white. With color or grayscale images, the halftone dots visually smooth out bitmapping. But the transition from black to white is stark enough to make pixellated edges stand out unless the pixels are tiny. So Hess scans her art at 400 dpi (her scanner's native resolution), saves it in TIFF format, and reduces the image later on the computer to increase the resolution.

To create this illustration for a direct mail piece for an organic food store, Lydia Hess scanned a scratchboard illustration and added color in FreeHand. Hess enjoys the production efficiency of the computer, but the most important ingredient in her imagery is the handwork. So she's careful to set the scan resolution high enough to prevent jaggies in her black-and-white TIFF scans.

Hess places the scan in FreeHand (File, Place) and adds color, drawing filled shapes on top of the image and sending the fills to the back (Command-B). To make the TIFF whites transparent, she chooses the object icon in FreeHand 4's Inspector palette and checks the Transparent box. (In FreeHand 3, the Transparent option is located in the Element Info dialog box, accessed by choosing Element, Element Info or Command-I.)

Trapping is no problem for Hess. She carefully draws the shapes to cover white areas and edge into the black, then sets the black to overprint by selecting the fill icon in the Inspector palette, changing the style from None to Basic, specifying black as the fill color, and choosing Overprint. (In earlier versions of FreeHand, Overprint is set in the Fill And Line dialog box, accessed by choosing Attributes, Fill And Line or Command-E.)

"Clients are thrilled when I can save them separation costs or modem the file to meet a tight deadline," Hess says. And working electronically has expanded her creative options as well. For example, when she created an illustration for the Names Project, promoting a showing of the AIDS Memorial Quilt, she wasn't satisfied with her scratchboard work. So she edited the art in Photoshop before placing it in FreeHand ❶.

Hess also used Photoshop to modify a scratchboard illustration for *Alaska* magazine, dividing the TIFF scan into two separate files so that the scratchboard elements could be filled with different colors ❷.

To illustrate an article about feuding restaurant owners for *Texas Monthly*, Hess combined solid colors with radial fills ❸. "When I first began working in FreeHand, I stuck to solid fills, the way I used to cut overlays," she says. "But now I sometimes use gradients and radial fills to add some dimension to the scratchboard art." ■

B&W Resolution

Bitmapping is more visible in black and white than it is in color or grayscale art. So when you print a black-and-white scan, you need to keep the resolution high. Most experts recommend 800 dpi, and some insist on 1200 dpi — although others say a resolution as low as 600 dpi is acceptable for absorbent stock like newsprint. You'll get the best results by using your scanner's native resolution and reducing the art to increase the resolution.

Scan	For 800 dpi scale to	For 1200 dpi scale to
300 dpi	37.5%	25%
400 dpi	50%	33.5%
600 dpi	75%	50%

❶

❷

❸

1 Hess wasn't satisfied in the eye and spiral designs in her scratchboard original. She edited the scan by copying elements from illustrations she had already completed and pasting them into her Photoshop file. "So the computer file is the 'original' for this illustration," she says. "Being able to edit an image is a big improvement. With scratchboard, once you make a line, it's there to stay."

2 Hess used Photoshop's lasso tool to select the clouds, then deleted them from the original scan and pasted them into a new file. After placing the two Photoshop images into FreeHand, she could select the clouds and apply a fill color from the Color List palette while leaving the angel black.

3 Hess drew a radial-filled background box, then traced around the bulls to create white-filled shapes that mask out the radial fill on the bottom layer. On top of the white shapes — and under the black-and-white scan — Hess placed solid-filled shapes to color the clothing.

To illustrate an article for University of California at San Diego's alumni magazine on how students were learning to create a virtual global economy, Court Patton of Patton Brothers Illustration (Spring Valley, Calif.) collected images from a variety of sources. To tie them all together, he used Photoshop to strip out the original colors and create a monochrome effect, then wrapped the resulting patchwork around a globe using Ray Dream Designer.

PHOTOSHOP / ILLUSTRATOR / RAY DREAM DESIGNER

Wrapping Up An Image

■ *by Sara Booth*

WHEN HE DECIDED to use a 3-D program to create an editorial illustration, Court Patton's greatest challenge was making sure that his "chessboard" (created in two dimensions) would be pleasing once it was wrapped around a globe in Ray Dream Designer. A test grid helped the Spring Valley, Calif., illustrator visualize the placement of each square in the chessboard without wasting a lot of time and effort.

Patton gathered a variety of illustrations for the collage — some from stock photos, some from other stories in the same issue of the magazine, some he built himself in Illustrator — and then removed the color from the images in Photoshop and colorized them ❶. ☞ *To remove all color from an illustration in Photoshop without changing its color mode, choose Image, Adjust, Desaturate (Command-Shift-U).*

To see where each image would fall, Patton built a grid in Illustrator ❷, saved it as a TIFF in

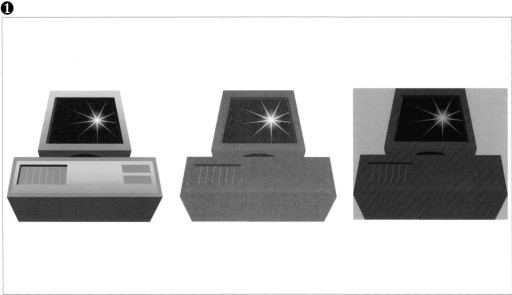

❶

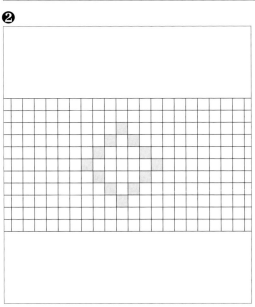

❷

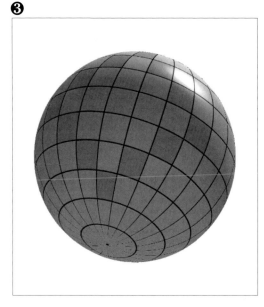

❸

1 The illustrations that were placed in the globe came from a variety of sources. To give them a consistent look, Patton took each illustration into Photoshop, removed all color, then filled the entire image with one of the approved colors, choosing Color mode in the Fill dialog box so that color would be added without disturbing values. If an image was too dark or too light, he chose Image, Adjust, Brightness/ Contrast and made some small adjustments.

2 Patton created a grid of squares in Illustrator. He filled some of the squares with gray, saved the grid in Illustrator, then opened it in Photoshop and saved it in TIFF format so he could use it as a texture map in Ray Dream Designer.

3 In Ray Dream Designer, Patton created a sphere (Edit, Insert, Sphere), set it to his desired size, and mapped his test grid onto it by choosing Texture Map from the Components menu of the Shader Editor dialog box. This allowed him to adjust the globe's size and position until the squares were where he wanted them and to identify the position of the most important squares based on where the gray boxes were. Then he made a laser print that he could use as a guide when he placed the images.

Photoshop, and mapped it to a sphere in Ray Dream Designer ❸. This test map helped him choose the best size and perspective for the sphere, and he used a printout as a guide to tell him where to place images when he created the final chessboard.

Patton then opened his grid in Photoshop and used it as a guide as he put together the colorized images. He needed to be sure the primary images would remain recognizable even with dramatic cropping and to work on balance and contrast within the whole composition — things he did mainly through trial and error. "It was just cut and paste, cut and paste, for a day or two," he says.

When the images were all assembled, Patton returned to his Ray Dream Designer test document to create the three-dimensional composition. He wanted to use chess pieces in his image,

and he found them in a file called Chess from the Dream Models folder of the Ray Dream Studio CD. He copied several pieces, placed them on his globe, and made small adjustments to the shapes of some of the pieces to make them look better at his chosen angle. When he had the chess pieces in place, he copied each one, pasted it into a new Ray Dream Designer file, and rendered it with an alpha channel so he could composite the image in Photoshop. ☞ *To align objects in Ray Dream Designer, first choose View, Preset Position, Reference (Command-0) to make it easier to judge directions. Then choose Arrange, Align Objects (Command-K) and set the objects' relationships (Align, Distribute, Contact, or Space) along any axis.*

After mapping the final Photoshop collage to the sphere in Ray Dream Designer, Patton set up

4 To create the red halo around the image, Patton put together all the parts of the illustration in Illustrator (including a tracing of the globe and chessmen) and made them into a single shape using the Pathfinder, Unite function. He decided how large he wanted the outline and added a stroke double that size (since the stroke would be centered on the line). He opened the Paint Style palette and chose a rounded shape for both caps and joins so there would be no sharp corners.

5 To create the empty spaces in the chessboard, Patton used Photoshop's pen tool to draw the sides of the gaps and filled them with shades of purple.

6 For a flying block, Patton first drew the block shapes in Illustrator, then copied them into Photoshop. He copied in the image that would be on the face of the block, then chose Layer, Transform, Distort to drag the image into the proper perspective. Finally he applied a motion blur.

❹

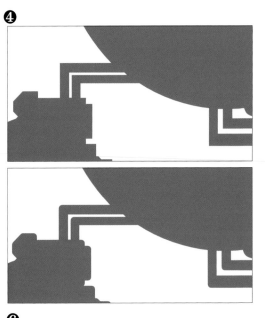

❺

❻

three light sources and rendered the globe with an alpha channel.

Other elements in the image were created in Illustrator. For the background, Patton drew a tan-filled rectangle, then drew a single white-stroked line and rotated copies of it around the center. To create the red stroke that surrounds the figures, Patton first placed the globe image in his Illustrator file, traced it with the pen tool, and deleted it. Then he selected all the shapes except the background and chose Filter, Pathfinder, Unite ❹. He assigned a dark red fill and stroke, then created a final Photoshop file where he pasted the image on its own layer.

Patton used Photoshop to put all the pieces together. When he had placed the background image in its own layer, he decided to divide it into light and dark quadrants. So he selected rectan-

gles at the upper right and lower left and lightened them in the Levels dialog box.

To create blocks that appear to fly out from the globe, Patton first used Photoshop's pen tool to draw the "empty" shapes on the grid where blocks were missing ❺. He went back to Illustrator for the blocks themselves, then applied a motion blur in Photoshop. To map the images to the blocks, he pasted the images, then chose Layer, Transform, Distort to adjust their perspective by eye ❻.

Patton used the red outline he had created in Illustrator to make a shadow: He copied the outline layer into an alpha channel, used the Offset filter to move it down and left by 30 pixels, and applied a Gaussian blur. He then displayed the background layer, loaded the channel as a selection, and filled with 30% black in Multiply mode to darken the background. ■

Putting Artwork In Perspective

■ *by Sara Booth*

FOR SOME ARTISTS, 3-D renders are final artwork; for Paul Johnson, they're raw materials. For a self-promotional collage, the Mequon, Wis., illustrator used Dimensions to add perspective to Illustrator contours, then simplified these 3-D objects into paths that he could use in Photoshop to create his final artwork.

MODELING IN DIMENSIONS

In Dimensions, fewer points means smoother results. So when Johnson drew his cross-sections in Illustrator, he based his shapes on ellipses and rectangles, then used the Pathfinder functions Unite and Divide to combine them and remove unwanted parts, adding connections with the pen tool and adjusting contours as he went ❶.

For rounded shapes such as glassware, Johnson brought cross-sections into Dimensions and revolved them ❷. ☞ *Dimensions automatically revolves a path around an axis that intersects its left edge. To revolve an object around a different axis, use Illustrator to create a guide that defines the axis of rotation.*

Johnson uses Dimensions to generate perspective, but he doesn't like the way it handles shading, preferring to add high-

"Some people watch TV," says Mequon, Wis., illustrator Paul Johnson; "I go online." His explorations of the World Wide Web paid off when he was researching a self-promotional collage: He downloaded low-resolution images from sites focusing on chemistry and used them as reference for a molecule, the periodic table, and other parts of his illustration.

1 The flask cross-section began as two circles, one for the body of the flask and one for the beaded rim. Johnson deleted part of the larger circle, then used the pen tool to re-connect the two shapes.

2 After importing the flask cross-section into Dimensions (File, Import or Command-Option-I), Johnson chose Operations, Revolve (Command-Shift-R), clicked the hollow icon in the Revolve dialog box, and revolved it 360 degrees.

3 Dimensions created shading by generating separate shapes, each filled with a different shade. Because Johnson planned to create his own shading, he simplified the artwork before placing it in Photoshop.

4 The computer shapes were created by choosing Operations, Extrude (Command-Shift-E), setting a solid cap and no bevel in the Extrude dialog box.

❶

❷

❸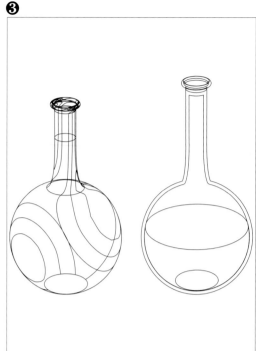

❹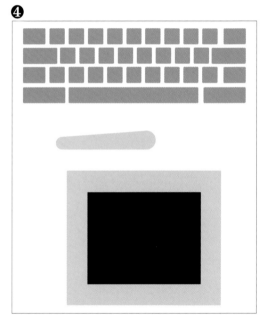

lights and shadows by eye. "Dimensions will give you all kinds of unnecessary stuff," he says. He opened each shape in Illustrator and deleted contours, or combined them using the Unite function, until he had only the shapes he would need in Photoshop **❸**.

To create the computer, Johnson first drew a series of rectangles for the keys and the monitor, then slightly rounded the corners by choosing Filter, Stylize, Round Corners, entering a radius of 2 points. After drawing the tapering shape of the keyboard cross-section, he copied each shape, pasted it into Dimensions, and extruded it, then dragged the shapes into their proper locations **❹**.

Johnson wanted all the shapes to appear in the same perspective. So before rendering each one, he chose View, Custom Perspective (Command-Option-P) and dragged the slider to 44 degrees, creating a perspective that was slightly more exaggerated than Dimensions' Normal perspective, but more subtle than the Wide Angle setting. Then he chose View, Draft Render (Command-Y) before exporting each file (File, Export or Command-Option-E) so that it could be opened in

❺

❻

❼

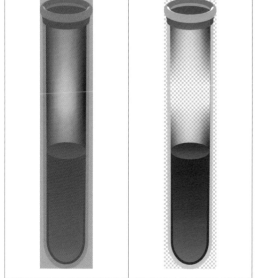

❽

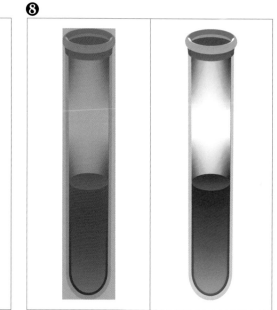

5 Johnson created a draft layout in Illustrator to determine the sizes of the elements before he did his Dimensions work.

6 In the final Illustrator layout, flat shapes were replaced by objects rendered in Dimensions. Johnson saved objects in separate files, so when he placed them in Photoshop, they landed in their proper locations.

7 To create a graduated selection in Quick Mask mode, Johnson first turned a subpath into a selection, then selected the gradient tool, set its mode to Darken Only and its style to Foreground To Transparent, and dragged two vertical gradients — one from top down, one from bottom up. Deleting the pixels inside this selection left a transparent area.

8 Another graduated selection was used to add red to the test tube: Johnson chose Image, Adjust, Hue/Saturation (Command-U) and dragged the Hue slider to change the color inside the selection.

Illustrator. ☞ *Because Dimensions' Draft render mode uses less-detailed shading, it results in a shape with fewer contours.*

CREATING A MASTER LAYOUT

He made an initial pencil sketch, but Johnson did most of his trial-and-error work in Illustrator, where he built a detailed sketch of the collage ❺. Then he refined his layout, working out the color, placement, and layering of each object in a master file in Illustrator ❻. "At this stage, I'm thinking ahead to how it will work out in Photoshop," he says.

To prepare to bring contours separately into Photoshop, Johnson placed each group on its own Illustrator layer. When the layout was complete, he saved each layer as its own file by copying the layout, then deleting all unwanted layers. When he placed the documents in Photoshop, each element dropped into its proper location.

REFINING IN PHOTOSHOP

In addition to placing objects in Photoshop as pixels, Johnson also pasted them in as paths, which helped him add details such as transparency and

Building An Electronic Reference File

In the past, if Paul Johnson wanted reference for an illustration or an element to use in a collage, he would have taken a photograph. But today he's more likely to build an electronic model using a variety of 3-D programs, from Adobe Dimensions to Strata Studio Pro. And once be creates these images, he uses them over and over.

Johnson has nearly 100MB of commonly used shapes and objects, from clock faces to human faces, on one of his hard drives. "I'm very systematic about this," Johnson says. "For instance, I've built all kinds of earth models — some stylized, some very realistic with transparency maps for clouds." He can give these elements a different look each time he uses them by altering color, size, texture, or viewing angle.

Johnson's self-promotional collage *Human*, right, shares some elements (for example, the atomic symbol, the molecule, and the squares from the periodic table) with the illustration on page 1. Other elements, such as the globes, the cells, and the many textures, come from his permanent reference collection. The heart and the human figure were created in Poser, then adjusted in Photoshop for better contrast and detail. "Poser gives you very crude renderings, but I use it fairly often to get positions right," he says. ■

reflection. To make a test tube fade gradually into transparency in the center, Johnson selected the subpath that defined the body of the tube and loaded it as a selection by clicking the selection icon in the Paths palette. Switching to Quick Mask mode by typing the letter *Q*, he created a graduated selection using the gradient tool. Switching back to normal mode by typing *Q* again, he feathered the selection, then pressed the Delete key ❼.

A similar technique was used to add a hint of red to the bottom of the purple test tube: Johnson made a graduated selection in Quick Mask mode,

feathered it, then chose Image, Adjust, Hue/Saturation (Command-U) and dragged the Hue slider to change the color inside the selection ❽.

To add a dark shadow on the right side of a test tube, Johnson loaded the subpath that defined the inner edge of the test tube and deleted some parts of it. He loaded the path as a selection, but kept it active as a path as well. Then he chose the airbrush tool, defined a dark-blue foreground color, and chose Stroke Path from the popout menu of the Paths palette. The airbrush line was clipped by the selection, appearing only inside it. ■

RAY DREAM DESIGNER / PHOTOSHOP

Going A Little Deeper

■ *by Sara Booth*

UNDERSEA CREATURES are not yet among Ray Dream Designer's primitives, so if Mark Siegel wanted an octopus and an ocean scene, he had to make them from scratch. The Canyon Country, Calif., illustrator used sweep paths and cross sections to make unpredictable organic shapes and bump maps to add texture. And he used Designer-generated channels in Photoshop to vary the filter and lighting effects, adding spaciousness to his underwater scene.

Siegel used many programs to create *Treasure Guardian*, which won first place in the non-commercial category of the 1995 Ray Dream Modern Masters of 3-D contest. He used KPT Bryce to generate landscape features; then, because Bryce cannot export 3-D information, he used a shareware terrain generator, Terrainman, to save a Bryce scene in DXF format so he could open it in Designer. Kai's Power Tools was used to create textures. And Photoshop's compositing tools brought it all together.

Alignment is one of the challenges of 3-D modeling. Illustrator Mark Siegel has a default Ray Dream Designer document with a variety of cameras already in position. He begins each illustration by opening this file, which makes it easy for him to view his work in progress from many viewpoints.

Electronic Design   **207**

1 Siegel made a plank for the chest by extruding a rectangle; he created others as instances (by choosing Edit, Duplicate or Command-D), which reduced file size and rendering time. Similarly, all the rivets are instances of a single shape.

2 In Designer's Modeling window, Siegel drew a circle (by clicking the rectangle tool in the toolbox and dragging out to the circle tool), then chose Arrange, Ungroup and adjusted curves. When Designer extruded this shape, he used the add point tool to add curve points to the sweep path, adjusting it into a long, curving tube (left). To taper it, he turned the endpoint into a cross section (by choosing Sections, Create), then reshaped it.

3 Siegel added cross sections by selecting points and choosing Sections, Create. When he rotated these cross sections with the rotate tool (accessed by dragging out from the virtual trackball in the toolbox), he pressed Option to twist the shape.

4 To add "veins" to his tentacle texture, Siegel opened the *Blistered Paint* texture (in the *Textures for Lighting Effects* folder on the Photoshop 3.0 CD) and copied part of it into a new channel. He created another channel of gradient-filled stripes, fading to white where he wanted the most texture. He loaded this channel as a selection, then chose Filter, Render, Lighting Effects. He chose a Directional light type, chose the *Blistered Paint* channel in the Texture Channel popout menu, and dragged the Height slider toward Flat.

5 To map the texture onto the tentacle, Siegel chose Windows, Shader Editor (Command-/). In the Color channel, he chose Component, Texture Map, selected *Tentacle*, and checked Tile and Seamlessly.

Siegel drew the chest in Illustrator. Then he opened Designer and dragged the freeform tool into the Perspective window to open the Modeling window, then chose File, Import to bring in his Illustrator files. After Designer extruded the shapes, Siegel resized the sweep paths ❶ before clicking Done to return to the main scene.

BUILDING ORGANIC SHAPES

To create a tentacle, Siegel extruded an irregular ellipse, then edited the sweep paths into a complex curve ❷. While he worked in the Modeling window, he used the virtual trackball to rotate the view so he could see many angles without moving the shape. He wanted a curve with even diameter, like a pipe, so he chose Geometry, Extrusion Method, Pipeline. ☞ *In Designer's Pipeline extrusion method, the cross section is perpendicular to the sweep path; in the Translation method, it is perpendicular to the ground plane.*

To make the tentacle twist, Siegel added cross sections, then rotated them ❸. When all the tentacles were finished, he arranged them in the chest.

TEXTURIZING TENTACLES

Textures slow down screen redraw, so Siegel usually builds and arranges all the parts of a scene before adding them. But he wanted the suckers to follow the twists of the tentacles, so he needed a texture as a guide to tell him where the bottom of each tentacle was. He worked on each tentacle in its own file to speed the work: He selected a tentacle, then opened the Numerical Properties dialog box (Windows, Numerical Properties or Command-I) and wrote down its x, y, and z coordinates before cutting and pasting it into a new file. When he finished it, he pasted it back into the main file, then entered the x, y, and z coordinates to return it to its original location.

Siegel chose a Kai's Power Tools texture and scaled it vertically in Photoshop. He used a channel filled with graduated stripes as a selection to fill the texture with two shades of pink, fading gradually into flat color. Then he added a veiny effect ❹ on the central part (which would become the back of the tentacle) and saved the texture as a PICT image called *Tentacle* to use as a texture map in Designer ❺. With the texture in place, he could see exactly where the suckers went ❻.

Placing one large sucker at the base of the tentacle, he repeatedly duplicated it (Edit, Duplicate or Command-D) and scaled it down for the length of the arm. Because he had already arranged the tentacles and chosen a camera, Siegel knew which

❶
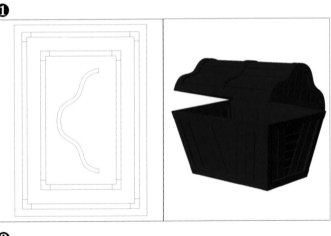

❷

❸
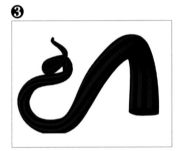

❹

❺
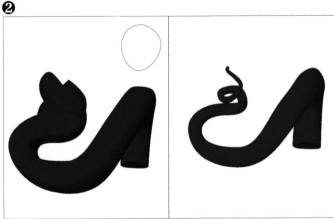

suckers would be hidden, so he left them off — "I'm not completely crazy," he says.

Siegel used the virtual trackball to rotate the tentacle into more accessible views as he positioned the suckers. It wasn't easy to get them into alignment, so to preserve that alignment, he linked the suckers to the tentacle as children by dragging their icons in the Hierarchy window onto the icon of the tentacle. Now if the tentacle was moved, its spatial relationship with the suckers would be maintained. As a finishing touch, Siegel added a starfish and a scatter of gold coins ❼.

BUMP MAPS AND PAINT SHAPES

Siegel scanned photos of a split rail fence and a rusted air conditioner for textures. His custom shaders also contained bump maps for a more realistic impression of an uneven surface ❽.

Rather than map an entire shape with the same texture, Siegel wanted to apply multiple textures to some shapes — for example, to create separate planks on the chest lid. Paint shapes allowed him to fill selections with textures ❾.

For the ocean floor, Siegel turned to Bryce, where he altered a preset terrain by choosing Objects, Edit Terrain ❿. A Designer bump map placed shadows on the sandy floor. Bryce was also used to generate two mountains that would become part of the background.

SIMULATING WATER

To add an underwater feeling, Siegel added a gel light overhead to project a wave pattern on the objects ⓫. To enhance the effect, he added fog to his Designer scene ⓬ by choosing Render, Effects (Command-Shift-E), displaying the Atmosphere channel, and choosing Distance Fog from the popout menu. He wanted to match his fog color in Bryce. Clicking More Choices in Designer's color picker allowed him to choose Apple RGB as his color picker and write down the RGB readings of the fog. Then Siegel opened the mountains he had created in Bryce and added a fog the same color (by choosing Sky & Fog from the master palette, clicking and dragging in the fog icon to choose a fog effect, and Option-clicking the color swatch below the icon to enter the RGB settings). The fog made it easy to combine the Designer and Bryce scenes in Photoshop with minimum retouching.

RENDERING AND COMPOSITING

Siegel wanted Designer to create channels to make Photoshop compositing easier. So he chose Render, Settings (Command-Shift-T). In the File

6 To build a sucker, Siegel extruded a circle and chose Geometry, Extrusion Envelope, Free. He added points to the scaling envelope, then edited it (right).

7 To build a starfish, Siegel extruded a flattened ellipse with a tapering scaling envelope, then made four duplicates and aligned them with a central object. For coins, he used the cylinder primitive; to flatten this cylinder, he chose Windows, Numerical Properties (Command-I) and reduced the z dimension. Then he created a shader that mixed gold and brown: In the Shader Editor, he chose Components, Operators, Mix. He dropped two colors on the color areas, then highlighted the Function area and chose Components, Natural Functions, Spots.

8 Siegel cropped his scans (top) in Photoshop and used them as shaders. To add a bump map, he opened a scan in Photoshop, converted it to grayscale, and increased contrast in the Levels dialog box (bottom left). To place the bump map in Designer, he chose the Bump Map channel of the Shader Editor, chose Component, Texture Map, and selected the grayscale file. The program interpreted lighter shapes as raised areas and darker ones as depressions (bottom right).

9 Siegel mapped the wood texture to the chest using paint shapes. After selecting the custom shader he had created, he used the rectangle paint shape tool to drag out a marquee, which was filled with texture.

❻
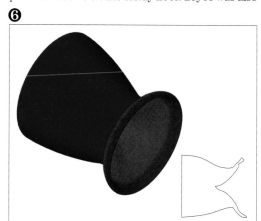

❼

❽

❾

10 Bryce exported the ocean floor as a grayscale PICT; value differences represent height differences. Designer can't interpret PICT terrain models as 3-D space, so Siegel opened his PICT in Terrainman to save it in DXF format.

11 To add a gel light, Siegel made a water texture in Kai's Power Tools and changed it to grayscale in Photoshop. In Designer, he dragged a light into position to open the Object Properties dialog box. In the Gel channel, he chose Map from the Gels popout menu and selected his grayscale texture. In the Light channel, he unchecked Shadows.

12 Designer creates fog along the active camera's view line. Siegel entered a Fog Start of 145 inches and a Visibility (the distance at which visibility reaches zero) of 75 inches.

13 Designer rendered a distance channel expressing depth in grayscale values, with white (fully selected) pixels in the background and darker grays closer to the camera.

14 Siegel loaded the distance channel as a selection and applied the Ripple filter (with large ripples and an Amount of 56), which had the strongest effect on distant areas. But after experimenting, he decided that inverting the channel gave a more realistic effect

15 To create the effect of light through water, Siegel filled a new channel with a gradient. He chose Image, Calculations and used Add mode to combine this channel with the *Water Mask* channel, naming the new channel *Water Grad Mask.* He loaded *Water Mask* as a selection and filled it with a blue-to-green gradient, then loaded *Water Grad Mask.* He created a Kai's Power Tools texture, setting its mode in the Texture Explorer to Procedural+, then chose OK to apply it inside his selection.

Format channel's G-Buffer area, he checked Mask (to create a background mask outlining the shapes) and Distance (to create a distance mask, a grayscale representation of distances) **13**. He rendered the file as *Octopus.*

Because the Bryce mountains wouldn't interact with other parts of the scene the way the ocean floor did, Siegel didn't need to open them in Designer. So instead of taking them through Terrainman, he rendered them in Bryce, naming the file *Mountains.* (He rendered a background mask separately by choosing Mask Render in the Render palette.) Siegel opened *Octopus* in Photoshop

10

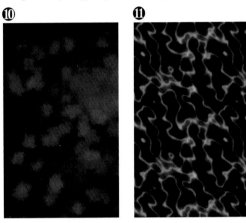

12

13

and retouched the tentacles slightly by cloning pixels with the rubber stamp tool to cover seams.

Siegel opened the *Mountains* file and loaded the background channel to select both mountains, then used Command and the lasso to deselect one. He copied the mountain to the clipboard and returned to the *Octopus* file, where he loaded the background channel and chose Select, Inverse to select only the background. Then he chose Edit, Paste Into to paste the mountain into the selection, so it would appear to be behind the octopus. While the mountain was still selected, he saved the selection. He repeated the process to add the second mountain.

ENHANCING THE WATER EFFECT

The Ripple filter intensified the underwater effect, with an unexpected bonus: The geometric suckers appeared more lifelike **14**. To select the space at the top of the scene, Siegel loaded the octopus background mask, then Shift-Option-clicked the two mountain masks in the Channels palette to select everything but the water. He saved this selection, then used it to add the appearance of sunlight filtered through water **15**.

Finally, Siegel drew paths in the shape of fish, filled them with a dark contrasting color, then blended them into the scene with the blur tool. ■

14

15

GLASS
ENVELOPE

PLATE

GRID

CATHODE

HEATER

BASE

Where 2-D Meets 3-D

■ *by Sara Booth*

HOUSTON ILLUSTRATOR CHRIS LOCKWOOD is known for 3-D work. But one key to his expertise is knowing when to supplement a 3-D program with other software. For a showcase book ad, he used Illustrator to create the background and raw materials. After rendering, he turned to Photoshop, where masks and channels helped him generate glass distortion and fade effects.

Lockwood combines two 3-D programs. For rendering, he chooses Alias Sketch for its richer rendering engine. But Sketch's modeling functions are limited, so he does modeling in Form-Z, which, in addition to lathing and extruding, supports Boolean operations for combining objects in complex ways. "The only problem is that because the two programs have different modeling methods, it takes forever to import a piece from one to

When Chris Lockwood designed this ad for a showcase book, his goal was to demonstrate his expertise in 3-D illustration. But to generate realistic glass, the Houston illustrator had to manipulate his 3-D rendering using Photoshop masks and channels.

1 Lockwood drew the parts of the tube in Illustrator, using vertical lines to define each axis of revolution. He imported the Illustrator file into Form-Z and extruded or lathed each piece.

2 To create the diagram of the tube, Lockwood reflected a copy of the outlines he had drawn for Form-Z. Strokes (shown in blue) represented sweep paths for the stems. To make the stems themselves, he assigned these strokes a heavy weight, then chose Filter, Objects, Outline Path. (Applying the Unite filter removed overlaps.)

3 To create the gear, Lockwood drew a circle plus a shape (shown in blue) that would take a "bite" out of it. After deciding how many teeth the gear should have, Lockwood divided that number by 360 to arrive at the angle of rotation, then rotated the shape repeatedly around the circle's center. Finally, he chose Filter, Pathfinder, Minus Front. Concentric circles (shown in red) were used for both the inside of one shape and the outside of another, so when the pieces were extruded, they would fit perfectly.

4 When Lockwood rendered the tube in Sketch, the background seen through the glass was darkened, but not distorted. (This rendering shows an earlier version of the background, which was replaced by the grid and diagram in the final image.)

5 Lockwood rendered the tube and its alpha channel twice, once with glass and once without. Opening the channels, he chose Image, Calculations, chose each channel as a source, set the mode to Difference, and chose a new channel as the result. This created a channel, called *Distort*, of only the background that showed through the glass. Then Lockwood manipulated this area to simulate glass distortion.

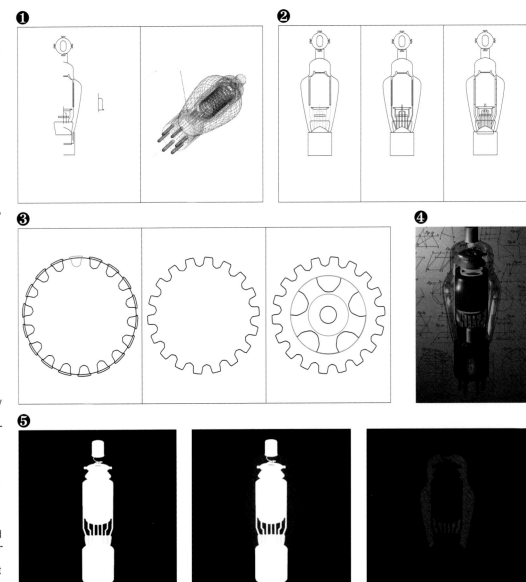

the other," Lockwood says. And because Sketch interprets objects differently from Form-Z, Lockwood must make some changes in his shapes before rendering them, such as breaking apart any object that has both rounded and flat surfaces so that Sketch can render them separately.

BUILDING BLOCKS IN ILLUSTRATOR

For the 3-D elements of his showcase ad, Lockwood drew many basic shapes in Illustrator, then used Form-Z's modeling functions to bring them into three dimensions ❶. For example, the plate at the top of the vacuum tube, as well as the gears at the top of the image, were extruded. The tube's base, glass, cap, screen, and many other elements were lathed (revolved). Below the screen are long metal tubes, which bend as they run toward the base. These were extruded along sweep paths, so

both the profile and the path had to be created in Illustrator. Only the spiral elements were drawn from scratch in Form-Z, which has special tools for creating helical and spiral shapes.

For each lathed element in the three-dimensional tube, Lockwood used Illustrator to create a cross-section from the center outward, plus a guide around which Form-Z would lathe the shape. When he began working on the two-dimensional diagram of the tube in the background, he could build the entire shape by reflecting a copy of the cross-section using the center guide as an axis. For elements for which he had drawn a sweep path, that path could be altered to represent the shape itself in the diagram ❷.

The gears could not be extruded in a single piece because the spokes were lower than the other parts. To be certain that the separate pieces

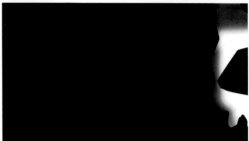

would fit together perfectly, Lockwood began with a series of concentric circles in Illustrator, so that a single circle could be the outer edge of one piece and the inner edge of another ❸.

CREATING GLASS DISTORTIONS

"Reflections are easy in a 3-D program," Lockwood says. "But distortions are hard." When Alias Sketch rendered the image, it distorted the components inside the glass, but not the background ❹. So he decided to create the distortion in Photoshop. To do this, he needed an easy way to select the part of the background that showed through the glass.

Like most 3-D programs, Sketch offers the option of creating an alpha channel of an object as it renders it. So Lockwood rendered the tube twice: once with the glass envelope and once without. A Difference calculation between those two

channels resulted in a single channel, called *Distort*, that selected all the background that would be visible through the glass ❺. He used this channel to create a distorted effect ❻.

FROM CHANNELS TO MASKS

To unify the 3-D and 2-D parts of the image, Lockwood wanted the gears to fade into a background drawing. After rendering the gears with an alpha channel, Lockwood brought them into Photoshop, along with a diagram of the same images ❼, then created the fade using a layer mask ❽.

A similar technique was used to make the black portion of the LCD panel fade into the background. Sketch can't make an object give off light, so to simulate the glowing numbers on the LCD display, Lockwood placed a red light near the object before rendering it. ∎

6 To save time, Lockwood rendered the tube against a low-resolution version of the background. He opened the rendering and loaded the *Distort* channel, floated the selection and placed it on its own layer, then used Image, Effects, Distort to slightly resize the selected background (shown in blue). The size difference, coupled with the slight blurring caused by the background's low resolution, created distortion. Lockwood clipped the distorted area within the glass shape by reloading *Distort* (shown in red), inversing the selection, and deleting.

7 Lockwood wanted to use both 3-D and diagram versions of the gear. For the 3-D version, he extruded Illustrator contours in Form-Z, but this changed the dimensions, so the two versions no longer matched. Opening the Form-Z gear in Photoshop, he saved a low-resolution copy, placed it in Illustrator, dragged the linework in front, and scaled the linework until the two matched as closely as possible. After adding details to the linework, he copied it into its own Photoshop layer behind the 3-D gear.

8 To make the 3-D gear fade into the diagram version, Lockwood added a layer mask to the gear layer. He Option-clicked the mask's icon in the Layers palette to display the mask, loaded the alpha channel created when the gear was rendered, inversed the selection, and filled with black to mask out everything except the gear. Then he used the airbrush (defining a large brush) and the eraser (with opacity set to about 15%) to alter the mask so the linework could show through.

Improving the View

■ *by Jay Stevens*

THE ADVANTAGES of working in a 3-D drawing program are obvious. But the disadvantages are equally easy to see: Once you've finished rendering an illustration (and even on the fastest computer, the rendering process summons all the patience you can muster), the surface looks like molded plastic. That's fine if you're trying to capture the look of plastic — or metal or polished marble — but if you have another effect in mind, you won't get it in a 3-D program. It seems that there's nothing natural about working in 3-D. True, the perspective is accurate in the rendered image. All the shadows fall in the right direction, and the highlights gleam where they should. But the overall effect screams "manufactured entirely with artificial ingredients."

The solution is to let the 3-D program do what it does best (build perspective and establish highlights and shadows) and use a program with painting tools to fine-tune the effect and create the look you want. But even that can be time-consuming. Many times I've found myself reworking a 3-D illustration entirely in Painter or Photoshop, using the rendering as reference.

Recently, though, I stumbled across a new technique that lets me work much more quickly. I stack up three layers of the 3-D image in Photoshop. The bottom layer provides the "base" color of the object, the center layer defines any sharp edges in the image, and the top layer is the selection that I paint into to build up the shadows. An added benefit is that I can work with a low-resolution rendering (150 dpi or even less), so I don't have to spend as much time watching the progress bar fail to progress in the 3-D application.

The first step is to create the 3-D imagery. When I set the lighting and choose the perspec-

1 Before I render a 3-D object, I take some time to preview it from several angles so that I can choose the most dramatic one (or the one that's easiest to identify, depending on the effect I want).

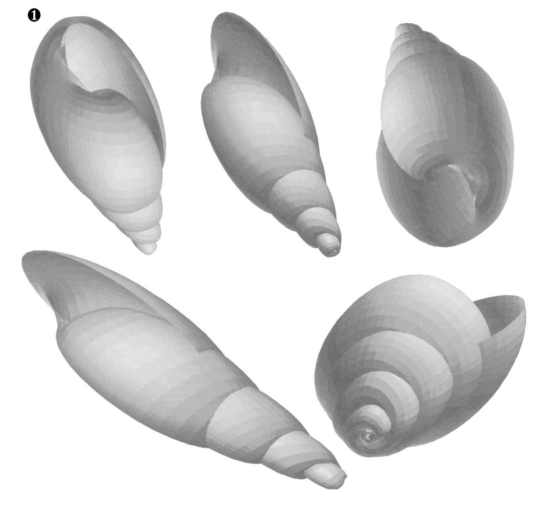

❶

tive, I like to experiment wildly, turning the object in dozens of different directions and changing the camera angle at will. Many times, unusual and dramatic views will present themselves — angles much more daring than I would have thought to try if I had been confined to two dimensions. One of the not-so-obvious benefits of working in 3-D is the way the program frees your imagination when it suspends your illustration in mid-air and makes it easy for you to explore it from every possible vantage point.

I work in Ray Dream Designer. So when I come across an angle I like, I save it in the Camera Settings dialog box (Windows, Camera Settings or Command-E) so that I can get that viewpoint back when I want to. Then I experiment some more. Finally, I choose my favorite camera angle from the ones I've saved, render the image, and save it in Photoshop format.

Because I render at a low resolution, the "struts" of the underlying wireframe show through the "skin" in a few places. But I've found it takes only a few minutes to give the surface of the 3-D image a rough "sanding" using Photoshop's blur tool. I only attack the most obvious bumps and ridges; I don't try to smooth out the image. On an image the size and complexity of the one shown here, the sanding process takes well under five minutes, only a fraction of the time I would spend rendering the art at high resolution.

Before I begin smoothing the art, I isolate it from the background (by selecting the background with the magic wand tool and choosing Select, Inverse). This keeps me from "pushing" color from the art into the background when I apply the blur tool — and it's essential for the next step in the process, when I place copies of the image on three different layers in the Layers palette. ■

2 Once I decide on the view, I render the image at medium resolution: 150 dpi or less. The "ribs" of the wireframe may show at this point, but I can correct that in the next step.

3 When I open the image in Photoshop, it is automatically placed on the background layer. I create a floating selection and place copies of this selection on two more layers. I apply the Blur filter to the image on the background layer to smooth out the bumps that show through the wireframe. On the center layer, I increase contrast before applying the Find Edges filter in the Stylize submenu. I set the opacity of this layer at about 30 percent. On the top layer, I apply the Noise filter (set to Monochromatic) and choose Darken as the mode setting in the Layers palette.

4 The final image has a hand-painted look, unlike the machine-made look of art that comes straight out of a 3-D application.

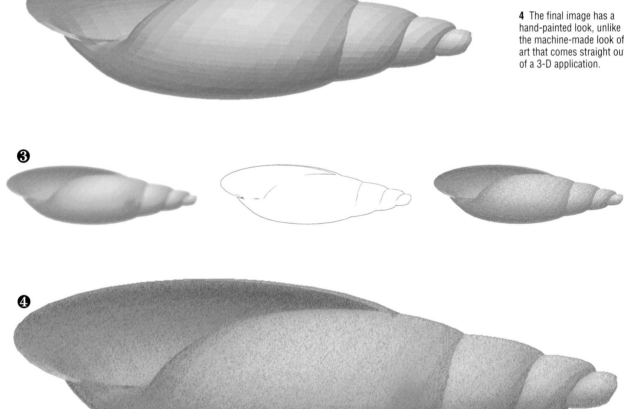

❷

❸

❹

FEATURED ARTISTS

PETER ALSBERG
33 Columbia Ave
Takoma Park, MD 20912
202.334.4552

LISA BELHAGE
Vildrosevej 20
Espergærde DK-3060
Denmark
45 49 170760

GARY BLAKELY
#118-350 E 2nd Ave
Vancouver BC
Canada V5T 4R8
604.708.1767

ELIZABETH BRANDT
35 1/2 W 8th St
Holland, MI 49423
616.394.4240

JIM CARROLL
Box 7
East Chatham, NY 12060
518.392.5234

MARGARET CARSELLO
Carsello Creative
516 N Vine St
Hinsdale, IL 60521
630.794.9120

RON CHAN
24 Nelson Ave
Mill Valley, CA 94941
415.389.6549

GARY CIRINO
Logos Studio
8611 Whippoorwill Ln
Cleveland, OH 44130
216.888.7870

TRACI O'VERY COVEY
682 South 700 East
Salt Lake City, UT 84102
801.363.6063

DIANA CRAFT
413 Creekside Dr
Richardson, TX 75081
972.235.1700

ELDON DOTY
9405 179th Pl NE, #3
Redmond, WA 98052
425.558.3993

STEVE GREENBURG
368 Congress St
Boston, MA 02210
617.423.7646

DAVID GUINN
Design One
26 1/2 Battery Park Ave
Asheville, NC 28801
704.254.7898

LYDIA HESS
1246 SE 49th Ave
Portland, OR 97215
503.234.4757

DAVID HIGH
405 Southeast 49th Ave.
Ocala, FL 34471
352.624.0088

CHARLIE HILL
7412 Meridian Hills Ct, Ste C
Indianapolis, IN 46260
317.257.5417

MIKE HILL
701 Estates Ct
Bel Air, MD 21015
410.893.7620

MICHAEL HOLMES
1701 N Market, Ste 400
Dallas, TX 75202
214.571.4024

JOHN HOVELL
513 Green Village Rd
Green Village, NJ 07935
201.822.5002

DAN HUBIG
4104 24th St, #240
San Francisco, CA 94114
415.824.0838

ROGER HUNSICKER
415 E. Frye Ave.
Peoria, IL 61603
309.494.1161

SI HUYNH
1613 Creekside Drive
Nanaimo BC
Canada V9S 5V8
250.753.7484

GRANT JERDING
6278 Levi Ct
Springfield, VA 22150
703.276.5334

PAUL JOHNSON
11412 N Port Washington Rd
Ste 202
Mequon, WI 53092
414.241.4484

ALBERT KIEFER
Gulikstraat 210
5913 CZ Venlo
Netherlands
31 77 320 05 80

MIKE KUNIAVSKY
660 Third St, 4th Floor
San Francisco, CA 94107
415.276.8400

SUSAN LEVAN
LeVan/Barbee Studio
30 Ipswich St #211
Boston, MA 02215
617.536.6828

CHRIS LOCKWOOD
1210 W Clay St, #19
Houston, TX 77019
713.524.1860

MAGGIE MACNAB
Macnab Design
400 San Felipe NW, Ste 4
Albuquerque, NM 87104
505.242.6159

JOHN MARSHALL
Beckett Interactive
15850 Dallas Parkway
Dallas, TX 75248
972.991.6657

DARLENE MCELROY
2414 Calle Zaguan
Santa Fe, NM 87505
505.471.8300

JAMES MICELI
155 Canterbury Rd
Rochester, NY 14607
716.271.8190

JUDY MILLER
801 N Shepherd Hills
Tucson, AZ 85710
520.296.5323

LORI OSIECKI
123 W 2nd St
Mesa, AZ 85201
602.962.5233

ROBERT OSWALD
112 Corley Woods Dr
Lexington, SC 29072
803.356.3203

CHARLY PALMER
7007 Eagle Watch Ct
Stone Mountain, GA 30087
770.413.8276

ELLIOTT PARK
The Art Source
2820 Rainforest Ct
Southlake, TX 76092
817.481.2212

COURT PATTON
3768 Miles Ct
Spring Valley, CA 91977
619.463.4562

DINO PAUL
Dino Design
4203 E Indian School #160
Phoenix, AZ 85018
602.952.0665

JEFFREY PELO
P.O. Box 5295
Larkspur, CA 94977
415.455.8617

RICHARD PUDER
Richard Puder Design
2 W Blackwell St
P.O. Box 1520
Dover, NJ 07802-1520
973.361.1310

MIKE QUON
Quon/Designation Inc.
53 Spring St, 5th Floor
New York, NY 10012
212.226.6024

NICOLE RAYNARD
2000 Broadway #711
San Francisco, CA 94115
415.921.8005

KEN ROBERTS
Canary Studios
600 Grand Ave, Ste 307
Oakland, CA 94610
510.893.1737

WAYNE ROTH
ChiselVision
712 Main St
Boonton, NJ 07005
201.402.0066

MICHAEL RYZNAR
#202-5652 Patterson Ave
Burnaby, BC
Canada V5H 4C8
604.501.5099

MICHAEL SCARAMOZZINO
DreamLight Studios
38 Montvale Ave, Ste 220
Stoneham, MA 02180
617.438.8575

MIKE SCHMALZ
1302 Rhomberg Ave
Dubuque, IA 52001
319.584.0172

JOANIE SCHWARZ
561 Bradford Ave
Westfield, NJ 07090
908.233.8615

TRISKA SEEGER
11570 Alkaid Dr
San Diego, CA 92126
619.566.1570

MARK SHAVER
2334 Oak St, #C
Santa Monica, CA 90405
310.450.4336

MARK SIEGEL
14648 Hydrangea Way
Canyon Country, CA 91351
805.578.3100

CHRISTOPHER SPOLLEN
Moonlightpress Studio
362 Cromwell Ave
Ocean Breeze, NY 10305-2304
718.979.9695

NANCY STAHL
470 West End Ave
New York, NY 10024
212.362.8779

AUGUST STEIN
3732 First Ave
San Diego, CA 92103
619.299.8999

CLARK TATE
115 West 4th St
P.O. Box 339
Gridley, IL 61744-0339
800.828.3008

MARINA THOMPSON
31 Willow Rd
Nahant, MA 01908
617.581.1725

LAURIE WIGHAM
209 Mississippi St
San Francisco, CA 94107
415.863.6113

PAUL WOODS
414 Jackson
San Francisco, CA 94111
415.399.1984

TED WRIGHT
4237 Hansard Ln
Hillsboro, MO 63050
314.827.2091

INDEX

To recieve *Step-By-Step Electronic Design* every month, one year (12 issues for only $48)

CALL: 800-255-8800 • FAX: 309-688-8515 • E-MAIL: sbspub@dgusa.com